The Elder Testament

The Elder Testament
Canon, Theology, Trinity

Christopher R. Seitz

BAYLOR UNIVERSITY PRESS

© 2018 by Baylor University Press
Waco, Texas 76798

All Rights Reserved. No part of this publication may be reproduced, stored in a retrieval system, or transmitted, in any form or by any means, electronic, mechanical, photocopying, recording, or otherwise, without the prior permission in writing of Baylor University Press.

Cover Design by Aaron Cobbs
Cover art: Andrei Rublev, The Trinity, icon showing the three angels being hosted by Abraham at Mamre

First issued in paperback format in November 2021 under ISBN 978-1-4813-0829-8.

The Library of Congress has cataloged the hardcover as follows:
Names: Seitz, Christopher R., author.
Title: The elder testament : canon, theology, trinity / Christopher R. Seitz.
Description: Waco, Texas : Baylor University Press, [2018] | Includes bibliographical references and index.
Identifiers: LCCN 2018006476 (print) | LCCN 2018027108 (ebook) | ISBN 9781481308373 (Web PDF) | ISBN 9781481308366 (ebook-Mobi/Kindle) | ISBN 9781481308304 (Epub) | ISBN 9781481308281 (hardback : alk. paper)
Subjects: LCSH: Bible. Old Testament--History. | Bible. Old Testament--Criticism, interpretation, etc.
Classification: LCC BS1130 (ebook) | LCC BS1130 .S45 2018 (print) | DDC 221.6--dc23
LC record available at https://lccn.loc.gov/2018006476

Contents

Introduction   1

PART ONE
ORIENTATION

1   Elder Testament: Introducing the Scriptures of Israel   13
2   Canonical Interpretation of the Elder Scriptures   21
3   Theological Interpretation of the Elder Testament   35
4   "Can we read this book?": Reader Response-ability   51

PART TWO
ENTERING THE ELDER TESTAMENT

5   The Strange Old Book: The Limits of Narrative   71
6   The Fate of JEDP: The Mysterious Disclosure of the Divine Name   85

7	YHWH and Elohim: The LORD God	97
8	Order, Arrangements, Canonical Shape, and Name	119
9	The Pentateuch	131
10	Prophets	139
11	Writings	161

PART THREE
THEOLOGICAL READINGS IN THE ELDER TESTAMENT

12	The Triune Name	183
13	Proverbs 8:22-31 and the Mind of Scripture	201
14	The Sun Also Rises: Time and Creation in Ecclesiastes and Genesis 1–11	221
15	"When Christ came into the world he said": The Scriptural Christ in the Letter to the Hebrews	243
16	Theophany and Trinity	261

Conclusion	271
Bibliography	281
Scripture Index	295
Author Index	301

Introduction

I have always been a voracious reader, from Hardy Boys books with a flashlight in the backyard tent to high school introductions to American novels and Latin history and French short stories to undergraduate courses as an English major. Especially there in college, reading Faulkner or Milton or Shakespeare or the metaphysical poets, I began to sense that it was the Bible, and often the Old Testament, that was the inspiration guiding great literature and great writers. I took a couple of courses from a very popular professor on Old Testament prophets and basic Old Testament and New Testament introduction. I was introduced to moderate forms of historical-critical method. The professor was a gifted orator, and it was a blow when he died before retirement—in the pulpit of the Presbyterian Church he was visiting as preacher. I went to the funeral, and his widow invited me and other students and teaching assistants to their house for tea afterwards. She wanted me

2 The Elder Testament

to have some of his books, which surprised me, as I was intending to go to law school. I had known the professor well enough that he knew my intentions. I picked out three books we had used in the courses he taught. His wife said she wanted to add one. It was a big Brown-Driver-Briggs Hebrew Lexicon, probably the most thumbed book in my present library after forty years of studying and teaching Old Testament, writing books, and directing doctoral students.

I have written biblical commentaries, technical studies on Jeremiah and Ezekiel and the Deuteronomistic History, monographs on the development of the book of Isaiah, a theological commentary on Colossians, books on hermeneutics and prophetic literature and the relation of Old Testament and New Testament, and scores of technical articles on Genesis, Job, Ecclesiastes, Isaiah, Jeremiah, Psalms, Exodus, and most of the material of the Old Testament. I have edited several books that cross disciplines.

As I now look back on my own education in biblical studies, I can reflect on the different experiences I have had. After university I even taught high school students "JEDP" and "Q" and "special Luke" and "authentic Pauline epistles" before attending seminary. God only knows what they took away from that. I had fairly standard introductory and advanced courses in seminary, and then attended the University of Munich for several terms. I was intrigued by the standards and the discipline of German biblical criticism. My first interest in Brevard Childs was via his Exodus commentary, which had appeared and was highly regarded as a model, if ambitious, deployment of critical methods so as to evaluate the final form of the text.[1] Provocatively, he said the text's prehistory had a counterpart in its reception history, which he spent considerable space evaluating, and both helped illuminate the presentation of the final form and its unique contribution.[2] At the

---

[1] Brevard S. Childs, *The Book of Exodus: A Critical, Theological Commentary*, OTL (Philadelphia: Westminster, 1974).

[2] "The section on the history of exegesis offers an analogy to the section on the prehistory of the text. The one deals with the period before the text's

time I did not understand much about what a canonical approach meant and did not know why he included a section on history of interpretation. I was far more interested in his command of source, form, tradition history, and the general development of the text from oral to written form.

I was privileged to study with him and in time to be his colleague and friend. Our offices were next to each other, and more generally it was an exciting time to be at Yale. A young James Kugel was teaching there then. The theological and historical faculty were impressive and engaged across their respective disciplines (Hans Frei, George Lindbeck, David Kelsey, Paul Holmer). Old and New Testament colleagues discussed each other's domains and read each other's books. Childs produced a New Testament introduction at that time.[3] I team taught with Leander Keck on several occasions.[4]

Yale was the first place where critical methods were taught with great rigor *but at the same time* were also the subject of an equally rigorous evaluation. I suppose it was the generally high regard that Yale had for history as a discipline as such. Critical methods had a history, they cast a shadow, they belonged on a longer timeline than those who proposed them often liked to think. Before Wellhausen there were Spinoza and Hobbes, Simon and Astruc, Reuss and Kuenen and Eichhorn. And before them all were Calvin,

---

complete formation, the other with its interpretation after its formation. Both have a significant, albeit indirect, relationship to the major task of interpreting the canonical text. The history of exegesis is of special interest in illuminating the text by showing how the questions which are brought to bear by subsequent generations of interpreters influenced the answers which they received. No one comes to the text de novo, but consciously or unconsciously shares a tradition with predecessors" (Childs, *Exodus*, xv). The present work will explore both of these dimensions as well though toward a slightly different end, as will become clear, it is hoped.

[3] Brevard S. Childs, *The New Testament as Canon: An Introduction* (Philadelphia: Fortress, 1984).

[4] See now his *Christ's First Theologian: The Shape of Paul's Thought* and his *Why Christ Matters: Toward a New Testament Christology* (Waco, Tex.: Baylor University Press, 2015).

Luther, Erasmus, Rashi, Aquinas, Cassiodorus, Augustine, Jerome, Theodoret, Theodore, Athanasius, Hilary, Irenaeus, and Origen. All of them were sophisticated interpreters who knew what history was, if in a register different than the one from the eighteenth and nineteenth centuries animating modernity.

I have had the opportunity, in addition to a year of teaching high school students, to teach Lutheran seminarians headed for the most part into parish ministry, inner-city Philadelphia pastors, nondenominational and international divinity school students at Yale, university students of varied backgrounds in Scotland, and most recently Ph.D. and M.A. students at Wycliffe College in Toronto, a school in the Toronto School of Theology. As one can see in the pages to follow, I have taught basic critical methods as appropriate to the strength of conviction with which they were held by the wider discipline of Old Testament studies. These were the methods in which I was trained, and the canonical approach I would come to adopt in time was deeply indebted to them for trying to understand the peculiar character of the biblical narrative as it presented itself, undeniably with a depth dimension of some kind that such methods sought to interpret and reconstruct. That has been the starting point for my interest in the Bible from the earliest moment of my formal study of it.

I have therefore thought of this present project as a commentary on critical method with an appeal to taking seriously the ontology of the Old Testament—its unique presentation of monotheism—as this opens onto theological formulation.[5] It is written in the light of my own long study of the biblical text and my experience over almost forty years teaching it formally, and examining students in accordance with the historical-critical methods said to be appropriate to its proper interpretation. But I have also written it in the spirit of my Yale years onward and my sense that the methods as passed on needed rigorous interrogation precisely to the degree

---

[5] The concerns that will arise here are anticipated in my "The Trinity in the Old Testament," in Gilles Emery and Matthew Levering, eds., *The Oxford Handbook of the Trinity* (Oxford: Oxford University Press, 2011), 28–40.

they were on the—just partially—right track. One version of the canonical approach resisted having it conflated with what was being called "canonical criticism" because the impressive series of nineteenth- and twentieth-century criticisms had done their appropriate serial work and now needed to be put in the service of something else.[6] Exactly because they had exhausted a certain kind of depth inquiry, appropriate in accordance with the canons of their investigation, to honor them would also be to let them stand in their integrity and do their work, so that another angle of vision that took them cumulatively seriously, though provisionally, might be brought into play.

In the first half of this book I try in a non-technical way to signal where new critical developments are at work in the field of Old Testament studies (the present state of Pentateuchal criticism; the Book of the Twelve; the Law, Prophets, and Writings; canon formation) with the hope of encouraging further study. I know this landscape as a student, teacher, researcher, author, and supervisor, and I respect it and what it means to contribute to it. My modest goal here is to take it seriously enough to turn it this way and that and see if its provisionality can be seen as an asset, and as leading to something finally truer to the way the biblical text places itself decisively before us and asks us to learn its ways of speaking. This will also include asking if we are worthy to be readers at all—those of us who come to the Old Testament by means of the Israelite who opened the sacred books for outsiders to the covenants, and without God in the world, showed them to be about him and so finally also about us (Luke 24:27-47; Eph 2:11-22).

Because I have touched upon what I write here in previous works and have labored to commend the same in the context of alternative approaches and views, I can direct the reader to those works and to the interlocutors I have judged most important in the present field of scholarship. I am writing a book for critical

---

[6] See my own evaluation in *The Character of Christian Scripture: The Significance of a Two-Testament Bible* (Grand Rapids: Baker Academic, 2011), 27–91.

readers who have already embarked on a serious, critical journey and may wonder if they are seeing the length and breadth of what it means to read the Old Testament critically and theologically. So I will not burden them with a long footnote discussion they may not know the precise details of, portions of which they will likely contact as their interest deepens or as they are forced to come to grips in the course of more advanced study. My concern is to keep things in perspective. Methods are meant to illumine interpretation and are not meant to be studied for their own sake. They are tools, not masters. The Old Testament is sufficiently masterful as it declares its word to us. I want to come alongside that and let its mastery master us.

The first part of the book will deal with conceptual and orientational matters, including what one should call "the literature." The term "Old Testament" has been rejected by many for not allowing the Jewish or historical dimension of this material sufficient scope in interpretation, and "Hebrew Bible" has been suggested as an alternative. Yet there is a particularly Christian appreciation of the character of the first witness of the Bible that is shared both with historicality and with Judaism more generally, but admits of extensional significance as well—not as a retrospective overlay but arising from the same literal sense displaying the concrete historical dimension as well as later Jewish sense-making as such. This in turn raises the question of just what such an extensional potential looks like, and how one grounds it in exegesis that is open to wider scrutiny and does not arise in the conventicles of theological preunderstanding. It is an extensional dimension arising from the historical and literal sense. The section ends with a question about whether one can be a reader of this "Elder Testament" on the terms that it presupposes, that is, as a privileged account to a special Israel in divine relationship.

The second part will engage modern critical approaches to the Old Testament/Hebrew Bible in the form that is likely familiar to more advanced students of the Bible. The perspective of canonical reading is introduced in part 1, and the way in which it handles the Law, Prophets, and Writings will be set forth in part 2. The canonical reading engages deeply with the findings of modern critical approaches but sees these are improperly attuned to theological evaluation focused on the peculiar character of the final form of the biblical canon. From time to time the late-modern reading proposed by canonical hermeneutics gives way to, and allows access to, earlier perspectives in the history of interpretation. Of particular concern is evaluating the potential of the canonical form for disclosing matters, not just of history/economy, but also of creation/ontology. The final form speaks of historical disclosures that themselves, due to the divine subject matter, correlate the theological identity of God across diverse dispensations.

The third part will pick up this concern more specifically through several important test cases, involving Proverbs 8, Genesis 1, Psalms 2 and 110, and other significant Old Testament texts notable for their appearance in the earlier history of interpretation. Lectionary pairings of Old Testament and New Testament texts, as these have arisen in the previous midcentury and are now widely read on Sunday mornings in Catholic and Protestant churches, actually operate with the same fields of association we can see in part 3 of this work. They frequently showcase typological and figural associations that in turn preserve theological convictions of the Christian church in shimmering dress. One wonders how often the genius of lectionary pairings—at least as a form of biblical theology—is truly appreciated in the life of the church for whom they have been prepared and who is confronted by them Sunday by Sunday. I hope that part 3 will introduce the reader to the ontological pressure exerted by Old Testament texts that gave rise to the earliest expressions of Trinitarian reading in the Christian church, indeed before a formally analogous scripture arose bearing the now-familiar name "New Testament."

In sum, the title of the book is meant to reflect three interlocking realities in respect of the Elder Testament, and the book unfolds along these same lines. First, "canon" refers to a literary reality with hermeneutical implications. The word points to matters of association and arrangement in the present form of the text as a literary feature. In the earliest use in respect of scripture, canon referred to "order" and "sequence" and "totality" and "the mind and thrust" of the biblical text in association with other texts, and it had a theological underpinning.[7] The earliest use of the term in this realm was generated for reasons of theological hermeneutics. Because the God of Israel was held to be the God revealed in Jesus Christ by the Holy Spirit, the theologically associative lens on scriptures' different parts followed naturally, was strongly defended, and finally held to be indispensable to proper exegesis and interpretation. So it is important to come to terms with this alliance between literary coherence, proper readership, and the subject matter of the Elder Testament as ontologically associative in character.

Part 2 will be devoted to exploring the canonical coherence of the final form of the Elder Testament, not by dismissing cases of alternative arrangements or by rejecting historical-critical readings, but by allowing these proper scope so to shed light on the achievement of the final form of "the Law and the Prophets." This section will allow us to look at the canonical achievement of the Old Testament as a way of introducing the major contours of the diverse library of biblical books it contains. Canon here refers to an "achievement of association."[8] Alternative orders as these arise in Jewish and Christian reception will also be evaluated.

---

[7] See my discussion in *Figured Out: Typology and Providence in Christian Scripture* (Louisville, Ky.: Westminster John Knox, 2001). Also, the important work of Frances Young, *Biblical Exegesis and the Formation of Christian Culture* (Cambridge: Cambridge University Press, 1997). On the semantic confusion associated with the word "canon" in the modern discussion over closure and stability, chiefly in the North American usage, see Stephen Chapman, "The Canon Debate: What It Is and Why It Matters," *JTI* 4 (2010): 273–94. For an evaluation of the different appeals to the term canon in respective European and North American contexts, see Brevard S. Childs, "The Canon in Recent Biblical Studies: Reflections on an Era," *ProEccl* 14 (2005): 26–45. I have discussed the problem of having the word "canon" refer primarily to closure and lists in *The Goodly Fellowship of the Prophets: The Achievement of Association in Canon Formation* (Grand Rapids: Baker Academic, 2009).

[8] The term is used in my 2009 work *Goodly Fellowship*; in *Prophecy and Hermeneutics: Toward a New Introduction to the Prophets* (Grand Rapids: Baker Academic, 2007); in *Character of Christian Scripture* (2011); and in relation to the

Part 3 will return to the driving concern of the book as a whole: the literal sense of the Old Testament with its extensional potential to deliver via the historical witness a larger sense-making at the level of theological ontology. Far from rejecting the historical dimension, it will be held that just this witness pressures forth the mature theological interpretation that emerged in the earliest Christian handling of it. Canon to theology to Trinity, then, is not a strictly sequential track but one ontologically calibrated through time by the One God who is the selfsame subject matter of its two main parts, Elder Testament and New Testament. Clement of Alexandria would then be correct in referring to canon as "the concord and harmony of the law and the prophets in the covenant delivered at the coming of the Lord" (*Stromata* 6.15).

I would like to thank Carey Newman for undertaking this project and for enlisting useful readers of the manuscript, alongside his own sage counsel. Diane Smith and her team at BUP did timely and professional work as well, which I acknowledge with gratitude. I have benefited from previous teaching with Mark Elliott in the history of interpretation, and seminars at Wycliffe with PhD students have given me the opportunity to become more conversant in this rich legacy. My colleague Ephraim Radner and I have run bi-annual conferences on the interface between scripture and theology over the past decade, and he is a constant source of encouragement and inspiration. Mark Gignilliat has been a helpful reader of this present work. Wayne Lott prepared the index. I would especially like to thank Don Collett. I always learn much from our conversations and from his own careful contributions in the area of ontology and the literal sense of scripture. I mention with gratitude the colleagues and supportive friends in Church and academy I have been privileged to know over the past years in France. Je rends grace à Dieu for the unfailing support of my wife Elizabeth.

Pauline Letter Collection in *Colossians*, Brazos Theological Commentary on the Bible (Grand Rapids: Brazos, 2013).

PART ONE

ORIENTATION

The goal of part 1 is to establish the proper bearings for exploring the contents and approach to follow in the main part of this book. Here we seek to enter the necessary compass headings for the reader. We hope also in consequence that the character of the title and subtitle will become clear.

The opening chapters will therefore introduce and clarify terms of reference. Chapter 1 will explain why the language of "Elder Testament" is being employed in our study as a wider conceptual lens over the more typical "Old Testament" or "Hebrew Bible." Chapter 2 addresses the use of the term "canon/canonical approach" as this has taken form in the recent period. The term has at ground a concern with theology and hermeneutics, as we will see from the example of Irenaeus we provide in the course of our evaluation. Unfortunately, the word "canon," as many will confront it in the modern period, is now primarily associated with questions of literary stabilization: the number of books, the sequence, institutional closure, and the sociological forces behind all this. We wish to free the word to operate in a different and more original context and so to highlight the theological concerns animating reflection on One Bible in Two Testaments.

Following these two brief studies, we can turn to the literal sense of the Elder Testament and how it may be said, from out of its specific historical situated-ness, to give rise properly to extended sense-making. We take up one prominent example of biblical theology from the recent period that has sought to give scope for appraisal of the subject matter to which the literal sense pointed as a legitimate part of the exegetical task of the Christian church.

In the final chapter of this section we look at a related concern. The examples of Christian interpretation from the early church, as these arise in non-Jewish circles, everywhere give evidence of commentators embarking enthusiastically on exploration of a book now available to them for the first time. The privileged character of the witness, as personal talk to a chosen people, is accepted as critical to how the witness does its theological work. Yet in the light of a dominical warrant to take up and read afresh, the chosen ones enter the world of Elder Testament as honored invitees, and reading with the grain see the theological portrayal of this One God as pressuring forth an extended sense deeply imbedded in how the Elder Testament speaks of God. Our concern is with keeping clear the conditions on which modern readers approach the Elder Testament, especially against a generalizing hermeneutic that said "read the book like any other book," without thinking very carefully about the special hermeneutics every book demands of us.

1

Elder Testament
Introducing the Scriptures of Israel

As noted in passing above, in the recent period new terms of reference have been proposed to replace the terminology "Old Testament." This has happened for a variety of sometimes complementary reasons: because the term "old" has been thought, in the English language, to be pejorative in character; in order to respect the existence of these scriptures within Israel prior to the church's use of and renaming of them; or to dampen these scriptures' traditional claim on and use within a specific ecclesial context.

I have in other places defended the traditional terminology. Here I want to broaden the scope of the inquiry by looking at a different cultural context in which the pairing *l'Ancien Testament* and *le Nouveau Testament* are the terms of reference. I will propose that in our present English language context where the word "old" suffers from consumerist connotations, "Old Testament" quite likely means something like "Elder Testament." This is not an argument for changing the terminology, but for widening our conceptual lens on what the term "old" likely meant when in Christian circles the emergence of a second scriptural witness caused a change in how the scriptures of Israel were referred to, as part one of a Bible with a second, "New" testament.

It is reasonable to open a section on orientation with the basic question of proper terms of reference, that is, what to call this literature that forms the large first part of the Christian Bible. In the present era, especially in North America, the terms of use have been under discussion, and several alternatives to "Old Testament" have been proposed. I want to consider the issue from the standpoint of the French language to get perspective on challenges presented by the English language in the present cultural context of modernity. It is hoped that recourse to a different cultural context will help to gain perspective on what are arguably serious losses in how the word "old" once made its force felt when the scriptures of Israel became the Christian "Old Testament."

In the French language there are three different lexical possibilities for the English equivalents "old," "aged," and "former": *vieux/vieille*, *ancien/ancienne*, and *âgé/âgée*. The first set can have a pejorative overtone in French, as in "worn-out," "bygone," or "outmoded." One does not call one's parents "old" but instead one uses the word "*âgée*." An "old car" (*une vieille voiture*) is not a nice new one, and it isn't a valuable antique car either. *Vénérable* is not a possible synonym of *vieux*.

The second set, *ancien/ancienne*, has some subtlety in its usage in French that lacks an exact English equivalent. The word changes its meaning slightly depending on whether it comes before or after the noun it modifies. An *ancien advocat* is a "former lawyer." *Les meubles anciens* refers to "old furniture" or antiques. The latter phrase can have a slightly negative overtone in some cases, but this depends on the context. *Vénérable* is a possible synonym of *ancien*. In the biblical context, the plural *les anciens* is in English "elders" with the nuance of "wise," *les sages*.

Placed before the noun, the word *dernier* can function as the coordinate of *ancien*, as in the English pairing "former/latter." Placed after the noun, *dernier* reproduces the English adjective "last"; so *dimanche dernier* is "last Sunday." *Le dernier candidat* is also possible, however, as in "the last candidate."

The pairing that corresponds to Old Testament/New Testament in French does not use the sets *vieux/vieille* or *âgé/âgée* but *ancien/ancienne*. Though the adjective precedes the noun for the term "the Old Testament," or *l'Ancien Testament*, one does not have a corresponding *le dernier Testament* but rather *le Nouveau Testament*. One would not therefore translate in English "the Former Testament" and "the Latter Testament." "The New Testament" is the obvious translation of *le Nouveau Testament*. But the first literature is not *le Testament vieux* or *le Vieux Testament*. In the pairing *l'Ancien* and *le Nouveau*, as the French language refers to the two parts of Christian scripture, absent is the nuance of "outmoded," "bygone," or "not new" for the first literature. One might therefore for the first literature render into English "Elder Testament" for "Old Testament" to avoid the English language problem suggested by "Old" and "New"—which, in the modern period at least, leans toward a movement from "outmoded" to "better," "up to date," or "improved." If one wanted to capture the nuance preserved by the pairing *l'Ancien Testament* and *le Nouveau Testament* in French, "Elder Testament" or "Older Testament" or "Original Testament" would serve the purpose better.

One is referring here to the problem of a modern English-language nuance and not one that is of necessity resident in the word "old." In antiquity the scriptures the church first possessed were only in time referred to as "Old" due to the emergence of a second literature. At that point in time, "Old" meant venerable, original, and time-tested.[1] The early church fathers routinely appealed to the antiquity of these writings as a warrant for

---

[1] See Gerald Bray, "The Church Fathers and Biblical Theology," in Craig Bartholomew et al., eds., *Out of Egypt: Biblical Theology and Biblical Interpretation* (Grand Rapids: Zondervan, 2004), 23–40.

diminishing the hold on culture that the philosophical literature of the age had. Clement of Alexandria writes page after page in the *Stromata* about the time-tested and prioritized character of the scriptural legacy inherited by the church; if the philosophical writings got anything right, they unknowingly had borrowed it from Moses.[2] We will discuss below the way in which especially non-Jewish interpreters judged their access to this Old Testament a great privilege and, consistent with the dominical excursus on the road to Emmaus, assumed it was a treasure chest awaiting disclosure of all manner of embedded riches. By contrast, the danger with the word "new" in "New Testament" was the possible nuance "novel" and "untested" measured against the original and ancient witness, and so specifically Christian claims had to argue for the balanced truthfulness and integrity of Old and New both.

I have written in defense of the traditional terms of reference used in English, as against substitutes, such as Hebrew Bible, First Testament, and so forth.[3] The former term has even led to the practice within certain circles of referring to the second witness as "The Christian Bible"—even Marcion realized to make this

---

[2] Clement (c. 150–c. 215) makes the point especially urgently in book 6. Origen is even more insistent in the next generation in his work *Contra Celsum*. A representative quote, from among myriad examples, comes from book 1, chapter 18: "And challenging a comparison of book with book, I would say, 'Come now, good sir, take down the poems of Linus, and of Musaeus, and of Orpheus, and the writings of Pherecydes, and carefully compare these with the laws of Moses—histories with histories, and ethical discourses with laws and commandments—and see which of the two are better fitted to change the character of the hearer on the very spot.'" Similar arguments continue through eight books. The Christian church has access to this enormously superior and truthful testament to God, which the second witness confirms, presupposes, and reiterates. Origen, *The Song of Songs: Commentary and Homilies*, ed. Johannes Quasten and Joseph C. Plumpe, Ancient Christian Writers 26 (Mahwah, N.J.: Paulist, 1957).

[3] "Old Testament or Hebrew Bible? Some Theological Considerations," *ProEccl* 5 (1996): 292–303; "On Not Changing Old Testament to Hebrew Bible," *ProEccl* 6 (1997): 136–40; *Word without End: The Old Testament as Abiding Theological Witness* (Waco, Tex.: Baylor University Press, 2005).

work one would have to take away 85 percent of the New Testament due to its dense reliance on the first witness to establish its claims about God and Jesus Christ. The term "Second Testament" seems like a demotion or an openness to "Third Testament." It is crucial for the Christian church, in my view, to have the same nominal term balancing both witnesses ("Testament") so that the covenantal continuity is center stage. The challenge, then, in the English language context of modernity, with its fascination with things "new," is how to avoid the pejorative overtones of "old" (fine for Scots whiskey and golf courses, but otherwise difficult). That the French language terms of reference have succeeded in large measure where English has not may be a simple accident of language possibilities across cultures, or it may have to do with different evaluations of what history continues to say and exhibit, in the Old World context of Europe and a France that highly values its *patrimoine*.

What this French language example shows, however, is that other possibilities exist for handling the character of continuity and of change the two terms "Old Testament" and "New Testament" bespeak. If "Old Testament" as a term suffers from misconstrual due to modern cultural realities in a New World setting, perhaps the best thing to do is offer a conceptual alternative less prone to misunderstanding. So the title of the present study, which will go on to explore the important character of the scriptures of Israel in other ways, may best open onto the discussion by using a fresh conceptual term—not to replace "Old Testament" and "New Testament" but rather to stimulate reflection on just how this Elder Testament is scripture of the Christian church.

There is another set of reasons why the term "Elder Testament" may properly resonate. One has been mentioned already. When one hears reference to *les anciens* in church in a French context, the phrase is almost universally positive. "The Elders" are revered leaders who serve in important roles due to their "life experience"—as we refer to it in modernity. In Israel and in the church birthed from it, the elders maintain memory, uphold norms whose veracity has withstood the test of time, and take responsibility for justice and proper stewardship of the past for the present generation. They are *les sages*, the wise. The Elder Testament is this kind of Old Testament. Its oldness is a fact that inheres within its own extended scope. It took time to be what it is in distillation and in aging over centuries. It says what it says, and then that finds a new point of reference in God's disposing through time. This typological or figural reality is confirmed in the Second Witness, with its language of fulfillment and accordance, but this patterning and associating impulse is deeply at work within the First Witness and helps explain its growth and scope as such.[4]

In addition, the Bible frequently explores the range implied by elder and younger in various ways across both testaments. The prodigal and the older son. Jacob and Esau. The young David and the young Joseph who nevertheless rise above older brothers. And most fundamentally, as Romans 9–11 has it, the original natural tree Israel and the transplanted church. Jacob tricks the elder Esau out of his firstborn birthright, but he must come to terms with that supplanting all the same and its costs of wounding and renaming (Gen 32:13–33:20). Or David supplanting the chosen Saul but learning at some risk to himself that the first king's office must be honored and respected, as well as the man Saul himself, indeed in his brokenness (1 Sam 16–31). Or a church that in its boastfulness would overthrow the very plan of God in bringing those far off to a nearness that is the domain of an elder relationship and an elder planting of love and commitment (Rom 11:1-36). And the cry of the Father, "Son, you are always with me and all that I have is yours, yet it was fitting" (Luke 15:11-32).[5]

---

[4] One thinks of former and latter things in the development of the book of Isaiah, for example, and kindred associative efforts within the Book of the Twelve and the Psalter, to choose some more obvious examples. See my discussion in "Isaiah 40–66," in vol. 6 of *The New Interpreters Bible*, ed. Leander E. Keck (Nashville: Abingdon, 2001) or more recently *Joel*, ITC (London: Bloomsbury, 2016).

[5] The provocative study of Jon D. Levenson comes to mind in this context: *The Death and Resurrection of the Beloved Son: The Transformation of Child Sacrifice*

So perhaps the word "Elder" has a certain fittingness for describing the character of the relationship between Old Testament and New Testament beyond seeking a more accurately nuanced term for the first witness given the yearnings of modernity. It is of course Jesus Christ who in himself is the elder and the younger, the old and the new, the Israel and the gentile graft; he is the covenant of an elder Passover celebration becoming the new covenant meal for the whole world at one and the same moment in time, crucified under Pontius Pilate and before the foundations of the world. The one who shared the "oldest possible life" with God and who said as well, "Behold I make all things new."

---

in Judaism and Christianity (New Haven: Yale University Press, 1995). Also, Gary Anderson, "Joseph and the Passion of Our Lord," in Richard B. Hays and Ellen F. Davis, eds., *The Art of Reading Scripture* (Grand Rapids: Eerdmans, 2003), 198–215.

2

Canonical Interpretation of the Elder Scriptures

As applied to matters of introduction and interpretation of the scriptures Old and New, the term "canonical" has had a bumpy ride. In North America particularly, the adjective and its noun form pushed one rather immediately into the realm of lists of books, their scope and sequence; into questions of closure and stabilization and the social and religious forces said to be critical of the emergence of a canon. Debates arose over whether one might helpfully distinguish "scripture" from canon, whether it is possible to speak of an "open canon," and how or if the two scriptures Old and New might be compared in the same domain concerned with canonical lists and institutional closure. With this context of discussion dominating, it would be very difficult to use the term for a different, hermeneutically primary purpose. At issue is how the term canonical might properly exist in the context of exegesis and hermeneutics, and only derivatively move us into material questions of the scriptures' literary stabilization.

In this chapter I will seek to ground use of the term in the earliest context of its circulation, that is, arising from reflection on how the scriptures' many-faceted pieces properly fit together, and how the One God of the scriptures' first witness is the same One Lord God of the church's confession. The canon of truth or of faith is what was appealed to in both instances, and it remains in that sense that we wish to use the term canonical with reference to our approach to the Christian Old Testament. That is, at stake here is the grounding of the term canonical, such as we will be using it in the present book, in the properly hermeneutical and theological context of its initial use.[1]

In the context of the New Testament (or the literature that will in time be referred to with that term), and in respect of the people who inhabit its pages, there is a single scripture. Modern debates about its scope and the character of its stabilization at the time leave untouched the fact that there is still only one sacred testimony, called variously "the Law and the Prophets," "it is written," "the oracles of God entrusted to the Jews" (Rom 3:2), "the scriptures" (Acts 17:2; Rom 15:4, et passim), "Moses and the prophets and the psalms" (Luke 24:44), "whatever was written in former days"

---

[1] A good recent discussion of terminology, and how much of the debate founders due to divergent starting definitions, can be found in Stephen Chapman, "The Canon Debate: What It Is and Why It Matters," *JTI* 4 (2010): 273–94. A full bibliography is available there and a fair evaluation of the positions of Ryle, Barton, Sanders, McDonald, Ulrich, Sundberg, Swanson, Gamble, van der Toorn, Ellis, Beckwith, and others. For a comparison of North American and European reference to canon in biblical interpretation, see Brevard S. Childs, "The Canon in Recent Biblical Studies: Reflections on an Era," *ProEccl* 14 (2005): 26–45. I argue for a core canon of Law and Prophets encircled by Writings whose number and character is less decisive and self-consciously so. This in turn makes the idea of "closure" far less central to a proper evaluation of canon and allows the hermeneutical and theological achievement at the heart of the Old Testament to find proper emphasis (*Goodly Fellowship*, 2011).

(Rom 15:4), "all scripture" (2 Tim 3:16), nor "sacred writings" (2 Tim 3:15). The earliest possible reference to the developing writings of the second witness being referred to with the nomenclature "scripture" is possibly the letters of Paul as referred to by Peter in 2 Peter 3:16.[2] When we read 2 Timothy and Romans 15, the situation is the same: the scriptures being commended as given by God to instruct in faith are the scriptures of the people of Israel. The creed of later church life uses the language of 1 Corinthians 15:3 when it speaks of Christ's life, death and risen economy as "in accordance with the scriptures."[3] Paul insists that Christ died for our sins "in accordance with the scriptures," repeating the phrase twice. In the Gospel of John these scriptures have been provided to give a clear window onto the present life and death and rising of Jesus Christ, but their meaning is not grasped.[4] When the "other disciple" reaches the tomb and believes, it is noted that this is what the scriptures were proclaiming despite the disbelief still in place amongst the disciples (John 20:9).

The situation for the earliest Christian commentators is the same. When they formally cite scripture, they cite texts which appear in what we now call the Old Testament. It would take more than one generation for the situation to change and for a second witness to be cited in parallel fashion.

---

[2] Alexander Sand, "Überlieferung und Sammlung der Paulusbriefe," in K. Kertelge, ed., *Paulus in den neutestamentlichen Spätschriften* (Freiburg: Herder, 1981), 11–24; Brevard S. Childs, *The Church's Guide for Reading Paul: The Canonical Shaping of the Pauline Corpus* (Grand Rapids: Eerdmans, 2008).

[3] Christopher Seitz, "'In Accordance with the Scriptures': Creed, Scripture and 'Historical Jesus,'" in *Word without End: The Old Testament as Abiding Theological Witness* (Waco, Tex.: Baylor University Press, 2005), 51–60.

[4] The difficulty of grasping what the scriptures plainly deliver is a running theme in the Fourth Gospel (John 2:22; 5:39; 7:38-39; 12:16) though the beloved disciple manifests his proper understanding at the cross (19:35-37) and empty tomb (20:8), and as omniscient narrator. See my discussion in *Figured Out: Typology and Providence in Christian Scripture* (Louisville, Ky.: Westminster John Knox, 2001), 91–101.

It is for this and for other reasons that one does not see use of the term "canon" in the New Testament writings, that is, as a formal term related primarily to the status and scope of scriptural literature. In the modern period, one may be inclined to hear the word canon as having to do with conciliar decisions related to order and number and scope and closure of those writings deemed to be central and sacred. But there are no such events or institutions when it comes to the scriptures of Israel and their status as scripture as modern readers may mean this with reference to the word canon.[5] It may further be dubious to freight the word with such events and institutions when it comes to the New Testament as well, though the usual practice is to say these institutional gatherings exist and then to assume that there must be an analogy in respect of the Old Testament. Yet it is the existence of a sacred literature held as such within the people of God, and making this claim about itself, that forms the basis for what will develop into a second sacred literature, in time to be referred to as scripture on analogy and cited as such in the same manner as the first testamental record.[6]

---

[5] It would be difficult to locate a contemporary scholar who believes in a "Council of Jamnia" (proposed by Heinrich Graetz in 1871) responsible for fixing the Old Testament canon, a notion rejected by Jack P. Lewis in 1964 and seconded by Frank Cross, Albert Sundberg, Sid Leiman and others. Lewis also wrote the ABD entry on the so-called Council where he reprised his earlier position (*The Anchor Bible Dictionary*, vol. 3, 634–37 [New York: Doubleday, 1992]).

[6] Even Adolf von Harnack understood this reality about the scriptural inheritance of the Elder Testament and its influence on the correlate New Testament. In commenting on Lessing he writes: "[Lessing] perceived that the New Testament as a book and as the recognized fundamental document of the Christian religion originated in the Church. But Lessing did not recognize that the Book from the moment of its origin freed itself from all conditions of its birth, and at once claimed to be an *entirely independent and unconditioned authority*. This was indeed only possible because the book at once took its place beside the Old Testament, which occupied a position of absolute and unquestionable independence because it was more ancient than the Church" (von Harnack, *Bible Reading in the Early Church* [London: Williams and Norgate, 1912], 145; emphasis original). As I described in my volume with coeditor Carl E. Braaten, *I Am the Lord Your God: Christian Reflections on the Ten Commandments* (Grand Rapids: Eerdmans,

In the modern period the use of the terms canon, canonical, or canonical interpretation, then, does not seek to seize upon some institutional warrant for how or why sacred scripture functions as such within the people of God.[7] Use of the term canon does not require one to develop and defend a complex theory of how the Law, Prophets, and Writings came to be, were stabilized, and their outer limits were set. Of course one can undertake to understand this process and to create a plausible reconstruction of its stages.[8] But it is crucial to understand that this modern interest in what is called "canonicity" is just that.

When the term canon appears in early Christian commentary—as noted, it forms no meaningful network in the New Testament or its language about the scriptures inherited and thoroughly appealed to in speaking of them or their relationship of accordance—it has a more hermeneutical and explicitly theological purpose.[9] The second century church father Irenaeus provides a classic example. He speaks of the "canon of faith"—*kanon* or *regula*—as "the foundation and support of our conduct." He is not using the word canon here to refer to lists of biblical books or institutional councils within which decisions might be rendered about books being sacred and set apart

---

2005), "This last quote is fighting on the main front of Lessing (the NT has authority only because the church gives it), but in so doing reveals a remarkable statement about why the authority of the NT took hold as it did, viz., because it followed and was paired with the authoritative scriptures of Israel, which already possessed this status" (37).

[7] See the perceptive essays of Stephen Chapman on divergent conceptualities in the canon discussion, especially in North America ("The Canon Debate"; and "The Old Testament Canon and Its Authority for the Christian Church," *ExAud* 19 [2003]: 125–48).

[8] I have my own accounts in *The Goodly Fellowship of the Prophets: The Achievement of Association in Canon Formation* (Grand Rapids: Baker Academic, 2009) and *The Character of Christian Scripture: The Significance of a Two-Testament Bible* (Grand Rapids: Baker Academic, 2011). Most recently, "Ketuvim and Canon," in Julius Steinberg and Timothy J. Stone, eds., *The Shape of the Writings* (Winona Lake, Ind.: Eisenbrauns, 2015).

[9] Leaving aside for the moment use of the term in respect of canon law, calendars, registers of clergy, and so forth.

or not. The rule or canon in fact consists of articles concerning God's character as God. Canon functions in an explicitly theological context. It concerns God the Father, the Word of God his Son, God the Holy Spirit, and the baptismal sacrament, which brings us into this life and in so doing regenerates us. It will be useful to have the text in front of us.

> This then is the order of the rule (canon) of our faith, the foundation of the building, and the stability of our conversation: God, the Father, not made, not material, invisible; one God, the creator of all things: this is the first point of our faith. The second point is: the Word of God, Son of God, Christ Jesus our Lord, who was manifested to the prophets according to the form of their prophesying and according to the method of the dispensation of the Father: through whom all things were made: who also at the end of times, to complete and gather up all things, was made man among men, visible and tangible, in order to abolish death and show forth life and produce a community of union between God and man. And the third point is: The Holy Spirit, through whom the prophets prophesied, and the fathers learned the things of God, and the righteous were led forth into the way of righteousness; and who in the end times was poured out in a new way upon mankind in all the earth, renewing man unto God. And for this reason the baptism of our regeneration proceeds through these three points: God the Father bestowing on us regeneration through His Son by the Holy Spirit.[10]

The role that scripture—here is meant the scriptures of Israel—plays in this theological and sacramental rule is crucial to grasp. This is spelled out by Irenaeus through the predications he assigns to each article. The Word of God, the Son, Jesus Christ "was manifested to the prophets according to the form of their prophesying and according to the method of the dispensation of the Father." It must be emphasized strongly, in line with the above, that the basis

---

[10] Irenaeus, *Demonstration* 6–7.

of this knowledge of God the Word, Jesus Christ, *is the scriptures of the Old Testament,* not yet referred to by that term, given the developing character of a second witness. Irenaeus is undoubtedly aware of apostolic writings, and one can sense allusions to them at times, especially to the degree they are speaking of the revelation of the scriptures of Israel in kindred terms.

Jesus Christ the Word is revealed as such by the prophets. This happens in accordance with the "form of their prophesying and according to the method of the dispensation of the Father." At issue here is that the witness of God the Father to the Son is varied depending on the prophetic voice—and here "prophets" is a reference not to one specific section of the scriptures but to their character as a whole as capable of disclosing Christ. These disclosures are not predictions of something to come in time, though that may be one of their "forms," but rather entails God's economic disclosures of Christ the Word in the scriptures' own literal sense. We know this very clearly from the way Irenaeus goes on to relate these in the numerous Old Testament examples to follow. The Hebrew of Genesis 1:1 is translated, "The Son in the beginning: God established then the heavens and the earth."[11] Jacob sees him upon the ladder.[12] The Word spoke with Moses out of the bush. The language Irenaeus uses to describe the ruled truth disclosed by the Elder Scripture is significant. He writes, "For in them the Word of God prepared and rehearsed in advance the things concerning

---

[11] Irenaeus, *Demonstration* 43. Jeremiah and the Psalter support this view as well, Irenaeus submits. *Bereshith* is heard as *en arche* which in turn is taken to be a title for Christ the Word. See the thorough and illuminating discussion of C. F. Burney, "Christ as the APXH of Creation (Prov. viii 22, Col. I 15–18, Rev. iii 14)," *JTS* 27 (1926): 160–77. Also, Christopher R. Seitz, *Colossians*, Brazos Theological Commentary on the Bible (Grand Rapids: Brazos, 2014), 86–101. An extended discussion of these matters is found in part 3 below.

[12] The figural significance is clear: "And Jacob, when he went up from Mesopotamia, saw Him in a dream, standing upon the ladder, that is the tree which was set up from earth to heaven: for thereby they that believe on Him go up to the heavens" (Irenaeus, *Demonstration* 45). This is not a predictive sense only but one already operative within the economy of Israel's life with God.

us." We can now see this clearly, as Paul noted, because the rock from which this water gushed pre-formedly (*promeletao*) is the rock himself. The Word gave us twelve springs (Exod 15:27), that is, the teaching of the twelve apostles, giving us an inheritance "who also delivers us from Amalek by the expansion of His hands, and brings us to the kingdom of the Father." This is what Irenaeus means when he speaks of the economies of God the Father disclosed in respect of the Son within the single scriptural testimony. The rule of faith is that which the church acknowledges as being disclosed about God the Father, Son, and Spirit from a single scriptural foundation. As Irenaeus puts it, "He set forth in types beforehand that which was to be."[13]

In the wake of the use of the term canon to refer to a species of biblical interpretation in the modern period, associated with the work of James Sanders, Brevard Childs, Rolf Rendtorff, and others, several objections have been lodged. To the degree to which the term in the modern period (especially in North American circles) refers to material questions of the scope and stability of the biblical writings under question, it tends to misfire as a way to understand the hermeneutical concerns resident in canonical approaches. As one can see in the writings of Irenaeus, it will also misfire when it comes to use of the term along the same lines in early church conceptuality. The word canon can and does have a role to play in evaluating—not just the final stages of a collection's stabilization but also the early and medial episodes of canonical shaping. But if this comes at the cost of misunderstanding the theological and hermeneutical dimensions that stand at the center of the term's historical use, the term will have become dislocated and distorted. The materialist question is simply too narrow a conceptual field on which to force the term to play its proper role.

As we see in Irenaeus, the term arises as a way to think about the character of the sacred writings as disclosing an ontological truth about God through the economies of his life with Israel. On this

[13] Irenaeus, *Demonstration* 46.

account, the character of God as triune—Irenaeus' three baptismal articles "as renewing man unto God"—is not a claim arising outside of the influence of scripture.[14] The "New Testament" does not yet exist as a correlate scriptural witness on analogy with those sacred writings Irenaeus gives attention to, given his place in time. Further, the early church did not possess a confessional conviction *ad extra* it then sought to find warrant for in an ancient source it invariably and anachronistically mishandled. The articles of faith and life are already pro-formed and bearing witness "set forth in types beforehand." The claims to antiquity and providential preparation are critical to support what God in the end times is doing and has done.

Even in the debates running up to Nicene formulation, the unavoidable terrain of God-talk was the words, sentences, paragraphs, books and testaments of a scripture held to be responsible for pressuring forth what the church believed.[15] We know that convictions about the single Elder Scripture being at least binitarian—God and the Word of God—were shared by Jews and Christians of a certain theological orientation when it came to the literal sense of the Old Testament at the period in question (the School of Antioch wrestled here, though the term *theoria* was used to acknowledge levels of sense-making across time).[16] Irenaeus and others of his

---

[14] Armitage Robinson's translation of this passage of Irenaeus reads, "God the Father bestowing on us regeneration through His Son by the Holy Spirit" (*Demonstration of the Apostolic Preaching*, trans. Armitage Robinson [London: SPCK, 1920]).

[15] The matter is taken up in detail in part 3 below, and especially in relation to the use of Prov 8:22-31 and other Old Testament texts in doctrinal debates of the period.

[16] Binitarian interpretation is discussed in chapter 15 below. On *theoria*, see the excellent survey of Bradley Nassif, "'Spiritual Exegesis' in the School of Antioch," in Bradley Nassif, ed., *New Perspectives on Historical Theology: Essays in Memory of John Meyendorff* (Grand Rapids: Eerdmans, 1996), 343–77. On Antiochene exegesis and *theoria*, see Christopher Seitz, "Psalm 2 in the Entry Hall of the Psalter: Extended Sense in the History of Interpretation," in Ephraim Radner, ed., *Church, Society, and the Christian Common Good* (Eugene, Ore.: Cascade, 2017), 95–106.

contemporaries did not believe the scriptures just pointed beyond themselves to a moment in time freshly to be regarded as Incarnational Time. Rather, the scriptures spoke of God in his personal life with Israel in time in ways that bespoke his eternal character as triune. The apostolic writings insisted on this in their own ways when it came to the critical role occupied by the scriptures of Israel as a witness fulfillable. But before there was a New Testament, the single scriptures disclosed the life of God, God the Word, and God the Holy Spirit in a way that belonged to its character as rule or canon. Precisely in this pre-formed form it became the center of determined efforts by Christians and Jews properly to understand the literal sense-deliverances it was held to convey.

The term "pre-formed" in Irenaeus, alongside use of the lexical stock associated with "figures" and "types"—sometimes by recourse to the word for other sense-making or *allegoria* for other commentators of the period—helpfully gets at another aspect of canonical interpretation more specifically relevant in the historical-critical environment in which it has risen more lately. Canonical interpretation has been viewed by some as a kind of synchronic, final form reading, perhaps best appreciated when the role and influence of the reader on interpretation is in turn factored in.[17] That is, it participates in a general shift away from objectivist readings, which held sway at the heyday of historical-critical reading. But to view canonical interpretation this way is to misunderstand the approach and its manifest location in time as arising from out of historically oriented reading. No one can read the Exodus commentary of Brevard Childs and come away with the sense that a new-critical, final form, reader-oriented approach has replaced

[17] John Barton's useful handbook does not confuse synchronic and canonical readings, though he views the latter without appreciation of the theological dimension ingredient in it (*Reading the Old Testament: Method in Biblical Studies*, 2nd ed. [London: Darton, Longman and Todd, 1996]). See my discussion in *Character of Christian Scripture*, 27–91.

older source-, form-, and tradition-historical methods.[18] What is being sought is a way to understand the complex final form of the text as itself arising from a myriad of historical and religious factors, whose probing is necessary if we are to appreciate the text as we now wrestle with it in the form that lies before us. Much of the present book will investigate the indebtedness of canonical reading to previous methods, which in their turn moved toward a higher prioritizing of stages in development and not appreciation of the final form as anything much beyond a starting point of reconstructing a history of religion.

When Irenaeus uses a term like "pre-formed" he is speaking about a providential overseeing by God whereby the revelation given to Israel in concrete times and places says what it says meaningfully but also bespeaks realities subsequently to be disclosed. Given his horizon of concern, this chiefly means accordances by type from the dispensation of Israel to the dispensation of the church, as the apostolic deposit holds that to be so, progressively pressured by the single scriptural witness. But given the unique character of this single "oracles of God entrusted to Israel" as consisting of a canonical testimony with a vast historical range and sustained life of hearing and rehearing within the people of God through time, the pre-formed and typological dimensions rise up already within the Elder Scripture itself in what has been referred to as the canonical process. So attention to the final form is attention to the entirety of a process of development, with appreciation for how the *tota scriptura* of individual books and larger canonical divisions are themselves commentaries on a rich prehistory of disclosure and rehearsal on the ground of Israel's lived life with God.[19]

Here is where Irenaeus' temporal and theological recourse to the term "recapitulation" finds its warrant. The quote from above therefore continues, "according to the method of the dispensation

---

[18] See by comparison the new commentary by Christoph Dohmen, *Exodus 1–18*, HThKAT (Freiburg: Herder, 2005).

[19] Part 2 will pursue this dimension more fully.

of the Father: through whom all things were made: who also at the end of times, to complete and gather up (*anakephalaiosasthai*) all things, was made man among men, visible and tangible, in order to abolish death and show forth life and produce a community of union between God and man." At issue here is not a reversal of Adam's fate by the New Adam narrowly conceived, but the entire drama of God's life with Israel being taken up by the Word who lived within that life, now in a form "visible and tangible" at "the end of times." God the Word is the living, pre-formed Word that is disclosed in the canonical form of the scriptures as a text conveying through its final form what God means to continue to use to disclose himself.[20]

In the present work when the term canonical or canonical interpretation is used, it refers to the providentially overseen character of the text, whose early and medial phases can be speculated on in ways, some more persuasive than others, so as to appreciate the ongoing form of the witness Israel has received, pre-formed through its rich life with God. The term canon will in the modern period participate in domains having to do with the scope and stabilization of two distinctive collections of sacred writings. But use of the term in the early church points toward concerns hermeneutical and theological as the overriding ones. In our use of the term here, we share these concerns. I have written several books dealing with the modern debate

---

[20] Irenaeus puts it thus: "The Son of God did not then begin to exist (at the incarnation), but was with the Father from the beginning; but when he became incarnate, and was made man, He recapitulated in Himself the long history of human beings, and furnished us, in resume, with salvation, so that what we lost in Adam—to be according to the image and likeness of God—that we might recover in Christ Jesus" (*Against Heresies* 3.18.1). John Behr glosses, "The Incarnation, therefore, is not an absolute beginning, but a recapitulation of the continual presence and activity of the Word" (Behr, "Scripture, the Gospel, and Orthodoxy," posted December 12, 2003, at Orthodox Christianity, http://www.pravoslavie.ru/english/7163.htm).

Canonical Interpretation of the Elder Scriptures 33

over canon formation and stabilization.[21] This is terrain that will be set to the side in the present work so to recapture the main lines of concern the term canonical interpretation has sought to foreground in our present season.

The title of an important essay by Kavin Rowe indicates the proximity to concerns to be developed in this book, "Biblical Pressure and Trinitarian Hermeneutics."[22] At the beginning of the discussion, he comments to the effect that the fight for the Trinitarian confession was a fight *for* the Old Testament. The historical dimension is not to be obscured for precisely it gives rise to levels of meaning that pressure the theological articulation of Trinitarian faith.[23] In what follows a canonical reading seeks to give proper attention to the findings of historical-critical labor precisely so that the theological heart of its canonical articulation can be appreciated as the final form of the text has set this forth.

To conclude, use of the term canonical points to theological hermeneutics that allow the proper subject matter of scripture to be disclosed.[24] As John Behr has stated it,

> The canon of truth, then, is not so much a list of obligatory beliefs, but a hypothesis or presupposition for reading Scripture as Scripture—to see in it the image of the King, rather than simply as a curious collection of ancient texts which might be interesting for what they say, but do not have much to do with our relationship to God. The canon, in this sense, and this is its

---

[21] In *Character of Christian Scripture* (2011) and *Goodly Fellowship* (2009) most recently.

[22] C. Kavin Rowe, "Biblical Pressure and Trinitarian Hermeneutics," *ProEccl* 11 (2002): 295–312. He notes the similarity of the comment by Brevard S. Childs to that made by Karl Barth, *Church Dogmatics* I/1 (Edinburgh: T&T Clark, 1936), 319.

[23] The essay of Rowe offers a superb and clearly articulated example of this dimension. We discuss the divine name in greater detail below.

[24] In *Against Heresies* Irenaeus uses the word canon to refer to baptismal faith as rooted "in the order and connection of the scriptures" (*tēn men taxin kai ton eirmon tōn graphōn*) (*Against Heresies* 1.8.1–1.10.3).

primary sense, is . . . seeing the whole of Scripture in the light of Christ and as speaking of Christ, the Old Testament invisibly in types and enigmas, the New Testament in a clear epitome." He then quotes the famous line from Clement of Alexandria, who defines canon as "the concord and harmony of the law and the prophets in the covenant delivered at the coming of the Lord" (*Stromata* 6.15).

3

Theological Interpretation of the Elder Testament

A major concern of the present work is the ontology of the Old Testament, that is, how the depiction at the center of the Elder Scripture—the divine life of the One Lord God YHWH—opens onto and indeed pressures a specifically Christian reading of the triune God as arising from this first scriptural witness. When the second testament uses the language of fulfillment or accordance it has in view the conviction that the Lord of the church's confession is both spoken forth from and somehow resident within the divine life as Israel has experienced and born witness to that in the scriptures.

Due to the preoccupation with a certain species of reading that emerged in the eighteenth century—focused on the historical origins and development of the Old and New Testaments and the original authors and their first audiences—an entirely new direction in exegesis was demanded.[1] Not the mature and aged product of the final form, but the barley, yeast, water, and peat of the original, prior to distillation, became decisive in offering up the religious dimension in its pristine, prescriptural aliveness. Earlier, medial, and later stages were all carefully set out, debated, recalibrated, debated afresh, and replaced. The "history of God" soon followed, as God's identity was understood on analogy to have developed from historically diverse influences available through archeological penetration into the comparative religions of the time. "God" was the religiously impulsed expression of peoples who thought this way and wrote down what they thought and passed it along. The referentiality of the biblical text was not a transcendent divine truth, but the history about which it spoke, to which it referred, and the human authors one could range within it, and their attendant ideas about the deity. These ideas required differentiation and proper historical specificity. "Anachronism" would refer to any confusion resulting in not keeping the historical specificity achieved through speculation and scientific method—akin to the natural sciences—strictly in observance. At times one might reflect on figural associations that seemed to arise and resurface even within the conceptual landscape of historical reconstruction, but care needed to be taken to avoid "reading later things back into earlier things" as the great faux pas most resolutely to be avoided. Human authors had single historical intentions, and the historical-grammatical approaches, conservative or skeptical, were calibrated to keep exegesis fixed on the target of historical specificity in time and the intentionality of an author—maximally identified with the canon's apparent referent (Moses or Isaiah or Paul) or minimally so brokered and instead to be critically excavated.

The problem with this focus on "authorial intention" was the evaporation of the presentation of the final form as having its own intentionality. And chief within this canonical achievement was the

---

[1] See the magisterial account of Hans Frei, *The Eclipse of Biblical Narrative: A Study in Eighteenth and Nineteenth Century Hermeneutics* (New Haven: Yale University Press, 1974).

Theological Interpretation of the Elder Testament 37

decision to make associations through time and across time at the level of human intention that provided a portrayal of rich historical signification all its own—indeed as lying at the very heart of God's acts and self in time with a people. The very signal achievement of the canonical form was ignored as accidental or obscuring or a neutrality waiting for reconfiguration. It was as if the scientist dismantled the clock to find out what time it was.

In this chapter I want to have a second look at a serious effort to rethink the relation between the biblical text and its referentiality, understood to be the divine life as such. The *littera* or letters of scripture—taken in the larger sense as its canonical achievement of coalescing generations of testimony into a coherent, if challenging final form—have a consistently theologically referential dimension, referred to on occasion as the *res* or subject matter to which the scripture refers. I will press the matter farther than its proponent was prepared to go, and then seek to test the theological subject matter as appropriate to exegesis in part 3 of the present work. This will be possible once the canonical hermeneutics in relationship to the shape of the scriptures has been set forth and evaluated.

The focus here is on a model for biblical theology set forth in 1992 by Brevard Childs. Our effort in this context is to move beyond some hesitancies he registered regarding the "discrete voice" of the Elder Scripture and extend other aspects of theological reading he adumbrated in that important work. His is one of the few recent efforts to link modern critical reading to classical dogmatic formulation from the Bible's long reception in the church's life, and so it is natural to work from this base.[2]

---

[2] A reformed proposal for Old Testament "christotelism" and varieties of narrative unfolding/story theology/tradition-history are popular alternatives. For a trenchant review of the first of these, see Don Collett, "Christotelism and the Old Testament," published as "Reading Forward: The Old Testament and Retrospective Stance," *ProEccl* 24 (2015): 178–96. See also Christopher Seitz, "Two Testaments and the Failure of One Tradition–History," in *Figured Out: Typology and Providence in Christian Scripture* (Louisville, Ky.: Westminster John Knox, 2001), 35–48. Walter Brueggemann and John Goldingay offer models that emphasize the distinctive theological/ideological contribution of the first

In 1992 an ambitious model for biblical theology was published. Both Old and New Testaments were covered. It was over five hundred pages in length.[3] It represented the culmination of serial efforts to think theologically and canonically about the Old Testament and New Testament.

One feature of the approach adopted by the author, which ironically summoned critical questioning, was his dedication to set forth what he called the "discrete witness" of the scriptures of Israel. One could see in this section the massive investment, over a lifetime of work, Childs had made in traditional critical scholarship. As in earlier works, however, this investment was geared to highlighting what he wished to describe as the canonical shape of the books of the Old Testament, which best yielded up what he saw as its theological contribution as Christian scripture. So the term "discrete witness" was not simply a rehearsal of historical-critical investigation, even as a reader unaware of Childs' earlier work or not deeply conversant with it might see this section as rather traditional historical evaluation, given Childs' penchant for wanting to evaluate the field on the terms that predominated at the time. One can read this section and see Childs the historical-critical scholar operating on the terms the discussion had called forth, and then giving his signature commendation of the canonical shape.

Here is where the term "ironic" comes into play, for many who read the work in its entirety wondered if the appeal to a discrete witness was in fact a brake on how the Old Testament might properly be read as Christian Scripture, which was manifestly what

---

witness and resist any wider coalescing on the grounds of critical economic differentiation. I discuss Brueggemann's model in *Figured Out*, and offer a brief response to Goldingay in "Canon, Narrative, and the Old Testament's Literal Sense: A Response to John Goldingay," *TynBul* 59 (2008): 27–35. A very ambitious effort to present a theology of Old and New Testament can now be seen in Reinhard Feldmeier and Hermann Spieckermann, *God of the Living* (Waco, Tex.: Baylor University Press, 2015).

[3] Brevard S. Childs, *Biblical Theology of the Old and New Testaments: Theological Reflection on the Christian Bible* (Minneapolis: Fortress, 1993).

Childs was arguing he was doing in this book.[4] Many argued that the Old Testament, even in Childs' winsome canonical evaluation, remained unacceptably discrete and too captive to the then-reigning historical-critical conceptuality.

The close reader of course would be aware that, as usual, Childs himself was conscious of this line of questioning, and indeed puzzled aloud about it himself. In a section in the middle of the work, before moving forward to do theological reflection on the double witness of Old and New Testament, as he had set this forth thus far, he raised the question of the relationship between the discrete witness and the subject matter to which it referred. In earlier works one can find much sober evaluation of the nature of the *sensus literalis* of the Old Testament and how this literal sense could never be immediately collated with what in the eighteenth century emerged as "the historical sense."[5] Appreciation of the *sensus literalis*, in all its characteristic richness, is the perennial challenge and theological duty of each age, and any account must be able to come to terms with the flexibility of this dimension of scripture and especially its openness to subsequent elaboration later in the canon as ingredients in what makes scripture what it is. This explains why some category of figural reading, including allegory, must be countenanced as proper to a grasp of the Old Testament's sense-making.

The distinction between letter and subject matter (*res*) is crucial to proper appreciation of what Childs in this work is seeking to do.[6] The subject matter of scripture, and this includes the Old Testament

---

[4] For a good example, see Francis Watson, *Text and Truth: Redefining Biblical Theology* (Grand Rapids: Eerdmans, 1997). My engagement can be seen in "Christological Interpretation of Texts and Trinitarian Claims to Truth," *SJT* 52 (1999): 209–26. See now Brent A. Strawn, "And These Three Are One: A Trinitarian Critique of Christological Approaches to the Old Testament," *PRSt* 31 (2004).

[5] Childs, "The Sensus Literalis of Scripture: An Ancient and Modern Problem," in Walther Zimmerli, Herbert Donner, Robert Hanhart, Rudolf Smend, eds., *Beiträge zur alttestamentlichen Theologie: Festschrift für Walther Zimmerli zum 70. Geburtstag* (Göttingen: Vandenhoeck & Ruprecht, 1977), 80–93. Compare Frei, *Eclipse*.

[6] He draws upon Gerhard Ebeling for this distinction, which in turn is found in Luther and in the history of biblical interpretation preceding (Aquinas).

most ambitiously, is, in Childs' conception, "Jesus Christ."[7] The issue I am raising in this chapter is just how one understands the dimension we might call "ontological referentiality," for it does not simply mean pointing from its place in time to a place in time commensurate with the incarnation as the New Testament records this.[8] The economic dimension is, to be sure, there; Jesus Christ was born under Herod and crucified under Pontius Pilate. He is the son of David, King of Israel, and the term "Christ" means to lay claim to prophetic talk from the Old Testament in which its ground sense is declared. But the literal sense's pointing to the subject matter Jesus Christ is more than an economic referentiality. There is an ontological dimension that must be given proper scope and authority, because the subject matter Jesus Christ is himself "God of God, Light of Light, very God of very God," of one substance with the only true God, who speaks and lives and acts within the covenant life of Israel and is attested to on the pages of its sacred scripture. Jesus Christ died and rose again in accordance with this scripture and in deepest ontological relationship to the God so declared there to be God.[9]

---

[7] "The challenge of Biblical Theology is to engage in the continual activity of theological reflection which . . . seeks to do justice to the witness of both testaments *in the light of its subject matter who is Jesus Christ*" (*Biblical Theology*, 79; emphasis added). Yet at a different place he will also remark, "The task of Biblical Theology in its theological reflection goes beyond that of seeking to describe historically how God was understood in both testaments, but seeks to move from the biblical witness *to the substance of the witness, which is God himself*" (*Biblical Theology*, 369; emphasis added). This movement from "Jesus Christ" to "God himself" may be a matter indifferent in Childs' formulation, or it may point to an area of possible confusion. My concern here is to explore this issue.

[8] See the remarks of Irenaeus in chap. 2 above.

[9] Childs will therefore also register this caution as he surveys the ground he is trying to claim. "Yet it was a fatal mistake of some forms of Biblical Theology when dealing with the identity of God to feel it could reflect on the subject matter only in terms of its historical sequence. This appeal to the so-called 'economic Trinity' would restrict the doctrine of God to the divine workings within a historical trajectory of past, present, future: God, Christ, Spirit . . . However, the attempts to describe God's identity merely in terms of his acts,

When one comes to this section of Childs' reflections, then, he must properly raise the question of how the substance to which scripture refers is to play a role in exegesis of the literal sense of the discrete witness of the Old Testament. Would it not be artificial to exclude it, having given it a proper and essential role in how one handles the literal sense richness that is a given in how the Old Testament speaks, and not just a retrospective overlay fighting for space where it does not belong, except as anachronism and theological contrivance? Elsewhere Childs speaks of the coercion of the literal sense and the pressure that it exerts at the level of its basic communication, prospectively.[10] Other scholars had picked up on this notion and usefully extended it as well.[11] New Testament scholars helpfully pointed to how the second witness is driven by the plain sense articulation of the first, precisely because the One

---

apart from his being, is not a serious theological option for either Biblical or Dogmatic theology. The subject matter itself requires that proper theological understanding move from the biblical witness to the reality itself which called forth the witness" (370). Our concern here is to press the matter further, assuring that "the subject matter" or "reality" is consistently trinitarian in character.

[10] See Frei's important observation about the *prospective* character of figural pressure in Calvin's exegesis. He is commenting on the character of biblical narrative more broadly when he writes, "The point is not really that the land of Canaan was a figure of the future inheritance at the time if, and only if, 'the Israelites' knew it to be such. More important is the fact that they enjoyed the land as a figure of the eternal city, and thus it *was* a figure at the time. It is not a figure solely in later retrospective interpretive stance. Calvin is clearly contending that figural reading is a reading forward of the sequence. The meaning pattern of reality is inseparable from its forward motion; it is not the product of the wedding of that forward motion with a separate backward perspective upon it, i.e., of history and interpretation joined as two logically independent factors. Rather, the meaning of the full sequence emerges in the narration of the sequence, and therefore interpretation for Calvin must be, as Auerbach suggests it is for the tradition at large, part of the flowing stream which is historical life" (*Eclipse*, 35–36; emphasis original). We take up the insights of Auerbach in more detail below.

[11] Especially C. Kavin Rowe, "Biblical Pressure and Trinitarian Hermeneutics," *ProEccl* 11 (2002): 295–312; "Romans 10:13: What Is the Name of the Lord?" *HBT* 22 (2000): 135–73.

God conception of the first witness is what pressures the claims being made about Jesus Christ as worthy of worship at his right hand.[12] Claims of literal sense pressure and the unique character of Elder Scripture monotheism, in other words, do not arise independently of scripture's theological legacy but arise perforce from within its own scope and testimony, as making sense of how the One God of Israel and the Risen Lord belong eternally in the same domain of being. Hence we note the awareness and conviction of Childs that ontology is not a subsequent theological icing but must be accounted for within the scope of scripture's own witness and sense-making. What the New Testament shows us of this dimension, moreover, is a critical but nevertheless partial view of what the Old Testament in its richness and complexity and range intends to yield up.[13] *Beginning* with Moses and the Prophets, Luke tells us, the Risen Lord explained the things about himself. The New Testament does not choose to spell out that first Easter Bible lesson but instead points to the warrant for our theological reading of the scriptures of the One God as grounded in the Lord who shares with him the divine life.

So when Childs proceeds to consider this dimension and its proper role in Old Testament sense-making, he speaks of the subject matter to which scripture refers with the term "triunity."[14] At issue is how properly to evaluate this reality and still permit the Old

---

[12] Richard Bauckham, *God Crucified: Monotheism and Christology in the New Testament* (Grand Rapids: Eerdmans, 1998); David Yeago, "The New Testament and the Nicene Dogma: A Contribution to the Recovery of Theological Exegesis," *ProEccl* 3 (1994): 152–64.

[13] I develop this point in my books *The Character of Christian Scripture* (2011) and *Colossians* (2014) as well as in "Jewish Scripture for Gentile Churches: Human Destiny and the Future of the Pauline Correspondence—Part 1: Romans," *ProEccl* 23 (2014): 294–307; "Jewish Scripture for Gentile Churches: Human Destiny and the Future of the Pauline Correspondence—Part 2: Colossians," *ProEccl* 23 (2014): 457–70.

[14] Cf. Childs, *Biblical Theology of the Old and New Testaments*, "full divine reality in its Triunity" (380) and "the substance of the witness, which is God himself" (369).

Testament to reside within its own critical, theologically providential historicality. Childs correctly judges simple imitation of the New Testament witness and its handling of the literal sense of the Old Testament as a threat to how the Old does its own work as Christian Scripture; it fuses the second witness with the first. The first witness speaks of the God with which the Son is one and so must be allowed its own literal sense declaration in order to grasp the second witness' claim. All this cautionary talk has a certain force working within the canonical framework of two witnesses speaking to one subject matter distinctively.

Yet there is another dimension to handling the subject matter to which the first witness refers. One can see this aspect in the way Childs does not restrict his comments to fusion of the literary witness of two different testaments. This is a larger question than the bald move to "read back into the story the person of Jesus Christ," which, in my view, he wrongly collates with a move "to interpret the various theophanies as the manifestation of the second person of the Trinity." For the first takes an economic reality disclosed in time and delimited by the cruciality of its earthly manifestation, and extrudes it into a previous economic time where it is does not belong. In Childs' compact expression, "theologically one cannot fuse promise with fulfillment."[15] Even allegorical reading did not function on this plane for the most part but saw rather the voice of Christ arising from the psalms, for example, as the psalms' own contribution and not a back-fusion of the earthly Jesus based upon a mechanical reinsertion. One can judge the conceptuality faulty, but that is what was at work all the same.[16]

But what is confusing in his comment is restricting the logos of God from having some active life within the covenant relationship, leaving aside for the moment whether theophanies are an appropriate

---

[15] Childs, *Biblical Theology of the Old and New Testaments*, 379.

[16] I discuss this issue in "Psalm 34: Redaction, Inner-Biblical Exegesis and the Longer Psalm Superscriptions—'Mistake' Making and Theological Significance," in Christopher R. Seitz and Kent Harold Richards, eds., *The Bible as Christian Scripture: The Work of Brevard S. Childs* (Atlanta: SBL, 2013), 279–98.

place to find this activity. Identifying an ontological reality at work in the Elder Testament is a different level of literal sense rendering than fusing the second witness and the first, because it proceeds on the basis of the theological pressure of the *sensus literalis*. I want to underscore this dimension of the literal sense in some respect in sympathy with what Childs himself elsewhere approves of, namely, an openness to a "multi-level reading of scripture." As he begins to conclude his careful reflections in *Biblical Theology of the Old and New Testaments* with the section "Reading Scriptures in the Light of the Full Divine Reality," he writes this: "Exegesis which comes to the biblical text from a larger theological grasp of God's reality [cannot] function apart from the various other historical and critical readings."[17] That is, one can properly speak of extensional sense-making if rooted within the literal sense, a mode of reading often termed figural or typological. The hyperbole of a realistic David (or "Psalmist") in Psalm 22, because it matches an economic manifestation in the New Testament, can be held to be divine intention via the literal and providential sense-making of the Old Testament *per se*. Calvin frequently noted the excess in expression uttered forth by the historical David in the Psalms ("I can count all my bones") or about his kingdom, and concluded this was providentially embedded so as to figurally anticipate through realistic historical portrayal the reality of Christ. Indeed this is what the New Testament means when it speaks of fulfillment or accordance across time, and it is a view it takes based on the literal sense deliverance of the first witness. This is not reading back Jesus Christ into Psalm 22 but hearing the passion in its light and as descriptive of the entire episode.[18] Undoubtedly this is why Childs concludes his own treatment rather elegantly, if provisionally, with a citation of John Donne on the literal and figurative God, following his own use of Isaiah 53 as explicative of Christ's passion due to what

---

[17] Childs, *Biblical Theology of the Old and New Testaments*, 379–83.

[18] Christopher Seitz, "Psalm 2 in the Entry Hall of the Psalter: Extended Sense in the History of Interpretation," in Ephraim Radner, ed., *Church, Society, and the Christian Common Good* (Eugene, Ore.: Cascade, 2017), 95–106.

Theological Interpretation of the Elder Testament 45

he calls its "immediate morphological fit."[19] One might have hoped for yet further examples, but the cautious evaluation of the section draws to a close.

That said, Childs has opened the door to some form of evaluation of the theological subject matter, even as he has shied away from greater specificity and illustration. He writes in the same section just quoted: "Rather, it is constitutive of true interpretation to move within a circle which encompasses both the movement from text to reality as well as from reality to text. That subtlety is required is obvious. The movement from *res* to witness dare not destroy the historical voice of the text" (381). So the real question that arises is just how the historical voice might be said properly, and *prospectively*, to be declaring a movement within the circle being described, from text to reality and from reality to text. We have mentioned typology already. There is also the ontological interpretation we see clearly at work in the early church, and especially in Irenaeus, Justin, and Tertullian. The logos of God is the active means by which God makes himself known within Israel, given the non-polytheistic portrayal that lies at the heart of the Old Testament's theological significance. So it can be argued that it is the literal sense of the Old Testament that is generating, within its own grammar and syntax, the theological design of ontology. The "morphological fit" is then not just at the level of economic figural intention but belongs to the ontology of One God who is "incarnate" by means of his Word to and with Israel.[20]

Irenaeus provides innumerable examples of this ontological identification, as he sees it, illumining the scriptures of Israel. Speaking of Christ as logos, he writes:

> This is He who, in the bush, spoke with Moses and said, "I have surely seen the afflictions of my people who are in Egypt, and I have come down to deliver them." This is He who ascended and descended for the salvation of the afflicted, delivering us

---

[19] Childs, *Biblical Theology of the Old and New Testaments*, 379–83.
[20] See the chapter preceding and especially part 3 below.

from the dominion of the Egyptians, that is, from all idolatry and ungodliness, and saving us from the Red Sea, that is, from the deadly turbulence of the heathen and from the bitter current of their blasphemy—for in these [things] our [affairs] were preformed (*promeletao*), the Word of God at that time demonstrating in advance, by types, things to come, but now, truly removing us out of the cruel slavery of the heathen, He caused a stream of water to gush forth abundantly from a rock in the desert, and the rock is Himself, and [also] gave [us] twelve springs, that is, the teaching of the twelve apostles; and killing the unbelievers in the desert, while leading those who believed in Him and were infants in malice into the inheritance of the patriarchs, which, not Moses, but Jesus <gave us an inheritance>, who saves us from Amalek by stretching out His hands and leading us into the Father's Kingdom. (*Demonstration*, 46)

At issue here is not the detail of Irenaeus' explication as much as the ontological perspective he operates with reflexively. The first witness is not being retrofitted, moreover, by means of a fusion with the second—to use Childs' language. Irenaeus is explicit that the first witness has been so formed by God in its literal sense in advance; it is pre-formed. We can find similar ontological reflection in Origen, Clement, and Justin. It is the very fact of the preformed character that gives them such confidence about what is being held in respect of the outcome the latter witness—the "New Testament" in time—proclaims. Without this anteriority, God is not consistent with himself in time and eternity, and fulfillment becomes novelty and one-off presentation only. Having possession of the oracles of God is of inestimable value because only by this means does the church have a way to say the One God has made good on promises lying at the heart of his own eternity, made economically known to Israel in advance.[21]

The early church interpreters were obviously emphasizing the ontological dimension in a way that, especially in the light of

---

[21] See the quote from Clement of Alexandria on this notion, together with commentary, in chapter 16 below.

historicism, is difficult conceptually for our age. The economic ("crucified under Pontius Pilate") delivers its sense and significance when seen rhyming with the ontological ("God of God, light of light"). The named God of Israel is, in accordance with its own morphology, the Triunity. And from this ontological perspective, the economic arises to close the circle via the literal sense of the first witness. The economic and ontological are mutually reinforcing and impossible to extricate or prioritize.

I want to draw attention to one further conceptual challenge. Childs does not want to fuse the second witness with the first. We have rehearsed several problems that can result from this sort of fusion, consistent with his canonical concerns and the character of a two-testament witness. One warrant he gives in his cautionary remarks is "the Christian church does not have the same unmediated access to God's revelation as did the apostles," followed by a dictum he repeats in other contexts: "we are neither prophets or apostles." What the dictum points to is the reality that God mediates his divine life to the Christian church by means of a canon of scripture, now in a specific form. The prophets and apostles had no canon in the form we have it but enjoyed a relationship to God differently mediated. My question has to do with use of the term "unmediated access." On my ear it tends to overstate the apostolic perspective and to flatten it across the New Testament range. The prophets and apostles had a different access to the divine life than does the church. For each in their own way, that access was privileged and special to their dispensation. In this book the tendency to speak in developmental or improving terms about any phase of that access will be held up to question. Such a move usually results in an "apostolic" privilege over the "prophetic," and also to the "privilege" of the church over them both, via higher spiritual insight or churchly superiority. Erasmus can write that scripture presents to us, in Old Testament and in New equally, a picture of Christ that is "better than if we gazed upon him with our own eyes." The canon is the means by which God raises up faith, perfectly attuned to the divine purpose. John Behr has usefully described the Risen

Lord, now at God's right hand, as the subject matter to which both testaments equally refer; he is not the unmediated Lord but is always known by Word and Sacrament, logos and sign, even in his Risen Life shared with a circle limited in its size and in similar manner known to Israel via sign and Word.

The church possesses a second witness in which the earthly Lord has come, and it reads this witness from faith to faith. It comes to us from faithful apostolic witness, testifying to something we do not have on the same terms. But to attempt to rank immediacy and mediatedness from prophet to apostle, to apostle to church could romanticize and confuse what it means to speak of the Living God in Christ, who is the only mediator of all covenant life and who makes himself known sufficiently in difference and distinction overcome. We know there was a "fullness of time," and its economic significance is everywhere registered. But the canon is the means by which that "fullness" breaks out upon us, setting us alongside prophet and apostle because One God is at work through all time to bring creation to his final salvific purpose. "Blessed are those who have not seen and yet believe," the Fourth Gospel insists. The main challenge this book sets for itself is allowing the first witness the scope to do its peculiar and distinctive work in the One God's economic and ontological life with Israel and the church and all creation. Not fusing the witnesses, not ranking them, but allowing their distinctive contribution to sound forth to those of us who stand outside the circle of their specially mediated life with God.

Theological Interpretation: A Brief Postscript

We are living at a time when the phrase "theological interpretation" is au courant.[22] The phrase may serve primarily as a placeholder

---

[22] Most recently, Craig Bartholomew and Heath Thomas, eds., *A Manifesto for Theological Interpretation* (Grand Rapids: Baker Academic, 2016). Compare Kevin J. Vanhoozer, ed., *Dictionary for Theological Interpretation of the Bible* (Grand Rapids:

for a new tentativeness about what the older critical methods were supposed to accomplish, whatever else it may mean positively in terms of a fresh approach. I believe critical methods served the purpose for their day that those who used them wished. They exposed dimensions of the present text that went back to developmental factors and sought to highlight and reconstruct these. The concern of the present book is to understand where they are useful and where they have sought to replace the canonical text with a reconstruction more decisive than it. In that sense, ironically, they are not unlike extreme forms of allegorical reading in the life of the church, obscuring while promising great results. The history of interpretation shows each age wrestling with this or that obscuring cataract as the effort to set forth the literal sense against such a wide backdrop of literature—crucially in a specific two-testament form—is undertaken. There is nothing like the form of Christian scripture. Christians come to the first part via a second part that issues them library cards so they may read, while the second part also makes the claims it does in relationship to and literarily deeply indebted to the first part, so at times it is unclear what the real direction of reading is. It is for this reason that one will recognize in the chapters that follow a resistance to "narrative" as the key to understanding how this two-testament scripture is to be read,

---

Baker Academic, 2005); Kevin J. Vanhoozer, Craig Bartholomew, and Daniel J. Treier, eds., *Theological Interpretation of the Old Testament: A Book-by-Book Survey* (Grand Rapids: Baker Academic, 2005, 2008); Kevin J. Vanhoozer, Daniel J. Treier, and N. T. Wright, eds., *Theological Interpretation of the New Testament: A Book-by-Book Survey* (Grand Rapids: Baker Academic, 2008). There is a *Journal of Theological Interpretation* (Eisenbrauns) started in 2007. For further on where the term appears, see Daniel J. Treier, *Introducing Theological Interpretation of Scripture: Recovering a Christian Practice* (Grand Rapids: Baker Academic, 2008); Stephen E. Fowl, ed., *The Theological Interpretation of Scripture: Classic and Contemporary Readings* (Cambridge, Mass.: Blackwell, 1997); A. K. M. Adam et al., eds., *Reading Scripture with the Church: Toward a Hermeneutic for Theological Interpretation* (Grand Rapids: Baker Academic, 2006); D. Christopher Spinks, *The Bible and the Crisis of Meaning: Debates on the Theological Interpretation of Scripture*, T&T Clark Theology (London: T&T Clark, 2007); Joel Green, *Practicing Theological Interpretation* (Grand Rapids: Baker Academic, 2011).

and care to reflect on the canonical form of the Old Testament and the parameters within which it operates as scripture, in time to be read by outsiders to its covenants and promises, and indeed without God in the world—as Paul states it briskly in Ephesians 2.

One may observe in the field of Old Testament studies one approach that holds the Bible to be a container of diverse and distinctive materials, whose present arrangement is either meaningless or a false compromise to be identified and renegotiated so that the truth of the matter can better be seen. Another approach accepts that the present text has a rich and complicated prehistory and that one cannot understand its present shape without acknowledging that what it is, it is due to this lived history with a people. But it does not see the development of the text as one of contested positions vying for (a messy, literarily) ascendancy. The development is one of augmentation, complementarity, and the drive to defer to the past while allowing a coherent final product to speak above the heads of any single moment in time. The aggregating of the tradition cannot be sketched out in specifics but only reflected upon as best one can as a provisional exercise; it is simply too much a part of the warp and woof of the literal sense presentation as we now have it. The refusal to give up a single convincing reconstruction that will persuade all and settle the matter is itself a tribute to the providential character of an assembling process that has let a final text speak meaningfully in the way the words go, while retaining all the evidence of a claim to have spoken once before and because of the fateful character of that speech, to have gone on speaking and re-speaking through time. Our approach does not operate with an understanding that the Bible is a container of materials that must go through a processing phase so that something raw may become cooked and made edible, but holds the final form to contain the nutrients needed to educate and sustain, precisely because the form and subject matter as they address us intend thereby to process us.

4

"Can we read this book?"
Reader Response-ability

As a critical response to objectivist readings of the Bible—we can refer to these as historical-critical readings—another school of thought pointed out that we find in texts what we are looking for. The subjective dimension cannot be so tidily isolated and assumed no longer to be a factor once we put on our lab coats and carefully lay out shiny historical-critical scalpels. The methods of source-criticism in which the final phases of the cult were held to be legalistic Judaizing, did not just happen to emerge because experts were dispassionately following the evidence where it was said to lead. This specialist view fit with what one needed if the New Testament was to be read as a hard correction of the history of Israel's religion the canonical scriptures yielded up after deployment of the source-critical evolutionary method. Method and predisposition are very hard to disentangle, and unsurprising was the tendency of a certain kind of Christian specialist to reconstrue the canonical deposit of the Old Testament in this manner.

That being said, a strong reader-response correction will need to think carefully about whether the objection to objectivist reading is correct for reasons not anticipated. The Elder Testament is a certain kind of literature that has the right to ask for a readership consistent with itself as literature. It is not just any kind of text that needs to be guarded against objectivist specialism, in the name of acknowledging predisposition. At issue here is what the word "predisposition" means to be getting at. One can ask this from the side of the reader concerned to guard against preemptive scientific methods that ignore what is being brought to the text by the reader. But equally one can ask whether what is being read has not just a predisposition of its own kind, *but a more strenuous version of this than modernity may be accustomed to accept.* This ancient scripture of Israel declares the sense of what it is saying about God and to whom it is saying it along narrower tracks than one will be accustomed who buys books of every kind at the airport stall. The Elder Scripture is a privileged lens onto God and a people he has chosen for himself.

So this chapter takes seriously the place of the reader vis-à-vis the Bible and vis-à-vis objectivist reading both. It does so in the name of attending carefully to just what kind of a book the Elder Scripture is, including its peculiar form of "authorship," its protagonists, main themes, and careful denominating of Israel, nations, and sojourners as ingredient in how it says what it says and is what it is as literature.[1]

In the early modern period the exhortation was issued: "Read the Bible like any other book."[2] On the positive side the appeal

---

[1] I have a related treatment from an earlier context of discussion in "'And without God in the World': A Hermeneutic of Estrangement Overcome," in *Word without End: The Old Testament as Abiding Theological Witness* (Waco, Tex.: Baylor University Press, 2005), 41–50.

[2] Often the remark is attributed to Benjamin Jowett, and it is certainly consistent with his concern to free the Bible from its history of interpretation or other theological enterprises, as he saw them. Yet his was also a romantic idea of

could be taken as: dig in, take this seriously, get engaged. Don't let a religious tone or use keep the Bible at a distance. Read it as you would read any challenging piece of literature. Don't pay an homage that prevents you getting involved with its substance.

Resident in the appeal, however, was also: interrogate its religious claims. Just as any literature that would purport to speak for God or speak uniquely about him ought to be critically evaluated, so too this book. Claims to special revelation, divine election, the wondrous, unique historical events—in short, anything that made the book different from the world as we presently perceive it, with its laws of science and its resistance to unique events or one-off speech in time—must be dissolved.[3]

More recently the exhortation has been questioned on the grounds that literature is of widely varied nature, and to read the Bible like any book would beg the question as to *what kind of book the Bible is meant to be like*.[4] Every book must be evaluated in

---

perfect intercourse with the authors or the characters of scripture, unfiltered as it were. "The true use of interpretation of to get rid of interpretation, and leave us alone in company with the author" summarizes one theme from "On the Interpretation of Scripture," in *Essays and Reviews* (London: Parker, 1860), 384. Another is "Scripture has one meaning—the meaning which it had to the mind of the Prophet or Evangelist who first uttered or wrote, to the hearers and readers who first received it" (378). Our relation to the authors or first hearers is a fully natural and universal one and springs from an undifferentiated humanity able to read and hear whatever it chooses or happens to cross its path. This is more akin to the experiential-expressivist hermeneutic that George Lindbeck described in his *The Nature of Doctrine: Religion and Theology in a Postliberal Age* (Louisville, Ky.: Westminster John Knox, 1984). An insightful essay from the recent period offers a very good introduction to the issues at stake. See Walter Moberly, "'Interpret the Bible like Any Other Book?' Requiem for an Axiom," *JTI* 4 (2010): 91–110.

[3] Jowett's own concerns were kindred but a bit different. He thought one could commune with the author or audience in some kind of direct way and thereby get out from under religious debates or theological formulations from a later period. This morphed in time to what was called "hermeneutics of suspicion," something he did not emphasize in his more optimistic mid-nineteenth-century frame of reference.

[4] As Moberly notes (p. 99), Karl Barth turned the axiom upside down. "Biblical hermeneutics is not so much an application of general hermeneutics

continuity with what it purports to be: poetry, manual, phone book, historical fiction, novel, antique biography, annals of Assyrian kings, sermon from a church father, Wesleyan hymnbook, scientific report, minutes of a meeting.

There is a different kind of question these various observations point to, be they early modern or more recent, having to do with whose book this is and what kind of readership it presupposes. Consider the rival question of whether it is possible to read *Moby Dick* by Herman Melville, and whether our readership is anticipated. The answer to the second question is not only Yes, but it is a Yes the author himself hopes will be on our lips. Melville's purpose, whatever else he may believe about high aims in writing, is to sell books and to gain as wide a readership as he can. That his work can be read is tied up with his hope that it will be, as widely as possible. His intended audience is as broad as he as author can imagine.

Here the Bible shows itself to be that very different kind of book that makes the exhortation above go awry. The author of the book is not easily determined and in any event cannot serve on direct analogy to Melville. So the more accurate question to pose is, Whose book is this? The answer is that it is a book whose main characters are one particular people, and to whom the literature has been entrusted. "The oracles of God entrusted to the Jews" is how a later voice characterized it (Rom 3:1). So let's unpack that claim and see how it coordinates with the literature's presentation of itself.

No matter where you fall on the "read the Bible like any other book" spectrum, anyone who reads the Old Testament cannot miss the fact that it has a dominant character in the people of Israel, and that dominant character is also the main recipient of what God has to say about himself. That there are exceptions to this, which we will discuss below, does not detract from the overwhelming impression that whatever else it is, the Old Testament is a book

---

but the pattern and measure of all others." See Hans-Werner Bartsch, "Rudolf Bultmann: An Attempt to Understand Him," in Hans-Werner Bartsch, ed., *Kerygma and Myth* (London: SPCK, 1962), 2:125.

in closest association—not with an intended audience of Melville, and a hope for universally acknowledged tribute for what *Moby Dick* is as literature—with a single people. To them God speaks in a manner unknown to others.[5] They are the bearers of his speech and the purveyors of it as well.

And there is a material, historical dimension that needs to be reckoned with as well. During the time of its transmission and eventual stabilization as literature, it did not exist as books do today. You could not buy it and read it. You could not have a private "copy" of it to consult. For the vast period of its coming to be, it was delivered specially and preserved specially, in ways that scholarship can speculate about based upon the few clues it gives up, but which everywhere show it as the literature, traditions, passed-on accounts of a people, by a people, and for a people. To ask "Can we be readers of this material?" during this time would have to be answered "No." We are not Israel. We could not, moreover, even if we were Israel, have a private book form of it. We might encounter, were we Israel, portions of it in the form of delivered speech, or memoirs of such speech in the form of later transmissions. Were we late enough on the scene we might have overheard larger sections of it read aloud in public assembly (so Ezra-Nehemiah), or later still in time, in worship time, in scroll form. But this still holds true not for Melville's hoped-for audience, but for a single people. In the case of Israel, one had to come to this "book." If its subject matter is centripetal (God, Israel, the nations), its material reality is centrifugal: it exists in rarity and in special physical housing. It didn't come to you. And it most certainly didn't come to a generic "us."[6]

---

[5] Psalm 147:19-20, "He declares his word to Jacob, his statutes and ordinances to Israel. He has not dealt thus with any other nation," summarizes the matter well.

[6] The generic "us" would include of course what the Old Testament calls "the nations." For other reasons, however, modern Jews also relate to this "Israel" of the Old Testament in differentiated ways. See "Old Testament or Hebrew Bible," in *Word without End*, 61–74.

Consider further its actual subject matter. It does not open with an exclusive focus on Israel (Gen 1–11), and one can regularly see how much as literature it insists that the God who has spoken specially to Israel is as well the God of all creation and the God of all nations on earth. God uses nations. He allows his people to bump up against all nations and insists this has its own purpose in making him known. On occasion we see this happen, as with Ruth, or the sailors with Jonah headed to Tarshish, or as the sojourners who come out with Israel from Egypt. The special literature of the Elder Testament tells of these more general occurrences. The man Job is depicted by the literature about him as before any special calling of Israel, and the literature insists he encounters the One True God even before the revelation of his personal name in a special way in the second book of the Old Testament. God makes himself known through or by creation, but it is a making known whose character is understood for what it is by contrast to the vast proportion of the literature's own special register of speech and life to Israel.[7]

The answer to the question of readership, given the above, is that we can be readers, we who are not historical Israel (nor arguably even a Jewish people who also have now to negotiate a different kind of "distance" from the Old Testament's own assumptions about itself as a "book not like other books"). We can, but we do so, consistent with the book's own parameters, *conscious of our place outside the privileged speech and life of God with his people, as the Old Testament describes this, as central to what it is as a book.* We do so, in other words, because over the course of time, and because of subsequent historical and theological realities, a literature that had a circumscribed life and did not actively seek out a readership outside its own circle, and in many ways did not anticipate this happening in the manner we mean when we say it is like other books—which, moreover, had as its main subject and object a special, named God

---

[7] What may not be clear to Job is certainly clear to us: It is YHWH whose created life is displayed in specific ways to Job "out of the whirlwind" (Job 38:1).

in relationship to a special, named people—got opened up to a readership that upon reading it, knew themselves to be over-seers and over-hearers of a special book whose specialness entailed its relationship to a people they were not and we are not either.

On my view we can be readers only if we understand the character of our place vis-à-vis the special people and special life being described by the Old Testament. Outsiders looking in. People being talked about, not talked to. That would mean to be readers of the Old Testament on the terms of its character as a book, which is like other books, precisely as it is not like other books. That people open the book and become readers on other terms is of course possible because every book is open to being read against the grain. We would be readers who do not understand or who dispute the literature's comprehensive sense of itself and how it has set the character of its message into time, and inside of time, so now as to include our time. Otherwise we would be unwinding a clock and misunderstanding how it is that we come to have access to this book at all. That is, how a dial tone became a party line for us, or how a library card got issued to us that was already worn and had someone's name on it previously.

Modernity has asked us to read the Bible historically, with historical precision, in its historical context, attending to historical authors and processes. Yet at one very basic level it has often failed to attend to the historical parameters and limitations the Old Testament presupposes are part of *what makes it an historically specific literature*, given the material realities that attended its coming to be and its life with an historical people in whose midst it consolidated and stabilized.

Our Vis-à-Vis

On historical terms, it is fair to reflect on how we have become readers over the course of time. Some will imagine ourselves as part of a long storyline and then describe the beginning stages so they match up with where we believe we now are in time, as a kind of drama headed to you and me.⁸ We could, and many do, think of the Elder Testament along these lines, as the natural Part One en route to our Part Three via the Part Two New Testament, but this preempts the actual means by which we in fact become readers. For this One Big Story approach assumes the Elder Testament is ours on general terms, and all we need do is find a past niche to place its chapters in so they head toward a book and a place we might properly declare is ours (New Testament). But it is that same New Testament book that says our access is not on these terms. In the New Testament we are described as "strangers to the covenants of promise, having no hope and without God in the world" (Eph 2:12) who have been brought into a story, not one we are sovereign over by means of dramatic redescription. "Go nowhere among the Gentiles . . . but rather to the lost sheep of Israel" (Matt 10:5-6) isn't an unreflective command from an otherwise general Lord but one reflecting the reality of the matter as God means it to unfold.

On the road to Emmaus Jesus opens the book and says it is everywhere about him. Even here, he opens the book for his own

---

⁸ Don Collett's essay tracks this instinct in a christotelic modality, but it pertains more broadly to story or drama accounts of how the two testaments are related. These are extremely popular reckonings. They reach from the Bartholomew-Gorman "drama of Scripture" model to N. T. Wright's prodigious serial offerings. I have an evaluation of the latter in "Reconciliation and the Plain Sense Witness of Scripture," in Stephen T. Davis, Daniel Kendall, and Gerald O'Collins, eds., *The Redemption: An Interdisciplinary Symposium on Christ as Redeemer* (Oxford: Oxford University Press, 2004), 25–42. Collett's essay "Reading Forward" is extremely penetrating in its effort to forefront the "prospective stance" of interpretation of the Old Testament in the early church and later reception history; "Reading Forward: The Old Testament and Retrospective Stance," *ProEccl* 24 (2015): 178–96. See Craig Bartholomew and Michael Goheen, *The Drama of Scripture: Finding Ourselves in the Biblical Story* (Grand Rapids: Baker Academic, 2004). The "plot line" emphasis is not wrong of itself—see Stephen's speech in Acts 7—but it often reduces the theological and trinitarian pressure from the first witness to a retrospective ("back to front") account. See the language in "thesis 3" of Richard B. Hays and Ellen F. Davis, eds., *The Art of Reading Scripture* (Grand Rapids: Eerdmans, 2003), 2.

brethren from the house of Israel. And Luke does not describe what "in all the scriptures the things concerning himself" look like, but only the agent of its being so. If the book of Acts is meant to describe something of what that might look like—and this is nowhere stated clearly—what we see is a gradual movement into the land we inhabit as Gentiles outside of the covenants with Israel. Proselytes and God fearers approach tentatively, with questions, "about whom does the prophet speak?" (Acts 8:34). When at last we find a clearer point of entry, the leaders of the Jewish-Christian assembly identify us as the sojourners in Leviticus, who came out of Egypt alongside the covenant people and were given a place for which the torah of God provided standing (15:19-20).[9]

If we wanted to be readers of this book at the time in question, we can indeed see how that transpired. Acts 15 says that in every city Moses has been taught, and of course he is not taught through general purchase at a local book stall, but within and through the company of those entrusted with the oracles of God. Standing in the hall of Gentiles, or finding our way into the company of the synagogue readers and hearers of God's scriptural address, is how our concrete address and inclusion might be imagined. So whether by the Israelite born of Mary or by decision to affiliate and hear, as invitees, as guests wanting to be a part of this story through Jesus, only by this historical means do we gain access.

When the book is then opened and we listen, we find that we are part of the story, in the role of the nations outside of a relationship, but one that was intended to include us in time. This is a mystery, Paul says, hidden but truly there from the beginning. One might wonder how would we see this fact if it were not for an Israelite like Paul, now in Christ Jesus, to help us see understand this properly: as an act of adoption, or transplantation. Yet even at this point, how it might be said that we identify with the protagonists

---

[9] Christopher Seitz, "Dispirited: Scripture as Rule of Faith and Recent Misuse of the Council of Jerusalem," in *Figured Out: Typology and Providence in Christian Scripture* (Louisville, Ky.: Westminster John Knox, 2001), 117–30.

has to be clarified. Israel, the nations, the sojourners are not generic realities but are clearly differentiated denominations.[10]

Surely at this juncture the proper stance for us as eventual readers of the Elder Testament is one of caution, humility, and respect before our status as invitees into a close and long personal relationship between God and his covenant people. The one move that must be resisted is to see this relationship as inferior to one we imagine to be our own, or one that is developmentally deficient, measured against a later, optimal one.[11] The Jesus who exists as divine Son and eternal Word and Son of David may declare himself the giver of and Lord of the torah of God and declare the law's deepest purpose through its letter (Matt 5:17-48). But that role is not our own. Any superiority we might feel Paul declares as false boasting born of misunderstanding (Rom 11:17-36). The Israelite Jesus opens the scriptures for his brethren and declares them everywhere about him, not everywhere about you and me. He is the Lord over both the Old and the New, equally.

Keeping clear the unique life the covenant people have with God, as we open the book we have been handed by the Risen Lord, means above all understanding that life as special and without analogy in its time. "He has not done so with any other nation" (Ps 147:12) is not a xenophobic assertion but doxology. And alongside it we hear, "Let us go with you, for we have heard that God is with you" (Zech 9:23) and the manifold refrains of Isaiah, "nations shall come to your light . . . lift up your eyes and see, they all gather together, they come to you" (60:3-4). This is our place of entry, "holding the robe of a Jew" as the same prophet Zechariah envisioned it (9:23).

Proper use of our library card also means keeping clear that the God of Israel is the only God and the creator of heaven and earth,

---

[10] Seitz, "Jewish Scripture for Gentile Churches: Human Destiny and the Future of the Pauline Correspondence—Part 1: Romans," *ProEcl* 23 (2014): 294–307.

[11] For an extended evaluation of "noetic surplus" and the selfsame ontological reality at work in both testaments, see Collett, "Reading Forward," 184–93.

of all peoples and nations yet to be born (Gen 1). As readers, our borrowing privilege accepts and appreciates that this claim is made by the named God of Israel, who has revealed his name and his most personal self in relationship to a chosen people, and through chosen and specific agents of his calling, without which there would be no book for others to read at all. This means that the claims of universal divine sovereignty, of God's life with all the world and all creation, are nevertheless predicated on this personal and specific life, of the One YHWH God. These claims arise from within the One divine life and do not float generally free. Because the Bible begins on just these notes, using a word for God available and in use (Elohim), is an act of condescension as much as it is a claim from within Israel that the named God is no tribal deity but rather the One God of all the world. This claim can also be taken as an evacuation of any other claim to know God except as he will be known as YHWH. It is only through this privileged knowledge that more universal claims are made, and these arise from the selfsame conviction, given by God, that "I am the first and I am the last and besides me there is no god" (Isa 44:6).[12]

The point here is that the universal claim of God as this arises as the scriptures open is not a warrant for thinking universally about our place in the book, or forgetting the special character of the protagonist Israel as like unto us but just living a long time ago. Even more deceptive would be the claim that the people of Israel lived not just a long time before us, whoever we may be (the chronologically improved), but also that their life with God does not truly partake of God as God is. It is at best *en route* to that. To say this is to imagine for ourselves as Christians a life with God that is not only distinctive, brokered through scripture and sacrament where once it was brokered through sign and word to Israel, but also outdistancing. Once this move is made we can no longer

---

[12] I have a discussion of natural law in the Old Testament in "The Ten Commandments: Positive and Natural Law and the Covenants Old and New," in Carl E. Braaten and Christopher Seitz, eds., *I Am the Lord Your God: Christian Reflections on the Ten Commandments* (Grand Rapids: Eerdmans, 2005), 18–40.

understand the Christ who is Lord over Israel and the church, and whose risen life was only comprehended in relation to just these scriptures and that life with Israel he shared. That he opens the book means the relationship he has as the Israel of God he is opening to us who come from afar. By means of his residence in this scriptural life we are cautioned to find him there and to find him on the terms of the scriptures' own literal and sacramental sense, and not as an inferior form of that as we would imagine to have it in our present Christian life. The same Spirit who gives life to the church, through word and sacrament, "spake by the prophets" and enlivened their life with Israel. So we go to read of that life as guests and as those who will learn about a life with God that is a figure overshadowing, guiding, and encouraging us even now. "For whatever was written in former days was written for our instruction, that by steadfastness and by encouragement of the scriptures we might have hope" (Rom 15:3). Now we are part of an "our" and a "we" when once we were not, and when once the Word came alive to others, but to us only by them through chance encounter.

The Speech of God: An Example of Specialness

There was a season in the middle of the previous century when the special character of the Old Testament was acknowledged by scholars and was thought to lie in the realm of acts of God.[13] The "mighty acts of God" were what made Israel unique and gave a special character to the Old Testament as a special witness. And there can be little doubt that the Old Testament does indeed report God's actions in her life in historical events in dramatic

---

[13] The best known anglophone contribution is that of G. Ernest Wright, *The God Who Acts: Biblical Theology as Recital*, SBT (London: SCM, 1964). See the evaluation of Langdon Gilkey, "Cosmology, Ontology, and the Travail of Biblical Language," *JR* 41 (1965): 194–205; also Brevard S. Childs, *Biblical Theology in Crisis* (Philadelphia: Westminster, 1970).

ways. The crossing of the sea was held to be the event par excellence whose centrality mirrored, though imperfectly, the centrality of the incarnation or the resurrection in the New Testament. The "creeds" of Israel were said to speak of God's action as "he who brought Israel out of Egypt."[14] The bestseller textbook of Bernhard Anderson, *Understanding the Old Testament*, ignored the canonical priority given to creation and started with the exodus.[15] Here the mightiest act of God was said to have started things. Secondarily the call of Abraham, the ancestors, the giving of the law, and especially though latterly creation as such were retrofitted and made to be settled scenes around this central act. If other mighty acts were held to be dubious legends, arising as etiologies or retrojections backward into time and space, the crossing of the sea remained to buttress the entire faith convictions of ancient Israel. There it was. The mighty act at the center of all historical significance.[16]

It was pointed out that there were problems if this depiction were made to carry so much weight. It is not obvious where the same mighty acts of our days are to be located, so that we could see the stories as relevant in some way and as interpreting our times as something other than metaphor or abstraction.[17] Belief in something and the something itself need mutually to reinforce each other in a way that isn't just a subjectivity of belief on the one hand, or a *bruta facta* that all ought to be able to see, Egypt and Israel both, on the other. What then accounts for its specialness would need explanation. A mighty deliverance at God's hand for some was for others a bad weather day or poor chariotry.

---

[14] Gerhard von Rad, "The Form-Critical Problem of the Hexateuch," in *The Problem of the Hexateuch and Other Essays* (Edinburgh: Oliver and Boyd, 1966; German original, 1938). See the detailed discussion in part 2 to follow.

[15] Bernhard Anderson, *Understanding the Old Testament* (Upper Saddle River, N.J.: Prentice-Hall, 1966). It is now in its 5th edition.

[16] As the cross was the central "act" in the New Testament, the sea crossing fulfilled this role in the Old.

[17] Gilkey, "Cosmology."

An alternative was proposed, though in many ways it never caught the imagination of biblical scholars in the same sense. The "mighty acts of God" slowly receded in importance, and the wider question of "what is history?" began to preoccupy the field. Books with titles like "can a history of Israel be written?" began to populate book shelves, with aggressive no and defensive yes responses.[18]

The alternative proposal was to place the speech of God at the center.[19] Quite properly it was noted that absent speech of God prior to an event, which promised it and explained its coming and its purpose, it would be difficult to know how wondrous events weren't just a kind of magic. The magicians of Egypt conjured up interruptions in the realm of events—to their own injury!—as did Moses and Aaron. The difference between their unspecial wonder working and Israel's special type would require explanation; both were acts mighty. But of course in the case of Israel, Moses and Aaron were instructed ahead of time by God's speaking to them, so that the events would be understood and would be "mighty," even in spite of their seeming failure to persuade the brass-foreheaded Pharaoh. "Then you will know that I am the LORD" when such and such happens. And through this speech-act link, others will know, and in time the whole world will know via the report we can now read about them as such.[20]

---

[18] Lester L. Grabbe, ed., *Can a "History of Israel" Be Written?* JSOTSup 245 (Sheffield: Sheffield Academic, 1997). "Yes" responses in serious form came from scholars such as Iain Provan, Phil Long, Tremper Longman, and others. Even the redoubtable James Barr entered the fray with *History and Ideology in the Old Testament: Biblical Studies at the End of a Millennium* (Oxford: Oxford University Press, 2005). See also Leo Perdue, *The Collapse of History: Reconstructing Old Testament Theology*, OBT (Minneapolis: Augsburg Fortress, 1994).

[19] James Barr's critique of "mighty acts" tentatively suggested that "speech" was a more obviously central emphasis. He averred, "A God who acted in history would be a mysterious and supra–personal fate if the action was not linked with this verbal conversation . . . In his speech with man, however, God really meets man on his own level and directly" (*Old and New in Interpretation: A Study of the Two Testaments* [New York: Harper and Row, 1966], 78).

[20] See my discussion in Christopher Seitz, "The Call of Moses and the 'Revelation' of the Divine Name," in *Word without End*, 229–47.

We have all heard a sermon in which the direct speech of God to Abraham, telling him to leave his country and go to a land God will show him, is taken to be a general kind of speaking, like unto the sincere responses to a "voice" we may make to take a risk and go out in faith in our time. And perhaps there is a reasonableness to making this association that belongs to their purpose as God's word to us today. But in what sense? If it is to evacuate them of a quite specific form of speaking (and hearing) that belongs to the way the stories make their sense, where the speaking is not intuition, or hunch, or even still small voice, but is said to be actual speaking from God to Abraham (the same word for me talking to my wife and God talking to Abraham is used in Hebrew), this would be to replace our religious sensibilities with the ones the Old Testament stories are reporting, using the different terms that belong to their specialness.

Instead the reader can acknowledge that here we are hearing about something we may have difficulty understanding in our frame of reference, without a form of translation or transfer, but which inheres with how the stories are what they are and that gives them the authority they have and have had in interpretation prior to our period. Instead of "domesticating" them in order to fit them into a story line that leads to us, or function as a kind of metaphor only, if they are left in the character of their scriptural form, they are then allowed to be strange and odd and different, and so to do their telling on just those terms. Perhaps there is really no category of "history" we can invent that allows them to be continuous with our own chapters in time, and that is not a loss but a gain. And what if that is exactly the point and is what makes Israel's life with God not just special, but meant in that specialness to baffle, probe, get attention, disturb, and otherwise call us to see ourselves as smaller or more in need of instruction than before? That is, it sets forth a species of history from Israel in which God is real and really present in speech and life so as to alert us to what that means in our dispensation now where we know God really and truly but through other means he has provided richly for us.

It certainly must not be the case that for a thing to speak to us, it can do so only on the terms we find congenial. And therein lies so much of the power and authority of the Old Testament, and that must be guarded by visitors to its landscape.

To reinforce this point one need only remember that within the landscape of the Old Testament itself the time will come when a sense of this kind of speaking begins to draw to a close. The Old Testament candidly announces that God's speaking has begun to take a new form, and it does not judge that a diminishment. It is rather the consequence of a rich, prior accumulation of speech and yet a lack of words finding their settled point of fulfilled reference. So they continue to "speak" but now through a changed medium (Zech 1). This does not detract from the reality of the past as betokening God's speaking or in any way mean to change the character of that speaking into metaphor or abstraction. It remains powerfully what it is in the form it is reported to us. And God said to Abraham. And God told Moses. The word of the Lord was to Amos.

As we close this section it may be important to note that the transition from live prophetic speech to the living-on speech of their written records may be different in nature from the speech we see reported in the early accounts of the Pentateuch. We can rightly wonder if the latest prophetic witnesses (Joel, Malachi, et al.) represent a new genre of prophetic "speech" different in kind to the viva voce of earlier prophetic voices, and note this movement inside a book like Isaiah as such, where the theory of three Isaiahs and a book growing over several centuries has proven persuasive.[21] What we are to make of the direct speech to Abraham or Jacob or Moses belongs to a period that is unique within the

---

[21] See my extended discussion in *Prophecy and Hermeneutics: Toward a New Introduction to the Prophets* (Grand Rapids: Baker Academic, 2007) and more recently *Joel*, ITC (London: Bloomsbury, 2016). See also "The Unique Achievement of the Book of the Twelve: Neither Reactional Unity Nor Anthology," in Heiko Wenzel, ed., *The Book of the Twelve: An Anthology of Prophetic Books or the Result of Complex Redactional Processes* (Göttingen: Vandenhoeck & Ruprecht, forthcoming).

canonical form, what one modern scholar has called "The Old Testament of the Old Testament," and what Luther referred to as the time of "patriarchal temptations."[22] He was referring to the experience of God before the giving of the law, and he spoke of the *Urgewalt* of God, much as Job experiences it in the framework the book associated with him and his trials presents it. Paul will seize on the uniqueness of this world before the giving of the law as a means to describe the life of the Christian justified before God by faith, and not by law. But however we think about it subsequently, alongside Luther or Paul or late-modern readings, it releases its force when we allow the relationship between God and the Israel of God to retain its peculiar immediacy and address.

In commenting on "the fact that Abraham Offered His Son Isaac," Origen says this in Homily VIII about Genesis 22:12:

> For now I know that you fear God. In this statement it is usually thrown out against us that God says that now he had learned that Abraham fears God as though he were such as not to have known previously. God knew and it was not hidden from him, since it is he "who has known all things before they come to pass" (Dan. 13:42). But these things are written on account of you, because you too indeed have believed in God, but unless you shall fulfill "the works of faith" (2 Thes. 1:11), unless you shall be obedient to all the commands, even the more difficult ones, unless you shall offer sacrifice and show that you place neither father nor mother nor sons before God (Mt. 10:37), you will not know that you fear God nor will it be said of you "Now I know that you fear God." The faith of the figure is a paradigm. "All these services are not asked of you" he remarks earlier, but all the same "be constant in purpose, at least, and mind. Offer your son to God, joyful, immovable in faith. Be the priest for your son's life."

---

[22] Walter Moberly, *The Old Testament of the Old Testament*, OBT (Minneapolis: Fortress, 1992).

He concludes the homily with reference to the other high patriarchal figure for the church, Job. "For he too, although he was rich, lost everything because of God. But he bore well the struggles with patience and was magnanimous in everything that he suffered and said: 'The Lord gave, the Lord has taken away; as it has pleased the Lord so it is done. Blessed be the name of the Lord.' Because of this, behold what is finally written about him: 'He received back twice as much,' Scripture says, 'as he had lost.'" We can be readers, but only as we respect the place we occupy and the place the high figures occupy as well in their specific dispensation with God. "A clear way of spiritual understanding is opened for those who know to hear these words."[23]

---

[23] Origen, *The Song of Songs: Commentary and Homilies*, ed. Johannes Quasten and Joseph C. Plumpe, Ancient Christian Writers 26 (Mahwah, N.J.: Paulist, 1957).

PART TWO

ENTERING THE ELDER TESTAMENT

"Order and Sequence" (*taxis kai eirmon*) are the equivalent English language terms for what the early interpreters understood to be key ingredients, alongside totality or "scope," for the scriptures' proper literary and theological apprehension.[1] I take them to mean, in our period, attention to "the way the words go" (*akolouthia*) when one carefully studies the shape and character of the final form of scriptures' address. In our period, apprehension of this dimension is sharpened by what has come to be called "historical-critical" reading.

---

[1] In *Against Heresies* Irenaeus uses the word "canon" to refer to baptismal faith as rooted "in the order and connection of the scriptures" (*tēn men taxin kai ton eirmon tōn graphōn*) (*Against Heresies* 1.8.1–1.10.3). See the comprehensive study of Frances Young, *Biblical Exegesis and the Formation of Christian Culture* (Grand Rapids: Baker Academic, 1997).

In the present section we will offer an overview of the contents of the Elder Scripture against the backdrop of historical-critical investigation. This allows us to appreciate its special literary character, its relationship to history, the nature of its claims to inspiration, and the peculiar way in which its reference to the divine takes form. A special area of interest—precisely because it bridges traditional historical-critical reading and just that peculiarly arranged divine truth-telling—will be the emergence of source-critical theories concerning the divine name in the Elder Scriptures. The next three chapters will look at this issue from the standpoint of the Pentateuchal criticism of the late nineteenth and twentieth centuries. The entry into the topic begins with an appraisal of the peculiar character of biblical narrative, with help from Eric Auerbach.

The Old Testament does not exist in a single, ordered form but in many. The one with which most Christians are familiar is in fact a latecomer, with Genesis first and Malachi last, the consequence of widescale dissemination of printed Bibles as this occurred in the sixteenth century. If we are to appreciate the canonical shape of the Elder Scripture it will mean appreciating the variety of forms in which this comes to us and the special nature of the Hebrew ordering preserved in the life of Judaism over time.

Our presentation of the contents of the Law, the Prophets, and the Writings is offered against the backdrop of modern historical-critical reading. We believe this critical reading legacy represents a strong background foil against which to see the achievement of Tanakh and Christian Old Testament in a variety of orders.

5

The Strange Old Book
The Limits of Narrative

In this opening of a series of chapters we will look at the appeal to narrative as a primary lens on understanding the scriptures of Israel. Narrative can mean here two things. First, an understanding of the Elder Scripture as of necessity en route to the New Testament, and so the beginning half of a story whose denouement lies outside of its own theological and chronological range. On this account the Christian Bible is a dramatic story composed of a series of episodes, some of which come earlier and set up the plot development. The Elder Testament comprises the first four chapters of a six-chapter book. Narrative can also mean the insistence that the final form of the Elder Scripture needs to be recast in a properly sequential account, where the earliest authors/traditions and life situations are culled out and place on a developmental grid leading to the latest phases of religious reflection and life. One might even hope that these twin instincts reinforced each other: The Elder Testament as a history of religion leading up to and into the

New Testament (crossing intertestamental terrain) with a dramatic exile in time to be reversed; and a broadly antecedent narrative storyline whose sense is declared via the retrospective lens of the latter episodes comprising the New Testament story, where exile is countered and overcome by resurrection.

Our view of the canonical significance of the Elder Scripture will seek to resist these instincts, in the name of balancing the economic and ontological dimensions at work in the testimony of Israel's scriptures. The same pressures to relate earlier and later traditions in a coalesced final form of that first scriptural witness are also at work in how the New and Old Testaments together do their combined theological work. But our attention here is the Elder Testament and its strange new world. This chapter will open onto a series of reflections in part 2 on how the diachronic reality of the Old Testament is to be appreciated via the final form.

In a provocative essay likely meant to be provocative, Karl Barth spoke of the "Strange New World within the Bible."[1] He was referring to the stop-and-start, surprisingly transitioned, divine-interventionistic dramatic rendering the scriptures, especially in the Old Testament, deploys. Modern diachronic reading of the Old Testament regarded this dimension as sufficiently strange that it required lining up portions of the text with different authors or sources or traditions so as to appreciate the final form. *The Bible in Order* was a publication whose title and purpose seemed self-evident. Historical criticism either judged the final form rendering empty of significance or a cataract on the far more interesting religious history of reconstructed authors and audiences that discrete levels of text disclosed, when properly reconfigured using literary and historical acids.

More recently the appeal has been made, over against this, to the highly narrative character of scripture.[2] The Bible is a story.

---

[1] Chapter 2 of *The Word of God and the Word of Man* (Gloucester, Mass.: Peter Smith, 1978), 28–50.

[2] See the representative works cited in chapter 4, n. 8 above.

It tells via an economic account attuned to its final form a long dramatic tale, beginning with creation, moving to patriarchs and law giving, to prophet and wisdom, and straight into the second testament's continuing and dramatically conclusive final chapters. We are part of the story. It opens up and includes us. The first part less so directly and more so as necessary background, the latter part more deeply and profoundly. You can't have an ending without a beginning, and a middle somewhere in between. The first episodes do their ballistic work and then like booster rockets fall into the sea, en route to the real payload where we stand, alongside the One to whom history has been moving. On this BC/AD conceptual grid, the Elder Testament is living in a time prior to something and has its significance only with reference to a denouement to which it points religiously beyond itself.

If we prescind from the question of uninterrupted narrative movement from first to second witness, and look at the first witness alone, we would not reflexively call what we have in the Strange Old Book "narrative." To be sure there is a beginning: the beginning of all beginnings, one might say, in Genesis 1. And before Moses there is Abraham, and after Moses there is Joshua and Ruth and David and Jeremiah and Zedekiah. In some translational presentations of the Old Testament, a temporal unfolding is better represented than in others, such as we see it for example in modern English language Bibles, which move from Genesis to 2 Chronicles without prophetic interruption. But in the history of translational presentations, this is not a frequently appearing form, and in any event, it does not account for the other significant blocks of the Old Testament, the prophetic corpus of fifteen books and the writings of the third final Hebrew language section—books that can migrate into new positions in fresh translations and that do, but not always in the same way.[3]

---

[3] For a helpful chart of orders in Jewish and Christian usage, see the appendix in Lee McDonald and James A. Sanders, *The Canon Debate* (Peabody, Mass.: Hendrickson, 2002). Never is Malachi the final book, and usually the prophetic writings are found toward the middle of the lists.

But even the Genesis to 2 Chronicles movement is not obviously narratival, as it contains a wide variety of genre, including law and poetry and exhortation and retelling (the books of 1 and 2 Chronicles are not necessary if we are looking for continuous narrative only). The prophetic corpus Isaiah-Jeremiah-Ezekiel isn't narratival in character, and the Book of the Twelve has chosen to give us witnesses that are not in chronological order and some of which appear to be disinterested in strict temporal location, much less being a part of a dramatic unfolding of anything.[4] The diverse collection of writings has been the subject of evaluation as to the logic of its order, but whatever else it may be, it is not part of a narrative story.[5]

So if we want to come to terms with the Strange Old Book we have to think in terms other than "story" or "religious historical reconstruction." The former is arguably an imposition made in order to leap the gap into a subsequent New Testament witness, and the latter is most generously a rearranging of chairs by a guest in a house not her own so as to suit her own purposes. The question becomes more acute, however, when we observe those portions of the Strange Old Book that most approximate narrative and ask, "What in the world does this material lie before us in this form and arrangement for?" It is precisely the force of the question existing as such that in turn led to clever and sometimes fruitful diachronic rearrangements. Whenever there is a temporal disjunction—scattering nations into many languages and tongues *after* we were told they had already been separated on kindred terms[6]—solve the "problem" by positing sources J and P and "restore" an order indigenous to them alone prior to the present (narratively confusing) form of the text. Take the minor prophets and put them in their proper historical order, previously paring them each down as necessary until we have the

---

[4] See the evaluation, and a full bibliography, in *Prophecy and Hermeneutics: Toward a New Introduction to the Prophets* (Grand Rapids: Baker Academic, 2007).

[5] See most recently Julius Steinberg and Timothy J. Stone, eds., *The Shape of the Writings* (Winona Lake, Ind.: Eisenbrauns, 2015).

[6] So Gen 10:1-32 before Gen 11:1-9.

"real prophet" before us.⁷ Put all this "in order" and we have a critical introduction that may then resemble something like a "narrative" retelling after all. But this "narrative" is an extrapolation. It is not the canonical portrayal whose history of effects never registered the storyline in this reconstructed way.

So it is even at the level of narrative qua narrative where the problem is not resolved but lies before us. We see the disjunctions and doublets and backtracking and sometimes obvious anachronism and what appear to be secondary supplementation and rightly note. If this be narrative, it is very odd indeed and takes some getting used to.

An illustration may be helpful from the book of Exodus, which like other Old Testament witnesses confronts the reader with a final form presentation that surprises us, confuses us, doubles back, leaves things out we might expect, and so forth. I regularly teach Exodus to Ph.D. students, and we work our way through major sections of critical commentaries alongside our primary task of moving line by line through the Hebrew text. They frequently question why they should spend so much time with diachronic questions, and are asked to follow closely the evaluation of oral stages, tradition-historical alterations, movement into sources, and amalgamation. They wonder about what is wrong with just reading the final form as it sits before us. Perhaps this is merely an exercise to establish that one knows what the state of the question is, and to confirm that one is a competent interlocutor, but really doesn't contribute much to the actual reading of the text as it sits before us. For if so, then they would prefer to accept the priority given to final form or the canonical shape otherwise so persuasively argued for by a commentator like Childs or Christophe Dohmen, and dispense with the preliminary sections.⁸

---

⁷ A similar procedure obtains in the case of the Pauline letter collection. See my comparison in *Colossians* (2014).

⁸ Brevard S. Childs, *The Book of Exodus: A Critical, Theological Commentary*, OTL (Philadelphia: Westminster, 1974). Christoph Dohmen, *Exodus 1–18*, HThKAT (Freiburg: Herder, 2015). The Internationaler Exegetischer

Yet a close reading of even Childs' stated intentions shows that he believes the diachronic evaluation is indispensable because it has seen something that truly exists in the text as it sits before us. It is an uneven, unusual, sometimes eccentric presentation, where things don't unfold as we may think they should, and where genuine problems arise if we believe we should expect that the text is simply mirroring a straightforward, single-author, one-thing-after-another narrative story. The diachronic efforts quite properly seek to account for this by positing oral origins, transformations due to subsequent rehearsals in situations-in-life of the people of Israel, later supplementation, and only after all that a final stabilization. These diachronic efforts are trying to make sense of a biblical text on the terms of its own givenness, and account for what genuinely makes the text what it is, and also appreciate just what an unusual and unique thing it is as it does its work of narrating. This is why Childs also includes precritical and more recent authors who believe other explanations can be given that would restore the single-author idea, or explain the text more straightforwardly as reporting history mimetically. Text and historical reference are the only real matters to be concerned with for many of these authors, and these two dimensions are perfectly aligned and admit of no social forces or theological filtering over time. The text is akin to a camera lined up on an object it reproduces. These options are, however, rejected as unsatisfactory accounts of how the stories do their work if we are prepared to follow them closely on the terms of their own strange unfolding.

The hesitancy to do diachronic evaluation as an end unto itself is that typically this evaluation is explanatory of something

---

Kommentar zum Alten Testament volume *Exodus 1–15* recently appeared, written by the team of Helmut Utzschneider and Wolfgang Oswald (Stuttgart: Kohlhammer, 2013). The first is responsible for *synchron* analysis and the second for *diachron*. It is fascinating for what it showcases, and where the two approaches simply cannot line up. The commentary is pedagogically useful in showing the effect of two people coming at the text fully aware of the discipline represented by each domain, but leaving the evaluations sitting side-by-side. This is instructive even if unintended when it comes to evaluating method.

coming-to-be, and so fails to appreciate the final consolidation as worthy of its own careful analysis. Over time, it may also betray its sense that the final form of the text is only a starting point for the true business of excavation, and then the religious redescription becomes the real interpretation, and the text as a complex and coherent statement of its own disappears like the dirt around so many shards of pottery. One begins to sense that the final form of the text is only an accidental and arbitrary stopping point in an otherwise more important history of religious debate and disagreement and development (depending on the predilections of the interpreter, with P vs. D or J vs. "non-J," or Moses tradition here and Aaron tradition there, etc.).[9] Ironically, for all the modern concern to reject allegory because it appears to substitute for the literal-sense presentation a "resultant system" that wants to coordinate different literary parts on a higher plane, in some ways the real analogy to allegorical reading is a strand of modern historical reading. The text as it sits before us is subsumed under an explanation of how it came to be. We see the alleged tensions and contradictions that inhabit the uneven and strange narrative unfolding and reify them and make them what the text says and is finally about, en route to its final form. Yet there is another way to evaluate them, as part of the theological logic of the canonical form, which as a total product makes its sense with just these uneven and odd juxtapositions.

The Angel in Exodus 23-34: Canonical Interpretation

Consider one example from among many across the landscape of Exodus. In Exodus 32-34 the people of Israel build idols while Moses is away, and in the fundamental act of covenant and law-giving they show themselves weak and vain covenant partners, led by Aaron

---

[9] See the works cited in chap. 6, n. 13 below for a glimpse at the complex world of Pentateuchal criticism in its most recent phases.

(32:2-6). God proposes to remove himself and leave the project with Moses (33:1-3). Moses intercedes and reminds God of promises made in solemn speech to accompany all his people (33:12-16). God relents. He reasserts his presence and his character: of great mercy, but righteous and he who will by no means clear the guilty (34:6-7).

Inside of this drama, which unfolds reasonably evenly, God makes a proposal to send instead of himself a surrogate (33:2). He cannot go up because his righteousness would ultimately consume his people. Moses objects to this, and God ponders. Moses accesses his tent (33:7-11), a temporally disruptive bit of detail—its construction is described only subsequently—whose point is to reassure us of Moses' longstanding posture of intercession. He then formally intercedes. Still at issue is whether God will accompany Moses only or all the people. God assures Moses of the latter and solemnly declares his ongoing presence with Israel. In this account the angel is a surrogate and an obvious alternative to the divine presence as such. It is proposed and withdrawn after Moses' appeal.

Back in chapter 23, after the giving of the covenant code, God proposes to send an angel to guard and watch over Israel (23:23-33). There is no hint of this being a surrogate or replacement, but instead the angel functions as a guarantor of Israel's safety in the context of what will be difficult adherence to him and his torah. The angel is a gift, commensurate with the challenge Israel will face amongst the nations. So Israel is solemnly cautioned ahead of time about the snares they will face, and an angel serves to signal just what kind of challenge this will be and how a divine initiative of aid is there to assist.

If one seeks to make these into the same angel, the difficulty is obvious. The text does not resolve this tension for us, any more than it worries over-much about a tent that comes out of the blue and has not yet been constructed. One could reconstruct the different cultic contexts in which tents and angels find their integrated purpose and differentiate them on logical grounds. A protective warrior angel. An angel of presence, but signaling lack of ultimate presence and instead of distance. Both are capable of righteous judgment, and indeed this seems to be an attribute both share. The first is introduced as on Israel's side against idolatry and the threat of loss of faith. The second stands in place of this aspect of God's own self, should pure divine justice be left to direct itself against a sinful people.

In the conjoined text, it is not possible to make them function exactly on the same plane. But that is precisely the point. The text is content for one to function in one way here and another in a different manner there, even as we can see some overlap. One possibility is that this goes back into the text's prehistory and tradition-historical setting. But that would not be a final but a preliminary piece of exegesis. At issue is the cumulative effect. When we read Exodus 23–34 the destructive potential of angelic presence may well be in our minds (see also 4:24-26 as well as the deadly plagues and the "destroyer" of Passover at 12:23). But what we discover is that in this place God proposes the angel as a means to avoid his righteous coming to terms with a stiff-necked people, and so destroying them in the manner of Exodus 23 vis-à-vis idolatrous nations. Moses intercedes because his place is with the people as a whole, even though this is personally threatening—and further means he doesn't get to adopt the special one-on-one role divinely proposed. God indicates that his character will hold in sovereign balance aspects of great mercy and righteous judgment against evil, even when he must go up with a people he loves but who are fickle and prone to rebellion. Whatever the text's prehistory, and however much it may not be possible to create a smooth, single-authored account of the life history of a single angelic figure, that is itself a provocation to think carefully about what we do have, and not to expect smoothness and one-to-one relationship between text and historical reference when it comes to the difficult business of speaking of God's character in time and relationship.

Here it is useful to consider the work of Eric Auerbach on biblical narrative and what makes it unique. I will quote a long section so as to focus on the last observation he makes, which carries more theological weight. The emphasis is mine.

> The Bible's claim to truth is not only far more urgent than Homer's, it is tyrannical—it excludes all other claims. The world of the Scripture stories is not satisfied with claiming to be a historically true reality—it insists that it is the only real world, is destined for autocracy. All other scenes, issues, and ordinances have no right to appear independently of it, and it is promised that all of them, the history of all mankind, will be given their due place within its frame, will be subordinated to it. The Scripture stories do not, like Homer's, court our favor, they do not flatter us that they may please us and enchant us—they seek to subject us, and if we refuse to be subjected we are rebels.
>
> Let no one object that this goes too far, that not the stories, but the religious doctrine, raises the claim of absolute authority; because the stories are not, like Homer's, simply narrated "reality." Doctrine and promise are incarnate in them and inseparable from them; for that very reason they are fraught with "background" and mysterious, containing a second, concealed meaning . . . Far from seeking, like Homer, merely to make us forget our own reality for a few hours, it seeks to overcome our reality: we are to fit our own life into its world, feel ourselves to be elements in its structure of universal history . . . *The greater the separateness and horizontal disconnection of the stories and groups of stories in relation to one another, compared with the Iliad and the Odyssey, the stronger is their general vertical connection, which holds them all together and which is entirely lacking in Homer.*[10]

Two conceptual realities are called attention to in this insightful observation from Auerbach that need highlighting. They are related. "Fraught with background" and "vertical connection." The first refers to the general observation that the stories of the Old Testament do not tell us things of general psychological interest but prefer to foreground the actions and dialogue as such. They

---

[10] *Mimesis: The Representation of Reality in Western Literature*, 50th anniversary edition (Princeton: Princeton University Press, 2003), 14–15, 17. German language original appeared in 1946 as *Mimesis: Dargestellte Wirklichkeit in der abendländischen Literatur*. The relevant chapter for our purpose is the first, "Odysseus's Scar."

avoid foregrounding what Abraham thought about the command to execute his son; or making clear it wasn't the same Abimelech who got duped twice in wife-sister scheming; or clearing up how long Israel was in Egypt, given that we seem to have rival estimates.[11] The first kind of example tells us that what we may expect in a good story will often be missing, and that is not accidental but the way the biblical narrative prefers to function. It pays attention to things that it believes matters and lets things that otherwise might matter to a certain kind of reader go undiscussed and even unnoticed. The second background fraughtness is of the kind we observed with the angel: the failure to coordinate fully, or the disinterest in anachronism as a problem, or the existence of doublets, or the mysterious appearance of items that are only fully developed later.

This lends a quality to the stories that there is more going on than is being accounted for. It gives us a sense that larger forces are somehow at work, and that we are being told what we need to know on the terms of the text's predilections even when strange or disconnected.[12] If it is true that they tend to be "tyrannical" in the substance of what they report, and not due to external theological requests that we hear them thus, but inherently, this is not only true of what they report but also in the manner of their reporting. We must come to terms with something. Or we must decide we aren't being asked that of the text because it is just a jumble and must be sorted out. Auerbach's point is to take very seriously the first option, because he judges the canonical text quite properly and adroitly to be doing what it intends in just the way it does that, and peculiarly so. He asks no more or less of the Iliad or Homer,

---

[11] Exodus 12:40-41 speaks of 430 years, and matches roughly Genesis 15:13. The end of Genesis and the beginning of Exodus appear to suggest the generation after Joseph is the subject of affairs with the "new king who did not know Joseph" (Exod 1:8). Exodus 6:14-25 counts four generations.

[12] That this is due to diachronic factors (diverse sources and traditions) is a reasonable explanation. At issue is whether this needs to be explained or whether the final form is content for other reasons to tolerate tensions and divergences as belonging to its unique character of presentation.

but sees them in strong contrast. The canonical reading follows the same instincts as Auerbach, even as it is prepared to evaluate the eccentricities as belonging to the text's real coming to be in the lived life of Israel. But this is better to understand the achievement of the final form as it invites us to follow its letter, and not for its own final significance.

Auerbach makes this compressed statement but does not follow it up with any explicitly theological explanation: "*The greater the separateness and horizontal disconnection of the stories and groups of stories in relation to one another . . . the stronger is their general vertical connection.*" The absence of strong connections throughout the narrative unfolding, offering a seamless and engrossing steady state of telling, would presumably call greater attention to the story itself as story. But the gaps and disconnection mean the storyline is at the service of something above it to which it refers, and that is not so much in nature or history or what we can call lateral ostensive reference— the text is talking directly about the events to which it refers as these exist in time and space—but exists by default as a "vertical connection." This would be our judgment of the conjoined effect of a certain species of presentation and the subject matter as theologically transcendant.

The observation of Auerbach would ground the theological authority and real divine presence in the character of the literature as the Old Testament presents this, and that is true so far as it goes. But it follows from the fact that of course the text speaks of God and allows God space as a speaker and real presence. It does not speak of gods or of refracted divinity but of the one true God YHWH. A "tyranny" of the One God who describes himself as of boundless great mercy and full authority to judge as God alone judges.

We will explore the significance of the divine name in Hebrew Scripture in a more extended manner below. For now it is important to register that alongside the insightful notes Auerbach provides about the literary character of the Strange Old Book, as constituting how it properly does its work in respect of gaps and disconnection, there is also the obvious gloss: that is because it speaks of God as

God is. This is presumably what it means for him to say earlier "[d]octrine and promise are incarnate in them and inseparable from them," because doctrine and promise are, respectively, God *in se* and God in relation. The "I am who I am as I will be with you and show myself faithful to my promises" is doctrine and promise at the heart of the God who speaks and who makes good on his speech in act, as vouchsafed to a people of his promising.[13] Exodus tells us of this God, and it does so through a narrative rendering Auerbach has identified as belonging to its unique portrayal, precisely where baffling and unusual and unexpected. It is as he is, but always of course much less so.

To conclude, what Barth called the strange world within scripture is that quality of the Old Testament that makes it different than straightforward narrative. The strangeness to which he refers is the ability, or proclivity, of the presentation to move briskly along and to contentedly live with gaps and silence and doubling back and failure to explain why we find ourselves where we do when this occurs. It disorients us just to the degree it is re-orienting us to its "new world" of providential history under God. Historical-critical method could see this feature and decide it needed resolution in the form of a properly sequential reconstruction that better conformed to what we expect our view of history to look like. In an ironic way, though it insisted it was dealing with the literal sense soberly, it sought to produce a master account of the Bible's coming-to-be that obscured the achievement of the final form. Rather than regarding the final form as an achievement at the end of a long period of gestation—for this is the dimension historical evaluation was good at identifying—it insisted that the only true way to appreciate the literal presentation was by recasting it in the form of a properly chronological re-telling. At the beginning of this process, it was the earlier phases that tended to be given priority, as original and closer to the events they reported and so

---

[13] Christopher Seitz, "The Call of Moses and the 'Revelation' of the Divine Name," in *Word without End: The Old Testament as Abiding Theological Witness* (Waco, Tex.: Baylor University Press, 2005), 229–47.

warranting the phrase "historical." As the method has evolved over several generations, the difficulty of extracting the earliest phases and correlating them with the events now more decisive than the canonical presentation itself has given new value to the final phases. But in either case, the phases are what become important and not the strange presentation itself. Historical-critical findings are to the literal or canonical sense what once excessive forms of allegory were: resultant systems that themselves gave signification to the literal sense, absent which there is no genuine literal sense presentation itself worthy of prioritizing.

But perhaps more fatal is the theological diminution. Auerbach is right to note, even at the level of literary theory, that it is the strangeness of the depiction that has given room for the vertical address, from a point of standing outside of narrative time or its historical-critical rearranged version, as more decisive than what is being referred to within time. Time is in God's hands. We will look at one very prominent version of the issue in the form of the use of the divine name in the Pentateuch. The variation of the divine name—YHWH, Elohim, El Shaddai, the El of PN—has been identified an an entry point on a developing history-of-religion, which includes as well development of God or authorially sequential ideas about him. Yet in the final form of the text, this development is nowhere foregrounded in the "way the words go." Instead, a different perspective on the divine life is set forth, with its own self-understanding of time and ontology, and indeed its own claim to describe "history" as under providential superintendence. On this account, later and earlier—as narrative or historical-critical views would have it—co-mingle and retrofit and project forward in the curious and strange world now represented by the theological achievement of the final form of the Elder Scripture.

6

The Fate of JEDP
The Mysterious Disclosure of the Divine Name

The next two chapters focus on the monumental theory from the nineteenth and twentieth centuries concerning the existences of sources in the first five books of Moses. The impact of this reconstruction—in incipient trial form and then in the mature expression/consolidation associated with Julius Wellhausen—has been undeniable in its scope and its lasting challenge. At issue was not simply the loss of Mosaic authorship—whatever the idea meant—but it was felt in the terms of literary critical reconstructions of enormous complexity that emerged over the course of now a century and a half, and how to make sense of them. But further, to the degree the theory in whatever form was associated with the idea of a disagreement over the disclosure of the divine name, the significance of a major theological index—God's name and identity—was also at stake. Do sources disagree and make that disagreement felt via their use of YHWH and Elohim in respective literary strata?

But more importantly, the literary/theological question is whether this is the only way to understand the variation of the divine name that makes its presence felt not just in Genesis but in the ensuing books, and indeed for different reasons in the remaining sections of the canon. The literary theory, in other words, to the degree to which it believes it is solving a "problem" by recourse to sources/traditions, may in fact be obscuring a significance to the alternation of the name even the alleged sources/traditions themselves could believe needs attention in the conjoined character of their residence now in the present form of the Pentateuch.

The present chapter rehearses the general theory and its form-critical adjustments and anticipates the newer models to be discussed in chapter 7. The main topic to be explored is whether another conception lies to hand by which to account for the divine name's disclosure in the present amalgamation of traditions represented by the final form of Genesis and the Pentateuch. If we are not talking about sources in disagreement, we may be talking instead about conjoined traditions that seek to set forth a sophisticated account of the relationship between YHWH, the named God of Israel, and Elohim, the God of Israel and of all creation. This in turn may open onto the broader theological question of ontology and economy. That topic is pursued in more detail in the chapter to follow this one.

When I entered seminary forty years ago the rite of passage in Old Testament (with its counterpart in Q and synoptic studies) was becoming familiar with the source-critical theory, or popularizations of it as it emanated from Julius Wellhausen and his precursors. To have gone to seminary meant emerging knowledgeable in the secret arts of "JEDP." I at least had some Hebrew and could roughly understand what was at stake in the criterion of the divine name, though my classmates without Hebrew were expected to track the logic and understand the parameters of this major plank in Old Testament studies, and understand it to be very important. It was even possible for the method to be given a theological gloss, and my teachers did this. J was hierarchical. Leaders were called by God. They saw his presence and ate with him. The tent gave them ongoing access to God on derivative terms. E/D leaders were sent by the congregation. They heard God's word but did not see him. The ark housed the covenant, and from its center came the voice of God. These impulses—Catholic and Protestant!—are in tension, but both do their important work. You could tell, however, which one was really on the right track, as the professor winked and gave suggestions of his preferences.[1]

What was "JEDP" according to a developmental understanding of law and cult in J. Wellhausen, it became with Noth/von Rad a creative tradition-historical combination of form and source observations. And it became in Rendtorff tradition-blocks without any source conception at last settling into contemporaneous P/J/D in vying postexilic camps.[2] The venerable J of my seminary days, or in the dress of von Rad's preexilic theologian par excellence, or in bequeathing traditions to the prophets in the southern kingdom or funding specific tendencies in the Psalms—all of this has vanished as the method underwent closer and closer examination. E was always ephemeral and with rare exception is pretty much gone (though see Propp's Exodus commentary).[3] Genesis and the ensuing books seem to have emerged and tracked along different and contrasting lines.[4] Deuteronomy was always on its own,

---

[1] Murray Lee Newman Jr., *The People of the Covenant* (Nashville: Abingdon, 1962). An allied perspective can be seen in Samuel Terrien, *The Elusive Presence: Toward a New Biblical Theology* (San Francisco: Harper and Row, 1978).

[2] Gerhard von Rad, *The Problem of the Hexateuch and Other Essays* (Edinburgh: Oliver and Boyd, 1966; German original, 1938); Martin Noth, *A History of Pentateuchal Traditions* (Englewood Cliffs, N.J.: Prentice-Hall, 1972; German original, 1948); Rolf Rendtorff, *The Problem of the Process of Transmission in the Pentateuch* (Sheffield: JSOT, 1990).

[3] William Propp, *Exodus 1–18*, AB (New Haven: Yale University Press, 1997).

[4] The view is widely held today but stated most exhaustively in a 456-page work by Konrad Schmid, *Genesis and the Moses Story: Israel's Dual Origins in the Hebrew Bible* (Winona Lake, Ind.: Eisenbrauns, 2010). Compare the more efficient

introducing the history to follow (Joshua to 2 Kings), and maybe serving some hermeneutical bridge function in so doing, or backfilling a prior tetrateuch sufficiently enough for us to see his hand (or just making him all non-P and moving J out entirely).[5] It is unlikely that, on the terms of its initial formulation and adaptation, any one theory can now gain full acceptance as resolving the question of sources or traditions within the Pentateuch along the lines of either Wellhausen or von Rad/Noth or Rendtorff and his students. Martin Noth once famously said that if we only had the book of Numbers, we would never have moved in the direction of continuous narrative sources at all. I have long wondered if the fiveness of the Pentateuch—the specific indigenous contours of each book, and the development of them in the direction of five books as such, and not ever existing much within the framework of continuous sources overarching the books—is where the problem with the theory and its adaptations lies. It would require a monograph treatment of its own to pursue this five-book factor as pushing back against the conception of longitudinal sources. I will make preliminary suggestions in chapter 9 below.

In the modern period the idea of sources emerged in the form it did with a central plank being the criterion of the divine name, that is, with two main sources disagreeing over when the name YHWH was revealed. The J source insisted that YHWH was a name revealed early in Genesis (4:26). The Priestly writer credited its revelation to Moses and stated clearly in chapter 6 of Exodus that the divine name was not known in the period preceding.[6] To

and more theologically driven account by Gerhard von Rad in his classic *Old Testament Theology*, 2 vols. (London: Oliver & Boyd, 1962, 1965).

[5] A classical treatment remains Martin Noth, *The Deuteronomistic History*, 2nd ed. (Sheffield: JSOT, 1991). For an evaluation of his legacy, see Steven McKenzie and M. Patrick Graham, eds., *The History of Israel's Traditions: The Heritage of Martin Noth* (London: Bloomsbury, 1994). On Deuteronomy's location and purpose, see Stephen Chapman, *The Law and the Prophets: A Study in Old Testament Canon Formation* (Tübingen: Mohr Siebeck, 2000).

[6] A typical translation reads "by my name the LORD I did not make myself known to them" (RSV). The Hebrew has a passive (niphal) in the first-person

be sure, Wellhausen's classic theory focused more on the evolution of law and cult from J to D to P, and in turn on de Wette's idea that the chronological fixed point was the "discovery of the law book" in the time of Josiah.⁷ Before that was J, and after that was P. The criterion of the divine name went much further back in time, and in one of its earliest forms was used to speak of sources available to Moses so as to exonerate him from making such a jumble of Genesis; he inherited the problem.⁸ In this older version, the "Elohist" used the generic divine name, the Jehovist used YHWH, and Exodus 6 pointed to a general disagreement between them over the revelation of the name. But both sources were ancient. The "E" of classical Pentateuchal criticism really only emerged as an expedience to account for uses of the name Elohim in Genesis once the Priestly writer was invented and his disagreement with J posited in a much later and now overshadowing post-exilic source. This was the JEDP paradigm as it emerged in the late nineteenth century, to be summarized and packaged by Julius Wellhausen after several precursor suggestions (Reuss and Kneunen most notably).⁹ The astonishing element was the shifting of the main Priestly/Elohist strand, the ground floor of the Pentateuch, into the attic of postexilic and postprophecy residence.

Of course the idea of disagreement between J and P over the origin of the divine as a strong criterion for dividing into sources

---

conjoined with third-person "my name," and not a causative verbal form or the preposition "by." See the discussion below.

⁷ *Prolegomena to the History of Israel* (Edinburgh: Adam & Charles Black, 1885; German original, 1883).

⁸ See the recent discussion of Michael Legaspi, *The Death of Scripture and the Rise of Biblical Studies* (Oxford: Oxford University Press, 2010). The name of the eighteenth-century Paris physician, Jean Astruc, is relevant. See his instructively titled *Conjectures sur les mémoires originaux dont il paroit que Moyse s'est servi pour le livre de la Genèse* (Brussels, 1753).

⁹ I deal with the topic as it seriously impacted the interpretation of prophecy in "Prophecy in the Nineteenth Century Reception," in Magnus Saebo, ed., *Hebrew Bible/Old Testament: The History of Its Interpretation*, vol. 3, *From Modernism to Post-Modernism* (Göttingen: Vandenhoeck & Ruprecht), 556–81.

always suffered some major problems. If it was so pivotal, once we pushed past Exodus 6, why wasn't there one settled agreement that then put the matter to rest? At this point, both "sources" no longer had any (allegedly substantive) disagreement. The name was revealed to Moses, P made his point clear in Exodus 6, and now J and P were on common ground. After Exodus 6 the sources no longer had any disagreement. On the other hand, we do on occasion see in P in Genesis what looked like clear J, or some combination of them both: "YHWH appeared to Abram and said, I am El Shaddai" (Gen 17:1). As noted, Genesis 4:26, in a verse half, cannot really intend to make the all-important declaration of a first-time appearance of the sacred name of YHWH.[10] The compressed nature of a memorial of such an important occasion, and the terminology "to call on the name," do not point in this direction. In addition, the question posed by Moses about his ability to produce the name to the people of Israel (3:13) makes no obvious sense if they don't know the name already so as to verify what he tells them.[11] One recent effort to understand the disagreement over the name from a different angle has argued that neither Moses nor the people of Israel know the name, and so both J and P actually agree that the solemn name YHWH is not revealed until this time.[12] Yet how odd then, for when one reads further into Exodus, this pivotal scene of the conveying of the new name to the people never happens. Rather, Moses simply continues to theorize about new objections they will pose, as if the name YHWH is not really at any issue but rather the known YHWH's new agent Moses (4:1). God doesn't respond on the

---

[10] A point made quite resolutely by Claus Westermann in his massive Genesis commentary. See *Genesis 1–11: A Continental Commentary* (Minneapolis: Augsburg, 1984; German original, 1974).

[11] See my summary, among others on this point, in "The Call of Moses," in *Word without End: The Old Testament as Abiding Theological Witness* (Waco, Tex.: Baylor University Press, 2005).

[12] Walter Moberly, *The Old Testament of the Old Testament*, OBT (Minneapolis: Fortress, 1992).

front of first-time name recognition but rather supplies signs and wonders and, exasperatingly, an agent to accompany Moses (4:1-17). When the encounter happens at last, Aaron acts as spokesman, signs are done, and the people believe (4:29-31). Not a word about the name revelation or its relevance.

The idea of a disagreement over such a significant thing as God's name and its disclosure would on its face seem odd. This would leave the much later source P primarily concerned to lodge the negative point at Exodus 6 that J was wrong. If the "sources" have now become postexilic contemporaries with new nomenclature, as is widely held in European scholarship, it's not clear what this debate is about or why it would matter.[13] Once P has lodged his strong objection to the use of the name before Moses by a different source, it remains unclear how or why the criterion might function in any meaningful way from then on. That is, the recourse to the criterion after Exodus 6 diminishes the idea that Exodus 6 was saying what it has been held it was saying and suggests rather that something else must be going on in that chapter. To say this is to wonder aloud about just what YHWH and Elohim alterations after this point in the story might mean at all.

There can be little doubt that in Genesis one can make the *general* idea of alteration of the divine name line up with certain *general* trends one sees in the material. So for example, von Rad successfully extracted J from the story line of Genesis 1–11 and set it in contrast with what was left—for the most part, P. He then saw a pattern. Fall and clothing (sin and divine mitigation); murder and a mark for protection (sin and divine mitigation); flood and rainbow (sin and divine mitigation); a tower's destruction and a scattering over the face of all the earth (again sin, but now no mitigation).

---

[13] Thomas B. Dozeman and Konrad Schmid, eds., *Farewell to the Yahwist?: The Composition of the Pentateuch in Recent European Interpretation*, SBLSS 34 (Atlanta: Scholars, 2006) gives a good overview of the shifting direction of Pentateuchal studies. See also Thomas B. Dozeman, Konrad Schmid, and Baruch J. Schwartz, eds., *The Pentateuch: International Perspectives on Recent Research* (Tübingen: Mohr Siebeck, 2011).

The next move from J became then all-important. The call of Abram would be the mitigation of all mitigations, the beginning of real history and of the first history writing, the start of God's work of rectification through election and all that portended for the nations scattered after Babel.[14]

Yet even von Rad, later in life, in the final edition of his own Genesis commentary, wondered about the propriety of working in this manner, even though it lay at the heart of his effort to make source criticism join up with form criticism at the service of theological reading.[15] This was his lifetime project: moving from the creedal forms of recitation (Deut 6 and 26) which provided the ground floor of oral tradition in annual worship settings, coalescing with other traditions, and then coming into Wellhausen's J and so forth. He began to acknowledge that Genesis 1–11 presents the primal history in which J was joined by P by a redactor, whose work also needed consideration. For the "fall" to have its real effect, it needed the "very good" of P's creation. And others pointed out that the flood story was far more central in the conjoined narrative for J and P both than would be properly accounted for if you extracted P and then posited a series of four things overcome by the call of Abraham.[16] God had threatened to un-create and reverse Genesis 1 in the conjoined narrative of the flood. But having done so, he indicates he will not ever do so again in this manner and places a rainbow in the sky as his solemn pledge. History is made possible because creation itself is preserved and made the theater of God's saving activity. History is the product of the generations

---

[14] See the further discussion below in chapter 14.

[15] I have an extended treatment in "Prophecy and Tradition-History: The Achievement of Gerhard von Rad and Beyond," in I. Fischer, K. Schmid, and H. G. M. Williamson, eds., *Prophetie in Israel: Beitrage des Symposiums "Das Alte Testament und die Kultur der Moderne" anlässlich des 100. Geburtstags Gerhard von Rads (1901–1971) Heidelberg, 18.–21. Oktober 2001*, ATM 11 (Munster: Lit-Verlag, 2003), 30–51. See also "The Historical-Critical Endeavor as Theology: The Legacy of Gerhard von Rad," in *Word without End*, 28–40.

[16] See references to Rolf Rendtorff and others in chapter 14 below.

of the heavens and the earth (Gen 2:4), and the ongoing fact of this is reasserted in Genesis 8:22. There can be no call for Abram to leave Ur and go to a land to be shown without the clear sense that such a place is a destination of God's sure providential care and purposing. To have "salvation history" without "a bulwarked creation" is an abstraction without adequate underpinning.

So even if there be grounds for thinking in terms of distinctive traditions in Genesis, the idea of a disagreement over revelation of the divine name overshadows all that in the end. It is hard to imagine what the point of a later source tolerating such a blatant contradiction in Genesis might be. When one can see clear cooperation in other places—I would put von Rad's observations about J and P in Genesis 1–11 in this category—and a conjoined narrative making more not less theological sense when different hands coalesce to produce the text before us, it becomes difficult to believe a kind of grudge is being held that shows a disagreement so it can be given a conclusively negative verdict in the sixth chapter of Exodus. Single verses like Genesis 17:1 look like something other than disagreement and more like mutual enrichment.

On my own reading, Exodus 3 and Exodus 6 don't disagree over this matter. The first account tells how Moses came to knowledge of the name, and also in so doing was gifted with knowledge of God's personal character in that name as he who makes good on promises. For the true disclosure of the name, then, he and Israel must suffer through hardship and difficult encounters and through that see that God is good to his word and name. The second account isn't a call narrative anyway (as is now recognized in commentary treatments). It is a solemn reassurance to Moses following an exacerbated and death-threatening situation. The promises made to the patriarchs are being fulfilled. God's work with Moses is rooted in his entire life project with his people. God does not say that he did not make his name known (that would require a causative verb) but that he was not known in his name when he appeared earlier as he intends now: as he who makes good on promises that were solemnly given but not seen to fruition. The distinction is between appearances to his people in promise and the fulfillment of that, whereby the true significance of a name they knew is disclosed. Rashi had argued for this view of matters in his own way in the pre-critical period by noting the strange use of the passive form of the verb in first-person with a third-person subject in Exodus 6:2: "My name YHWH I was not known."

What then of the account of first-time revelation of the name? If Exodus 3 does not tell this (how could the people ask for a name they do not know, and learn anything when the air waves produced a name in their ears? "Ozymandius" would do) and neither does Exodus 6, it is hard to see Genesis 4:26 bearing this kind of weight. In my view Genesis 4:26 is important, but not on the terms being requested. *In my judgment the Old Testament neither asks nor answers the question about a time before which the divine name YHWH was not known.* It does not ask this or answer it because it has no answer God has provided in his life with them. As Westermann noted, the point of Genesis 4:26 is not to say "at this point in time I made my name know to humanity"—which would exactly fit the criterion of revelation of a divine name (causative verb from *yd'*). To "call upon the name" is the technical language of worship. It means, in the era of primordial time, the God being worshipped by humanity was and is YHWH.[17] Moberly spoke of the omniscience of the author responsible for the divine name in Genesis, who strictly speaking was introducing the name into a period long before it had been revealed for the very first time to Moses and so accepted the burden of historical anachronism in the name of theology. Because it is not the case that either account in Exodus speaks of first-time revelation, it would not be proper, then, to describe this as a studied anachronism by an omniscient narrator who knows the name is not revealed until much later. Rather, what Genesis 4:26 is saying is, the only true worship of God that happened and will happen will be of YHWH. To call on Elohim God is to call on YHWH. And so humanity in primordial time and the ancestors

---

[17] Westermann, *Genesis 1–11*, ad loc.

in God's history following Babel have relationship with and hear from and call upon YHWH.

We would need to locate the Elder Testament's decision to provide an account that explained: before now no name but rather an appellation, after that the declaration of the personal name. But none is to be found. Again, in my view the before no/after yes declaration of the name on these terms simply took on no special purchase within Israel's encounters with the living God. What we do know is that with Moses and the people of the exodus, the personally revealed YHWH is the "I am who make good on promises before your very eyes," whereas before this humanity lived in promise and faith in relationship to YHWH God. Perhaps it was viewed as blasphemous to probe for more in the form of what would rightly be called be "the etiology of all etiologies": that is, the report of an historical disclosure of the very name of God before which God had not been called upon as YHWH. One man—the antediluvian Job—may be said to have encroached on terrain like this. The God El Shaddai answered with might and fearful disclosure. This El Shaddai, the narrator tells readers observing the drama, was in fact YHWH (Job 1–2; 42:7-17). And he allows Job to utter a properly pious declaration of blessing of YHWH (1:21). Yet for the bulk of the drama he is not dealing with the God of promise and fulfillment and torah giving—YHWH as he is who he is in Exodus—but with an alien and strange YHWH God inside of unbearable suffering. And just so, the narrator prefers to share with us who this alien God is, we who oversee and in our own anguish observe, but who rightly close our mouths as those who seek not to be false friends in the encounter between YHWH God and the man Job.

It is not my point to suggest that the book of Job offers an example of what it means for the Elder Scripture not to have included an account of the signal disclosure of the Hebrew word YHWH from the mouth of the Living God now to be known by that name. Its themes are rich enough without asking Job to be probing for an answer to this theological paradox as well. Clearly he does not. But the book offers an interesting example of what it means to pursue the protagonist portrayed as a contemporary of Noah (Ezek 14:20) into the hoary time of what Luther called patriarchal temptation, when God in his *Urgewalt* dealt with a people before the Law. This God is always YHWH, as the folktale surrounding the main drama of Job makes clear (Job 1:6-12), even when the same YHWH will make himself known as the fulfiller of promises to the Patriarchs, including Job, when he is "I am who I am as I make myself known in the events of your deliverance" at this later time.

7

YHWH and Elohim
The LORD God

In this chapter I will stay with the Pentateuchal source problem but move more toward the theological potential latent in what it means for different terms of reference for God to exist in the opening book of the Elder Scripture. The issue has a long history and did not always head in the direction of the classical JEDP formulation. In the modern period it was challenged in the context of disputing sources entirely, in favor of a single authorial hand. That is not a view I share, even as it did take seriously another possibility for explaining the name variation so obviously in evidence in the text of Genesis.

Many recent specialists in Pentateuchal theory have rejected the idea both of sources and of thinking of them as discrete and only secondarily combined by redactors. This still results in two different models: one that sees a second level of tradition working directly on a previous one, and asserting a variant position in strong terms, and another that views the augmentation less combatively, and more on the order of complementation. I will not engage the proponents for these two positions directly or in detail, as it is beyond the scope of the present study. Instead I will give an example of a reading along the latter lines in the context of the opening chapters of Genesis. The point of this exercise will be to show that the interchange of the divine name may function more coherently than is held to be the case. I am not trying to overreach and "solve a puzzle," which in any event the final canonical presentation retains for other important reasons as discussed in chapter 5 above. My goal is to offer an alternative to the idea that the variation is of no significance, indicates disagreement, or can be attributed to a more abstract idea of single authorial alternation and predilection. The final horizon, however, is the possibility I entertain that the different names function in the realm on ontology and economic disclosure. That is, a very significant theological issue of transcendence and immanence is at work in the way the final consolidation of the Elder Scripture has thought about and set forth its presentation of YHWH Elohim.

This chapter, then, begins to edge toward the more sustained ontological evaluation that will be the focus of part 3 of this book. To give something of a sample of that at this point makes sense to me. It will also allow me to bring in an example from art: the depiction of the burning bush in the works of Derik Bouts, Nicholas Froment, and Marc Chagall. The issues raised at the close of the chapter are the subject of focused development in chapter 12.

Generally speaking, three movements mutually reinforced one another from the sixteenth to the eighteenth centuries: the production of vernacular translations of the Bible; the release of the Bible into popular cultural imagination, in consequence; and the emergence of nation states. The figure of Moses loomed large as nation states sought venerable models of law and statecraft.[1] One

---

[1] On this, see the engaging reflections in Michael Legaspi, *The Death of Scripture and the Rise of Biblical Studies* (Oxford: Oxford University Press, 2010).

thinks of the formidable statue of Moses by Michelangelo (1513) and fascination more generally with him and his writings in the next centuries, including criticisms of his written art in Genesis (so Hobbes and Spinoza in the seventeenth century). There were also critical introductions to the Old Testament that understood Genesis in particular as composed of sources (the Roman Catholic Richard Simon's work was translated into English in 1682). Jean Astruc (working in the eighteenth century) fought back against Hobbes and Spinoza by arguing that Moses composed Genesis in four different columns, much like the Gospels, but an editor clumsily combined them and produced a work that then gave rise to wrongful criticism. In all of this the alternation of the divine name was central in reconstructing these putative sources.[2]

As the legacy of this kind of investigation migrated into the late nineteenth and early twentieth centuries, most felt there were two main sources, not just in Genesis but also in the Pentateuch or even further: the Elohist and Yahwist. This corresponded to the use of Elohim and YHWH respectively in these documents. The Elohist was the main source and the Yahwist a supplementary source or supplement as such. In point of fact, the great "discovery" of the documentary hypothesis such as we now refer to it was not the argument for sources. As noted, this went back into the seventeenth century at least (earlier still, Rashi spoke of YHWH as the promise fulfiller and Genesis as a period not of fulfillment but of promise, under Elohim). It was the conclusion that the Elohist source was in fact a later, postexilic source, which imposed upon older traditions an understanding of priesthood and sanctuary that had no place in ancient Israel's life. P was thus birthed as we now

---

[2] For detailed discussion, see now the volumes in the three-volume work edited by Magne Saebo, *Hebrew Bible/Old Testament: The History of Its Interpretation* (Göttingen: Vandenhoeck & Ruprecht, 1996–2014), esp. vol. 2, *From the Renaissance to the Enlightenment*; vol 3, *From Modernism to Post-Modernism*, part 1, *The Nineteenth Century*. Still valuable as well is Henning Graf Reventlow, *The Authority of the Bible and the Rise of the Modern World* (Philadelphia: Fortress, 1985).

mean the term. The fact that so minimal reference was made to this material in the former and latter prophets convinced Wellhausen (and predecessors Reuss, Kuenen, and de Wette) that the former prophets and those they addressed knew nothing of it. It was in fact a late work and in his view one that sought to pass itself off as "early" and "historical" according to the lexicon of the day, and so was a fraudulently detailed poseur. As such it represented a deteriorative phase, one properly to be called a "Judaism" from which Jesus and the New Testament sought release and against which they levelled harsh and appropriate criticism.

In our present period the theory is under massive reconstruction, though some "neo-Wellhausians" continue to ply their trade.[3] The "new documentary critics" are unsure what to label things. J isn't the same as previous accounts held, so what to call it so as not to confuse has become a question. It is an exilic/postexilic epic. Some think it ought to be lodged alongside or called what had been called D. If the former P writing is now its contemporary, some prefer to speak of it as non-J. Genesis is a distinctive book in the Pentateuch as its presentation of promise and blessing seems not to presuppose a delay in the descent into Egypt, or so it is maintained. (Where this appears it is a minor theme and has been edited in.) Equally, most of the following books say very little about the ancestors as critical to God's "mighty act" in bringing Israel out of Egypt. (Where this appears it is a minor theme and has been edited in.) So the new documentary work proceeds.[4]

It is not our goal to say more about these trends, except to indicate that what went by JEDP forty years ago is by no means the

---

[3] Notably, and exuberantly, Joel Baden, *The Composition of the Pentateuch: Renewing the Documentary Hypothesis* (New Haven: Yale University Press, 2012). For a popular account in his own words, see http://www.bibleinterp.com/articles/bad368008.shtml. He writes at one point: "For scholars trained in the Documentary Hypothesis, as most Americans still are, there's a feeling that if you blinked at the wrong moment, you missed the sudden emergence of a radical new wave of scholarship." This has as much to do with the balkanization of scholarship as it does with blinking at the wrong moment.

[4] See the above note on newer Pentateuchal studies.

obvious rite of passage it once was for seminary and religious studies students, on those same terms. Some have broken away entirely and simply prescind from this kind of developmental theorizing, preferring to work with a synchronic model of interpretation that focuses on the present text and the reader's anticipated status as a reader. So it has become unclear what we are now to make of the interchange of the divine name, which certainly in Genesis was seen to require evaluation and explanation of some kind going back now for several centuries. One might wonder if in this kind of a model a theological disagreement over a properly ancient revelation of the divine name would be a false trail. An "author" might just shuttle back and forth, taking turns with various divine names as it were. Yet to say this would seem to imply that there is really nothing very much at stake in the revelation of the divine name, when in fact the text itself insists on its centrality, however we come to terms with this.

One recent effort to resolve the question of the divine name I referred to above, and versions of this have appeared in previous guises. This is the view that Exodus at all points agrees that only with Moses did knowledge of the name occur, and from him to Israel. As to the obvious question of why the name YHWH appears in Genesis, the answer given by Walter Moberly is: it is an anachronism introduced to make the point that the Elohim who is a character in Genesis is and can only be YHWH.[5] A fact known later in time is nevertheless a fact that should sound forth previously. The additional point is then made that the two testaments function this way analogously. What is known of God in Christ is assumed to be true of the God of Israel essentially. Of course the fact that this has not been registered as a Christian gloss of the Old Testament in its literary form, on analogy, must be registered as a difference; we do not read in Psalm 22, "My God, my God he said

---

[5] Walter Moberly, *The Old Testament of the Old Testament*, OBT (Minneapolis: Fortress, 1992). My engagement is found in *Word without End: The Old Testament as Abiding Theological Witness* (Waco, Tex.: Baylor University Press, 2005), 229–47.

from tree," nor have Christians placed "the Logos" next to specific occasions in the Old Testament where such a gloss might be fitting, like Genesis 1:1.[6] On his view, Genesis is "the Old Testament of the Old Testament" but also has received an omniscient glossing to make sure we know Elohim in the Genesis Old Testament to be the YHWH of the Exodus and following "testament."

I have mentioned problems with this view when it comes to reading Exodus 3 and Exodus 6 above. If to be taken seriously, moreover, one might expect direct discourse to be a place where use of the divine name is avoided. Yet Genesis quite happily allows the characters in its portrayal to speak of YHWH realistically and as imbedded fully in their pre-Exodus lives.[7]

There was a different approach to the problem of the divine name that should be mentioned, which arose as an objection to the documentary hypothesis altogether when at its heyday. One and the same author—presumably even Moses himself—alternated between YHWH and Elohim. Helpful here would be an explanation for why that happens. U. Cassuto sought to do just this in his arguments against the source-critical approach.[8] YHWH was the personal God of Israel, and when the author used Elohim, his horizon was widened to be consistent with the subject being related, on a more universal plane. Genesis 1, then, uses Elohim because the text is speaking about the creation of the whole world. Similarly Cassuto sought to find a consistent application of notions like this to explain the alternation of the divine name not just in Genesis but more broadly through the Pentateuch (where after Exodus 6 such a procedure might even make more sense, given the now consensus of J and P forged at Exodus 6, according to the theory).

[6] Part 3 looks at this dimension.

[7] For Abraham and his generation only, see direct discourse at Gen 15:2, 7; 16:2, 5; 18:14, 27, 31, 32; 20:4; 24:3, 12, 31, 35, 40, 42, 44, 48, 56; 26:28-29.

[8] Umberto Cassuto, *The Documentary Hypothesis and the Composition of the Pentateuch: Eight Lectures by U. Cassuto*, trans. Israel Abrahams (Jerusalem: Shalem Press, 2006; Hebrew original, 1941). The Pentateuch was a unified and coherent composition produced in the tenth century and unaltered thereafter.

One can have a certain sympathy for the approach of Cassuto as at least raising the question of alternation of the name if one does not believe Exodus 6 says what the documentary hypothesis claims: that here P asserts the view that J is wrong and no proper use of YHWH prior to its point in time is genuinely warranted. If Exodus is not saying this, as we hold, then asking why an alteration happens makes a good deal of sense. In my view, however, one can ask this question quite independently of asserting a single author is at work in the Pentateuch, which was certainly an agenda item of Cassuto. If we think of different levels of tradition in Genesis and the ensuing books of the Pentateuch; and we think of secondary supplementation in a more complementary fashion; and we try to understand the canonical presentation at work within a multi-leveled text whose tensions have not all been tidily resolved with erasure and redaction, which may reflect different emphases and concerns—including the use of the divine name—we can certainly seek to understand that apart from the conceptions of Wellhausen or Cassuto or some of the more recent efforts of Pentateuchal interpretation. We may even find ourselves back in something of the terrain of pre-nineteenth-century evaluation!

Looked at from the standpoint of the present state of the field, the perspective of Brevard S. Childs, in spite of reception of him in the 1980s, appears very traditional when it comes to source analysis. Traditional J and P are pretty much up and running, with the former passing from oral forms and a tradition-history into what the consensus of the mid-twentieth century held, and the latter equally, though perhaps more in the form of a supplement that a strictly independent "source" spliced in with difficulty by yet another hand. In a way not unlike the later von Rad, Childs was however interested in the cumulative effect of a text in which these two sources had been meaningfully combined. A good example, and one that became a hallmark of the 1979 *Introduction to the Old Testament as Scripture*, was the "seam" verse between the creation account (classical P) and the fall story, now appearing at Genesis 2:4a. Childs noted that "these are the generations" rubrics in

Genesis unfailingly introduce material, yet here, for the "P not J" source theory to work optimally, it would be useful to let 2:4a be the final refrain of what precedes and so P *in toto* (1:1–2:4b). Then we have a (roughly transitioned) altogether new start at 2:4b and a consistently J account running to the close of chapter 3.[9]

He argued instead that the verse's purpose could not be explained within strict documentary logic. We expect it to introduce and not conclude, and so, he argued, it does. The generational activity of "heavens and earth" includes the creation of humanity, and so that theme as introduced in 1:26-31 is here enlarged and extended in what follows. The Bible has no trouble picking up a thread and returning to it, and will make that move more decisive than what we might want in one-after-the-other temporal rigidity (the classic example in Genesis 1–11 is the Tower of Babel and Table of Nations juxtaposition).[10]

This insight can help us understand the way the divine name functions. Genesis 1 begins, as Cassuto argued, with the divine name Elohim as appropriate to its horizons, as dealing with all creation. Whatever priority von Rad sought to give to J, moreover, in his brilliant theological extraction and interpretation, it remains the case that we hear this tradition level through the lens of what has been called the Priestly writer. Childs notes the careful amalgamation accomplished literarily at 2:4a, but he will go further and indicate that the sequencing means history is viewed through the lens of ontology.[11] This requires careful articulation, so let's move more slowly now.

---

[9] See Childs, *Introduction to the Old Testament as Scripture* (Philadelphia: Fortress, 1979). See now Sarah Schwartz, "Narrative *Toledot* Formula in Genesis: The Case of Heaven and Earth, Noah, and Isaac," *JHS* 16 (2016): 1–36. Our discussion follows on in chapter 14 below.

[10] Jon Levenson, "The Eighth Principle of Judaism and the Literary Simultaneity of Scripture," in his *The Hebrew Bible, the Old Testament, and Historical Criticism* (Louisville, Ky.: Westminster John Knox, 1993), 62–81.

[11] Brevard S. Childs, *Biblical Theology of the Old and New Testaments: Theological Reflection on the Christian Bible* (Minneapolis: Fortress, 1993). The scholarly priority given to acts and "history" over creation (Bernhard Anderson's

It might be useful to recapitulate what we have been saying this far. (1) Let's say there are different tradition levels in Genesis and throughout the Pentateuch and that these can be identified in part as having a predilection, though not exclusively and not in disagreement with one another, for YHWH and Elohim. (2) These levels work to provide a complementary account in which their conjunction is theologically important. (3) The Old Testament does not ask or answer the question of first-time disclosure of the divine name YHWH. (4) Instead, Genesis opens with the generic name of God. (5) The generic name is a name Israel knows is used throughout the world, in Hebrew for them, and in approximate equivalents in Semitic cultures within which it lives. (6) The personal name for God, which Israel knows, admits of important enlargement and signification precisely because the name exists in a relationship initiated by YHWH God, maintained by him, and bearing a people through history and time. Decisively in Exodus and in promises in Genesis, YHWH makes himself known as the Elohim who created the heavens and the earth, all peoples, and who lives in personal relationship with Israel as named LORD.

When we read the account attributed to J (2:4b-3:24), following the introduction in P of Elohim (1:1-23), Elohim is now exclusively YHWH Elohim (2:4, 5, 7, 8, 9, 15, 16, 18, 19, 21, 22,; 3:1, 8, 9, 13, 14, 21, 22, 23). The repetition (20 times in 46 verses) is striking almost to the point of tedium. It is the snake who refers to the deity as just "Elohim" (3:1, 5) (and Eve once in the context of his questioning). The intimate life Adam and Eve share under the divine name YHWH God they alone share. After the departure from the garden YHWH is the name used for God in the following story of Cain and Abel. Genesis 5:1 recapitulates Genesis 1 and so speaks of Elohim. From then on, we have the alternation of the name, having been assured that worship of God in primordial time and thereafter, if it is worship of the one true God, is worship of YHWH in point

---

popularization in *Understanding the Old Testament*, which begins with the Exodus) is here critically questioned given the canonical portrayal's emphasis. See our discussion below.

of fact (4:26). As Westermann noted, the compact phrase means: worship of YHWH was proper worship from time immemorial.[12]

The old source theory and its modern permutations need proper, proportional evaluation. In my view the biblical text must be read on a case-by-case basis, and no single universal theory can be made to account for all the evidence. One level of tradition prefers to say that in Genesis—and perhaps more broadly—the divine name YHWH constitutes the character of appearance to Israel. This is true appearance and real presence by means of the name. But for this tradition, the *making known* of God as YHWH is a distinct act in time (*usemi YHWH noda'ti*). Prior to this, the narrator prefers to guard something of the historicality of a previous dispensation, and so while as narrator he may speak of YHWH to the reader (Gen 17:1), in direct discourse various forms of El are frequently deployed (El, Elohim, El Shaddai, the God of X person or Y place). A corollary tradition level does not labor as hard over this distinction. The only God is always and forever YHWH. Since both levels of tradition agree at this point, a successful manner of reading will not operate from the basis of disagreement but from the measured lens of complementarity. Inside of that, surprises may still be in store.

In conclusion I want to return to the observation that a decision has been made to give priority in the tradition process to ontology over economy, or what we mean by historical or temporal disclosure.[13] I have explained it above as a movement focusing on gradual recognition, as against a once-upon-a-time, single-event revelation: "I am now YHWH." Rather, Genesis purposefully moves from the generally used and recognized name Elohim to YHWH Elohim to YHWH and Elohim both. Yet more may be said. Israel's personal life with God and YHWH's knowledge provision of himself in time and in relationship are the economic manifestations of the one God of all time, before time, the creator in time of heaven

---

[12] Claus Westermann, *Genesis 1–11: A Continental Commentary* (Minneapolis: Augsburg, 1984; German original, 1974).

[13] Brevard S. Childs, *Biblical Theology of the Old and New Testaments*.

and earth. "In beginning God created the heavens and the earth" means that the one and only God is God *in se* before he is God in relationship to time and space, and before he is YHWH God and YHWH who is as he is as he is made known to Moses and Israel in salvation and with Pharaoh in judgment, and through the account of this to us today.

It has long been noted that the Hebrew *bereshith* is unusual in form and might be rendered "when God began to create" thus dampening a stronger sense of creation from outside of time, into time, or creation *ex nihilo*.[14] In my view the matter would turn far more on something other than a grammatical oddity. What can be noted, however, is that both Jewish and Christian tradition were perfectly able to think about "beginning" as much in terms of agency as a strictly temporal category. "In a first X" God created. For Philo this X was the perfect manifestation of God in his economy, or Torah. God created via his Word, his Torah, the supreme expression of himself. For one line of Christian thinking this beginning or *arche* was also the perfect expression of God's self, through whom anything that was made was made, the Word of God.[15] "In beginning was the Word, and the Word was with God, and the Word was God, all things were created through him and without him was not anything made that was made" (John 1:1). The light created was of his life.

In speaking of the ontology of Elohim and the economy of creation through Torah or Logos, the tradition was trying to come to terms with the pressure exerted by the Old Testament's literal sense, a pressure that was the consequence of belief in one God as before and above the things he made, but also as radically and personally active in making those things and making himself known reliably by his word and by his appearing, in personal

---

[14] In the beginning God created (RSV, KJV, ESV); when God created/began to create (Living Bible; Common English Bible); when God began to create (NRSV).

[15] A fuller treatment follows in part 3. We want simply to introduce the matter here in the narrower context of modern source-critical readings.

relationship. YHWH is Elohim, and as YHWH he is the most personal manifestation in time of God as is possible, to the point of risk and shared suffering with a people who will fail him. Here we have explanation for why it is that Irenaeus and the early fathers saw Christ *in* the Old Testament and not just pointing ahead to him. The dynamic "monotheism" that insists there is but One God and no other, and yet also insists this God is truly disclosed in the life of a people, meant that the Old Testament had its own distinctive kind of "incarnation," though under signs and figures.[16] For one line of Jewish interpretation all this was equally true. God had a shekinah, a word, a torah, a wisdom that was truly himself but that also pointed to an ontology before time.

In my view the failure to think theologically about the interchange of the divine name, especially in the opening chapters of Genesis, and instead to think of historical sources and authors in disagreement, has meant a wrong turn or too-long detour. It has pursued an aspect of the matter in literary and historical terms but failed to think about the canonical shape of the same text and its own theological achievements. When latter Isaiah and Ezekiel again speak of YHWH Elohim, we should be alert to something. We will take that matter up below. In the final section of the present work we will return to explore in more detail the implications of Genesis 1:1 for divine agency. For now, I want to turn to a second example of how the Elder Testament in its narrative form seeks to correlate economic and ontological perspectives in such a way that the literal sense rendering is also open to larger theological significance.

Moses at the Burning Bush

Art can be an effective way to explore the dimension of ontology in biblical depiction and how an economic portrayal can also refract a

---

[16] Christopher Seitz, "The Trinity in the Old Testament," in Gilles Emery and Matthew Levering, eds., *The Oxford Handbook of the Trinity* (Oxford: Oxford University Press, 2011), 28–40.

second level of meaning. Like narrative, it can differentiate between the viewer's perspective and what is happening in what is being depicted. The story of God's appearance to Moses at the burning bush was a favorite place to introduce a wider perspective while at the same time realistically painting what Exodus 3 related. Let's rehearse what the opening verses of that chapter describe.

Moses is tending the flock of his father-in-law. He drives the flock to the "back" of the wilderness (sometimes rendered "west," but the Hebrew sounds a bit more ominous).[17] This is a place out of the ordinary. He has come to the mountain of God. We know that Moses sees before him a burning bush. The narrator tells us this, and he says so himself. It is a great sight, he says, insofar as something is burning but does not burn itself up. The narrator explains to us that an angel of YHWH appeared to him in the flame of fire, yet we cannot be sure whether Moses has this same sense of affairs. He does not refer to an angel but to a bush on fire. What we then learn is that when he turns aside to look, or because he has already done so, God speaks to him and addresses him by name twice. Moses gives a standard Hebrew response: "Here am I." The narrator makes sure we know that YHWH is this God. Moses is told that he is on holy ground and must remove his shoes. God then tells Moses he is the God of his father, and the God of the ancestors. Moses' reaction to this is to hide his face for fear, now that he knows, as we already do, that God is the one addressing him

Most art picks up on the details of removing his shoes and further shows that his gaze is averted. The burning bush invites central and impressive rendering and is usually but not always the focus of the canvas. Fire is of course alive and makes for dramatic depiction. Because we are given to see that what the artist chooses to show us in respect of the bush, Moses has guarded himself from seeing, consistent with the details of Exodus 3, this can enable a wider lens than the strictly economic. Yet even here we must be clear that when we speak

---

[17] See William Propp, *Exodus 1–18*, AB (New Haven: Yale University Press, 1997).

of God as he is—and this most surely is the main subject of Exodus 3's "I am who I am"—and God as he appears, we are entitled to this wider lens.[18] The economic and the ontological have come alongside one another. Moses hears a voice and turns aside because it is God's and because God has so cautioned him. But what then will the artist choose to show us, as he who knows a wider account of who the eternal God is based upon a textual frame of reference greater than Moses', but derived all the same from the details of Exodus 3 and Moses' unique and significant encounter?

Marc Chagall, with his spare, evocative, imaginative style, shows Moses (with his horns) rapturously staring into middle space.[19] The angel hovers above the bush and the kneeling Moses, behind whom are the sheep of a shepherd. His feet are already bare. The bush is the largest thing painted, colorfully on fire. Above the bush we see the Hebrew letters *yod, heh, wav, heh*, the sacred consonants of the divine name. They seem to exist in a kind of penumbra, encircled, with beams of light emanating toward heaven above. Maybe this is glory or effulgence, such as Exodus will frequently mention under the topos of *kabod*. We see that Moses is in the presence of YHWH, and the economic manifestation of that is glory and Hebrew consonants, the latter which we read who know Hebrew, and which are directed to us even as Moses also seems to be looking our way.

A fifteenth-century Catholic version in the school of van Dyke and art from the Low Countries of the period, rendered by the Louvain painter Dieric Bouts, is more realistic in character. It shows a preliminary stage of Moses removing his shoes and then the main in which he is shoeless before the bush. His staff lies at his feet. Sheep graze on the hillside. In the distance is a mountain, or a range of mountains. Bushes like the one before Moses dot the

---

[18] On perspective and omniscience in biblical reporting, see the magisterial account of Meir Sternberg, *The Poetics of Biblical Narrative: Ideological Literature and the Drama of Reading* (Bloomington: Indiana University Press, 1985).

[19] The depiction of Moses with horns goes back to Jerome's Latin rendering of Hebrew *keren*—usually taken to be radiating beams—as *conuta* or "horns."

Moses and the Burning Bush, from The Story of Exodus by Marc Chagall

landscape, presumably to say that this was a bush of normal type. But from this bush, from the flames that top it, appears to be God Almighty. The angel bit of the story has not been rendered by Bouts. Moses is diverting his gaze from the God who stretches forth in human form from the bush. The right hand of the God-man is extended in benediction, like that of a priest. In his left hand he holds what appears to be a translucent globe. This is a curious detail. Perhaps the painter is showing off his craft. This is a detail we do not have in Exodus 3.

Bouts is said to have been interested in lines of intersection in his painting and a focal point. In terms of scale the largest figure in the painting is the gaze-averted Moses in the foreground. The divine figure is smaller. Though God Almighty can be depicted as an elderly man with a beard, that is not the universal practice. The hand in benediction, the clothing, and the beard resemble in this case Christ, though we are on firmer ground in taking the figure to be the Vicar of Christ, the Pope, who holds universal

112 The Elder Testament

Moses and the Burning Bush, with Moses Removing His Shoes
by Dierick Bouts the Elder

dominion in the place of Christ or on behalf of him. The detail of staging the removal of shoes is frequently noted, but is this just an eccentricity of the painter in this work? Why depict this? One could argue that the benediction is directed as much to the world behind Moses as to him as such. Benediction isn't a detail in Exodus 3 of course. The Vicar of Christ is blessing the world at large: the Flemish countryside; Moses at work, slowly removing his sandals; the villages of our common life. As such he is holding the world in his hand. We know from the fourth century onward that the globe with a cross is the symbol of universal sovereignty, and so Bouts depicts it here. God Almighty is not depicted because the only form in which we can view him, as the Catholic painter would know, is as he has been made known in the Son, and in the church via the blessing he bestows through the petrine office. Moses averts his eyes. This "great sight" is not his to view, in his dispensation, but is seen under a sign or figure that the later perspective of Bouts feels free to display.

The last example is the most amplified. It is part of the altar tryptic of the Cathedral of St-Saveur in Aix-en-Provence, painted by Nicolas Froment. He is a French painter from the Gard (Uzès) and paints a bit later than Bouts and under the influence of Flemish artists. Here the bush is the center of attention and fills the top half of the canvas. It sits upon a mountain of God, one supposes. Flames of fire can be seen emanating from the top of the bush, but the main theme is Virgin and Child. Here the angel of the Lord has a main role, and stands in the position of concerned cautioner, left hand raised in warning. Sheep (and sheep dog) surround Moses as he is in the act of removing his shoes. His gaze is averted, and he shields his eyes with his right hand. With the bold depiction of Virgin and Child—a theme Froment inherited with a long legacy before him, including eastern iconic depiction—we are here confronted with the boldest form of what historical-critical conceptuality would call anachronism.[20]

---

[20] "Moïse vit un boisson ardent que la flamme ne pouvait consumer et au milieu duquel Dieu lui apparût. C'est là une figure de la Saine-Vierge, car elle porte en elle la flamme du Saint-Esprit sans brûler du feu de la concupiscence" (Marcel Brion, *La Provence* [Artaud, 1960]). The quote comes from Honorius d'Autun, and it captures the traditional interpretation. Moses sees, and God speaks to him. The bush is what it is realistically/extraordinarily and as such is a prospective figure.

114   The Elder Testament

Triptych of the Burning Bush, Aix Cathedral, by Nicolas Froment

Popular interpretations emphasize things like the Holy Spirit as fire; the promise from the Angel that the Holy Spirit would come upon Mary (Luke 1:35); the perpetual virginity of Mary; the Holy

Spirit Fire that comes upon her but does not consume her; and so forth. More intriguing for our purposes is the place in Luke's Gospel where all of this is stated in Luke's terms, in the context of the nativity. Shepherds—like Moses—are keeping their flocks. An angel appears to them, and they are afraid. They are told not to look away, but to have no fear, and indeed to go and behold. And so in haste they do. They find Mary and Joseph and the baby. Mary kept all these things in her heart. If we look very closely in Froment's painting we see a small painter's conceit. It looks like a miniature rendition of the center of the painting we are viewing, of Mother and Child. It is in fact a mirror—the figures are obverse—which the smiling infant holds in his tiny hand. Perhaps this is Froment's idea of Mary's memorial, which her son holds up for her to see.

Moses does not see all this in his economic life with God. His gaze is, as in all renditions and true to the text of Exodus 3, averted. All he has seen is what the narrative has him refer to as "this strange sight." But he has indeed heard the true voice of God, and that voice makes God known fully in his time and space, as God wills to be known, sufficient and true, evoking worship and praise. Chagall captures this moment best with his raptured Moses and flying angel. Bouts sees this encounter as universal in intention and in final accomplishment, if not so grasped by Moses in his time, true all the same. Froment sees in his mind a kind of dyptic—a figural sign—in which angels, flocks, fear, and the most dramatic interventions of God in time are properly—in Elder and New disclosures—to be correlated for them both to be understood fully.

YHWH and Elohim and Christian Ontology

Irenaeus provides innumerable examples of this ontological identification, as he sees it, illumining the scriptures of Israel. Speaking of Christ as Logos,

This is He who, in the bush, spoke with Moses and said, "I have surely seen the afflictions of my people who are in Egypt, and I have come down to deliver them." This is He who ascended and descended for the salvation of the afflicted, delivering us from the dominion of the Egyptians, that is, from all idolatry and ungodliness, and saving us from the Red Sea, that is, from the deadly turbulence of the heathen and from the bitter current of their blasphemy—for in these [things] our [affairs] were preformed (*promeletao*), the Word of God at that time demonstrating in advance, by types, things to come, but now, truly removing us out of the cruel slavery of the heathen, He caused a stream of water to gush forth abundantly from a rock in the desert, and the rock is Himself, and [also] gave [us] twelve springs, that is, the teaching of the twelve apostles; and killing the unbelievers in the desert, while leading those who believed in Him and were infants in malice into the inheritance of the patriarchs, which, not Moses, but Jesus <gave us an inheritance>, who saves us from Amalek by stretching out His hands and leading us into the Father's Kingdom. (*Demonstration* 46)[21]

Philo likewise understood the ontology of God to be manifested in the literal sense of scripture, in the way depictions of theophanies and other texts balanced God's eternal life *in se* with the disclosures of his "real presence" vouchsafed to his saints. In light of the present discussion of the divine name alternation, it is interesting to note how Philo understands the three visitors to Abraham in Genesis 18. He notes the distinction the text maintains between the LORD (singular) and the three men, while at the same time clearly relating them as agents of divine disclosure; the three men are not ordinary men. Philo puts it this way in *Questions and Answers in Genesis* 4.4, where he speaks about the curious staging of Genesis 18:

---

[21] This translation is from *On the Apostolic Preaching*, trans. and intro. by John Behr (Crestwood, N.Y.: St. Vladimir's Seminary Press, 1997).

Now his mind clearly forms an impression with more open eyes and more lucid vision, not roaming about nor wandering off with the triad, and being attracted thereto by quantity and plurality, but running toward the one. And He manifested Himself without the powers that belong to Him, so that he saw His oneness directly before him, as he had known it earlier in the likeness of a triad.

Philo clarifies that the triadic representation entails God *pater ton 'olon* with his two powers. The first corresponds to Elohim or he who is (*'o on*) as God in creative power (*poietike*). The other is royal (*basilike*) or YHWH *kurios*. Philo pursues a similar logic to explain the theophanies of Exodus 25, Isaiah 6, and Ezekiel 1, and this tradition we can see in Clement of Alexandria and elsewhere in Christian circulation.[22] Philo notes that Abraham was not drawn by one or another but saw them as three, and concludes that this was so he "was not able to see just which of them was likely to be the true one." This coheres with his understandings of "powers" over against God qua God—or however one might track this logic. Obviously Philo and other Christian exegetes will see the matter differently, but striking is how for them all the literal sense is pressuring some accounting at the level of ontology.

To conclude for now, YHWH and Elohim are not just favorite names for God that different sources deploy in the light of a disagreement over when God made his name known. The use of them tracks a logic that belongs to the universal and creative Elohim, a name not restricted to the people of divine disclosure, and YHWH, the name above every name (Isa 45 and Phil 2), the personal "I will be with you and make good on promises through time with you" (Exod 3), YHWH sovereign, personal, providentially covenantal. Here the analogy with God the Father and God the Son of Christian theology needs exploring. We will take this up in part 3 below.

---

[22] See Bogdan G. Bucur, "Clement of Alexandria's Exegesis of Old Testament Theophanies," *Phronema* 29 (2014): 61–79.

8

Order, Arrangements, Canonical Shape, and Name

We move now to that section of the book where we look at the canonical presentation of the major blocks of the Elder Scripture. Because these blocks are not the only ones represented in Jewish and Christian contexts, and other sequences and arrangements can be found, it is important to be clear about the significance of this fact—in addition to becoming better acquainted with the variety that exists more basically. Our view is that the most important factor to be grasped is the rationale behind the orders and not necessarily a strict argument for the priority of one over another. The matter of correct translation into a vernacular forms an analogy here. Translations of the Elder (and New) Testament are dynamic and living realities, and no amount of scientific hard work, or ecclesial fiat, will produce a final text that defeats all alternatives. The character of the Hebrew and Greek tradition is such that the further back one searches for the "trunk" of the tree, one begins to encroach on the root system and its complexity. Still, judgments can be made about better and worse claims to a stable text tradition and what appear to be alternatives to it.

To be avoided in all cases are global evaluations that do not do justice to the orders as we find them. To take a prominent example, the final location of Malachi as the last book of the Old Testament, with its reference to Elijah, next to the first book of the New Testament, Matthew, would seem like it accommodates a view that the "Christian Old Testament" leans forward, is prophetic, and opens directly onto what follows. In this it is to be contrasted with the Hebrew Bible, which ends (sometimes) with Chronicles and so is more "historical" in character and back-to-Torah looking.[1] A look at the lists in Christian usage, however, shows that Malachi was never the final book for the long history of Christian reception—it is typically Esther or Daniel—until relatively recently. And it wouldn't likely have affected the appraisal of the theological and hermeneutical significance of the first Elder witness even if it had appeared in this final position. The present chapter ends with reflections on this matter.

One of the few stable conclusions of historical-critical scholarship is the idea that the final book of the Pentateuch coheres meaningfully with the books that follow, traditionally called "former prophets" (Joshua, Judges, Samuel, Kings). On Noth's view one could even

---

[1] Serial essays by Marvin Sweeney have sought to argue this, unsuccessfully; see my comments in *The Goodly Fellowship of the Prophets: The Achievement of Association in Canon Formation* (Grand Rapids: Baker Academic, 2009), 48. The full bibliography is there. For a sample, however, see Marvin Sweeney, "Tanak versus Old Testament: Concerning a Foundation for a Jewish Theology of the Bible," in Henry T. C. Sun and Keith L. Eades, eds., *Problems in Biblical Theology: Essays in Honor of Rolf Knierim* (Grand Rapids: Eerdmans, 1997), 353–72. At one point he acknowledges that Malachi's final position "appears to have been set only after the widespread use of printed Bibles in the Western World" (360). Luther may have picked up the order from humanist translations such as those produced by Jacques Lefèvre (i.e., Lefèvre's 1528 translation of the Old Testament).

speak of a single overriding purpose linking the otherwise disparate five-book assemblage. The Deuteronomistic History's single editorial purpose was to explain the demise of the monarchy.[2] Von Rad saw a glimmer of hope in the final reference to Jehoiachin's rehabilitation, and Wolf pointed to the theme of prayer, penitence, and forgiveness on the other side of anticipated judgment.[3] And though more recent scholarship continues to debate the existence of versions and editorial expansions, the general picture of a Deuteronomy-to-Kings coherent presentation has remained intact. Childs emphasized the hermeneutical bridge function accomplished by the decision to allow Deuteronomy the final place in a five-book Pentateuch. Every generation to come is placed on the banks of the Jordan and participates in the decision to obey the law of God as revealed to Moses, as if they were themselves eyewitnesses with him on the mountain.[4]

The decision to affiliate these writings comes then not as a later development, but according to critical theory it exists at the very root system and trunk of the tree. What in time will be termed "former prophets" was at its inception a collection of Joshua, Judges, 1 and 2 Samuel, and 1 and 2 Kings. The decision to identify Moses as prophet and to speak of a following succession of prophets after him leads congenially to the idea that the law will function into the generations to come and prophetically govern the life of Israel and King. Prophets will emerge and be so called in the Deuteronomistic History,[5] Elijah and Elisha and Samuel most notably, but also a host of minor prophetic figures, enabling the refrain that

[2] Martin Noth, *The Deuteronomistic History*, 2nd ed. (Sheffield: JSOT, 1991).

[3] Von Rad's position is found in *Old Testament Theology*; Hans Walter Wolff's contribution (in English) is "The Kerygma of the Deuteronomistic Historical Work," in Hans Walter Wolff and Walter Brueggemann, *The Vitality of Old Testament Traditions* (Atlanta: John Knox, 1975), 83–100.

[4] Brevard S. Childs, *Introduction to the Old Testament as Scripture* (Philadelphia: Fortress, 1979), 221–24. See also Dennis Olson, *Deuteronomy and the Death of Moses*, OBT (Minneapolis: Augsburg Fortress, 1994).

[5] Stephen Chapman, *The Law and the Prophets: A Study in Old Testament Canon Formation* (Tübingen: Mohr Siebeck, 2000).

Israel was warned in every generation by those God would call to this office (culminating at 2 Kgs 24:2).

The printed Bibles with which many are familiar adjust this picture by placing Ruth between Judges and 1 Samuel and continuing past the dire ending of Kings. We see the history expanded and retold by the Chronicler and then extended beyond exile to return in the books of Ezra-Nehemiah and Esther. This historical portrait ends and we jump somewhat abruptly into Job. Psalms, Proverbs, Ecclesiastes, and Song of Songs follow, giving us a five-book collection of what can be termed "lyrical" or "poetical" books, now positioned after what looks like a continuous historical account starting with the Deuteronomistic History plus Ruth. Then we have the prophetic books bringing up the rear, including the book of Daniel (who is never called a prophet but rather a wise man).

One is often told that this fourfold order of law, history, poetry, and prophecy is a "Christian order" and is to be contrasted with a Hebrew, threefold one (law, prophecy, writings). Doesn't Malachi introduce Matthew so effectively? The Christian Bible's Old Testament ends with prophecy and so "leans forward" toward the New Testament. The Jewish Bible "looks back" to the Torah, it is sometimes held, and the prophetic books orient themselves there as well, and not toward the future so much.[6] Then we have a miscellany that could be in any order, including the just mentioned Ruth, Chronicles, Ezra-Nehemiah, and Esther, and what has become the "lyrical book" section in certain Christian orders. Often forgotten in this take on things is the equally compelling ending of Chronicles in such an arrangement, rivaling an alleged significance of Malachi (about which more in a moment). After describing the edict of Cyrus and the charge to build a house, made by the LORD God who has given all kingdoms on earth into his hand, its final verse reads, "whoever is among you of all his people, may the Lord God be with him. Let him go up." The genealogical emphasis of Chronicles is unmistakable in Matthew

---

[6] Roughly the position of Sweeney, as discussed above.

as is the "let him go up" movement to Jerusalem for a Passover like no other previously.

When we look closely at the lists of Old Testament books in Christian circles, several things are notable. First, there is a wide variety of ordering and no consistency as compared with the threefold Hebrew Bible's sequence and arrangement. Second, Malachi is never in final place.[7] Typically the Book of the Twelve (Minor Prophets) is paired with Isaiah, and may follow or precede it, but the two are never last. The order of the Major Prophets varies, just as we have an ancient Hebrew order of Jeremiah, Ezekiel, and Isaiah (B. Batra 14b) alongside the more familiar one of Isaiah, Jeremiah and Ezekiel. Third, a grouping of "historical books" as in modern printed English Bibles is not attested frequently, so the idea of a fourfold canonical alternative is misleading. The same is true of a consistent "lyrical" section. What we may deduce from a close examination of the history of Christian listings is that a threefold ordering of law, prophecy, and writings can find its way into Christian sequences, but it is not followed as consistently as we see it in the Hebrew tradition. Certain groupings seem to catch on that depart from the Hebrew (Jeremiah with Lamentations; Judges with Ruth) but not with any strong regularity. Some traditional Hebrew groupings ("Major Prophets"; "Minor Prophets") are also maintained, and books like Daniel and Esther resist what we see in how they are organized in modern English Bibles; they move around a good deal, like Hebrews in the New Testament lists.

Translations into daughter languages like Greek and Latin came with the concomitant possible shuffling of books and groups of books. But the lack of any one single pattern is telling. No claim was being lodged of a strong, rival, comprehensive order as of specific Christian significance. Reading the history of Christian interpretation one also fails to see any major significance attached to

---

[7] See the helpful appendix in Lee McDonald and James A. Sanders, *The Canon Debate* (Peabody, Mass.: Hendrickson, 2002).

a single rival ordering, even as we know that men like Jerome and Augustine disagreed over how recourse to a Hebrew Verity ought to be evaluated theologically. Augustine felt that the Greek translation was traditional, gave rise to a common Latin Bible that was in use in the church, and went back to strong claims to wondrous production (made by Jews, not Christians in the first instance). But in the end the translational effort of Jerome in accessing a Hebrew corrective moved forward. There is no record of a disagreement over a distinctive Christian order and arrangement as against the one found in the Hebrew tradition. A variant order of the first six Minor Prophets can be found in certain translational versions, for example, but no commentator claimed there was anything theologically significant about this.[8]

This points to the question of how the student of the Old Testament should think about the order of the books, if not also the scope of the canon (Greek translations in use in Christian circles frequently include additional Jewish books not written in Hebrew). It would be our position that he should avoid the idea of a strong rivalry between single alternatives and should instead acquaint himself with the variety that exists in Christian circles. By paying attention to groupings that emerge one can begin to appreciate the character of arrangements as such and how grouping books together produces a wider effect. On my view the stability of the Hebrew arrangement deserves a particular kind of respect precisely due to that fact, in contrast to translational alternatives. And there is of course the very clear significance of a translation into another language being just that, and not the reverse. The Old Testament comes to us in a language that carried its own people along with it. Beyond this one cannot be doctrinaire. The Bible exists in relationship to the communities that have treasured it,

---

[8] The superscripted books Hosea, Amos, and Micah are followed by Joel, Obadiah, and Jonah in one Greek language translation. It was not a focus of attention as such by interpreters, and the early commentary by Antiochenes and Alexandrians gives no evidence of it. See the discussion in my *Goodly Fellowship*, 82–99; *Joel*, ITC (London: Bloomsbury, 2016), 22–24.

and this includes Jews and Christians both, the former maintaining a more stable tradition in respect of order and the latter less so.[9]

A course that purports to be an introduction to the Old Testament or Hebrew Bible will have to make decisions about the order in which individual books are treated. Does Ruth find its treatment after Judges and before 1 Samuel or within the five-book collection along with Lamentations, Song of Songs, Ecclesiastes, and Esther? The answer is simple: "Both." An explanation should be provided of why the books appear where they do. Proverbs ends by extolling the virtuous woman, and Ruth follows to give a stellar example (compare the *eset-hayil* of Prov 31:10 with Boaz's commendation in Ruth 3:11).[10] Judges ends on a hopeless note, with no king in the land as well, and Ruth comes to establish the line of David, and bring a ray of hope in the darkness, anticipating the Song of Hannah in 1 Samuel to follow.

The same basic lesson applies to what we call this collection of books, in whatever order we find it. Hebrew Bible, Tanakh, Old Testament, Jewish Scripture, First Testament have all been proposed. Some possibilities seem misleading or foreclosing. To say "Jewish Scriptures" raises questions about what the word "Jewish" means, since the people of Israel and Judaism are not directly equivalent. To say "Jewish Scriptures" to refer to the Old Testament in Christian circles and then "Christian Scriptures" as referring to the New Testament would be a fatal error, and one that not least completely distorts the New Testament's own sense of itself. As with different orders, the important thing is to be aware of what one is doing and what the wider implications are. The beauty of

---

[9] See Brevard S. Childs, "The Search for the Christian Bible," in his *Biblical Theology of the Old and New Testaments: Theological Reflection on the Christian Bible* (Minneapolis: Fortress, 1993), 67; Christopher Seitz, *The Character of Christian Scripture: The Significance of a Two-Testament Bible* (Grand Rapids: Baker Academic, 2011), 70–79.

[10] See the exhaustive evaluation in Julius Steinberg and Timothy J. Stone, *The Shape of the Writings* (Winona Lake, Ind.: Eisenbrauns, 2015). Previously, Timothy J. Stone, *The Compilational History of the Megilloth*, FAT (Tübingen: Mohr Siebeck, 2013).

Old and New Testament is the symmetry the term "testament" allows, emphasizing the covenants as continuous though different. The modern problem is the loss of a sense of "old" as revered, original, and authoritative because of trial through time, so that paired with "new" in our age of science and technology we can only hear "outmoded."

One thing that all lists agree on is the order and priority of the Law, or Pentateuch, in whatever dress we may find the totality of these scriptures as a whole. The decision to include the former prophets under a designation that appears to be "historical books" is not one we can track as consistent in orders other than the Hebrew, even though we may be familiar with it due to the printing of modern English Bibles. The problem here is that it breaks up the rubric of "prophecy" under which it has circulated, followed by the three (Isaiah, Jeremiah, and Ezekiel) and the twelve, or what has been termed "latter prophets." It is important to think through what the decision to group this disparate material together as prophets (former and latter) intends to convey. Once that has happened, then one may be free to reflect on how other orders move in other directions. One answer may be: for no particular reason at all and just by happenstance of translation and loss of context.

Yet there is more going on, in my view, in this discussion than a hopefully more sympathetic awareness of and evaluation of variant orders, with an eye toward proper appreciation of the Hebrew canon's central panel of prophecy. We live in a season of history and progressivism. One popular way of handling the Old Testament within the wider canon of Christian Scripture is by visualizing it as several acts in a drama headed toward the New Testament. Or from the New Testament side, thinking of it as essential background for locating an external piece of plot development by selecting out a theme like "Exile and Return" in order to make the subsequent denouement work. Or by declaring that the Old Testament is itself "Christotelic" or otherwise "leans toward" the New Testament. Malachi's final words about the return of Elijah anticipates the John the Baptist who awaits around the corner. We have discussed the matter in earlier chapters.

By thinking carefully about prophecy without a narratival lens only; by refusing to locate one half of it within a historical rubric leading to Ezra-Nehemiah and beyond, and the other half poised before the horizon of the New Testament so as to give it sense, we may slow the movement down and force ourselves to consider it more carefully as it addresses us in the form it does. It is a different thing to speculate that Matthew feels he has a key to open up the logic of Chronicles' creation-to-Cyrus movement than to say the Writings as a whole are "leaning toward" the New Testament. Indeed, by viewing the miscellany of the Writings, as well as the variety of orders in Christian circles themselves, the idea of a forward march toward something outside of itself is hopefully forestalled. This is said not in the spirit of "appreciate the Old Testament on its own terms and in its own time as now past" but rather in trying to understand how it evaluates the temporal categories with which it works on their own terms.

Let me try to give an example of what I mean. One way for Christians to understand the Old Testament is to think of all its characters on a flat plane, existing in a time long ago, before the New Testament and before our own time. The New Testament ushers in a new era in which the Lord and Son and Messiah has arrived. The language "Lord" and "Son" and "Messiah" we understand, as did New Testament people, to come from this previous period. But in the previous period a people knew these things provisionally, as we are given a ruler outside of its frame of reference to measure such a thing. On this account the decisive disclosure happens in the New Testament for those who witnessed the incarnation and stood with Jesus, and for some, witnessed his resurrection. They have an epistemic higher-grade octane of knowledge. We outside of the New Testament, but temporally after it, identify with their epistemic advance and noetic acquisition. On this account, the Old Testament properly discloses its frame of reference via the term "old." Old can mean prior to, outmoded, incomplete, insufficient, and so forth, all measured against something else that has arrived, that completes or suffices. This is calibrated with reference to the incarnation and earthly appearance of Jesus of Nazareth.

But on closer inspection this primarily chronological account runs into problems. The incarnation is as much an act of obfuscation as it is of disclosure for those who walked with or encountered Jesus. The same could be said of the resurrection. Who is this Risen Lord, and how is he to be known? In both cases we are told that the scriptures are critical, indeed indispensable, to noetic grasp. "You search the scriptures, and it is they that speak of me." "Beginning with the Moses and all the prophets, he interpreted to them in the scriptures all the things concerning himself." Proximity to incarnate or risen Jesus is not chronological privilege at all. Jesus Christ is who he is by disclosure of the Holy Spirit, who spake by the prophets. And as for our identification with those New Testament people on an alleged advanced point on a timeline, this too is not so clear on inspection. "Christ Risen" makes no sense as an isolated fact on the ground, looked back to as something dramatic "in time." "Christ Risen" always declares its truthful character in relationship to the testimony of the scriptures—for the apostles, Elder Scripture, and for the church, prophets and apostle, Old and New Testaments, via the Spirit's agency. "Christ Risen" is made known under a sign, again by the Holy Spirit, in the sacramental life of his Body in Eucharistic presence.

Now at this point it is important to grasp that in the very same way Israel "knew" the Lord, that is, under the signs and sacramental presence appropriate to their own day. This did not happen on a flat plane, shared with others, but in consequence of being witnesses to his word and life: Israel, disobedient and dull of mind, yet elected as others would be adopted, and like unto the earthly witnesses Jesus raised up around him, needing their eyes and wills and hands and hearts opened, daily.

There is of course temporal movement, across two testaments, as well as inside them individually. Pentecost is after Easter. But the careful Gentile reader must not insert a chronological index of understanding and knowledge that misunderstands the way the two-testament Bible actually works, when left to describe itself and its life with God, as Israel, as the apostles of Israel with the Son of Mary, and as adopted sons and daughters by his grace. Making the Old Testament function as chapters in a drama that heads to Jesus and us misunderstands how he is already at work within them and within the people of Israel, long before in the fullness of time he is born of a virgin and opens time onto a people far off but now brought near, who were once outside the covenants, without hope, and without God in the world.[11]

---

[11] Again, see the insightful remarks of Don Collett in "Reading Forward: The Old Testament and Retrospective Stance," *ProEccl* 24 (2015): 184–93.

9

The Pentateuch

We begin our overview of the canonical shape of the Elder Testament with the Pentateuch. We have, however, already spent substantial time evaluating the older source-critical notion and its successors and offered an alternative conceptual model. I will not cover that ground again. My goal here is more modest. It is simply to argue that, in the same way that the twelve books of the minor prophets must be taken seriously as individual literary works, in the sequence we find them, so too the Pentateuch is at ground five books, with marked beginning and endings.[1] The Pentateuch, in other words, is not longitudinal sources overriding

---

[1] See most recently, "The Unique Achievement of the Book of the Twelve: Neither Reactional Unity Nor Anthology," in Heiko Wenzel, ed., *The Book of the Twelve: An Anthology of Prophetic Books or the Result of Complex Redactional Processes* (Göttingen: Vandenhoeck & Ruprecht, forthcoming).

this fivefoldness, nor is it essential as a diachronic theory for describing the way the idea of a five-book presentation came about in time. There are five poems of lamentation comprising the book of Lamentations. There are five books of praise so demarcated in the book of Psalms by doxological rubrics. There are three works associated in some way with Solomon. These numerical realities (12, 5, 3) are important indicators of how the works are to be evaluated: as linked and associated in some way (so "the Five Books of Moses") but also as having markers of distinct beginnings and endings for five different works. This ought to seem like a simple thing, until one sees the provision of very different contexts for interpretation (four sources, the variety of *sitz im leben* of Psalms, the "wisdom literature" comprising Proverbs, Job, and Ecclesiastes).[2] More critical to the *diachronic* appreciation of Genesis, Exodus, Leviticus, Numbers, and Deuteronomy is not what may be said to be capable of identification across them in sources or levels of tradition but rather what helps us understand what they are individually as five different works.

It has been noted that the main themes and the ending of the book of Genesis do not all that naturally move us into the book of Exodus. The role of the ancestors and the promises made to them are not obviously critical to the way the book of Exodus makes its voice heard, and vice versa. Linkages that seek to resolve this are argued to be later and less deeply imbedded in both works. But this could be precisely the point. That is, the tradition-building process at work within individual works was more deeply operative in them as distinct works than anything to be claimed as functioning at the level of a Pentateuchal source or a continuous tradition said to be functioning in and across them all.

The idea that the Pentateuch as a literary classification had a self-evident claim to be taken seriously hermeneutically and theologically, in that form, fell to the side in the last century. This did not

---

[2] On the category "wisdom literature" see the discussion in chapter 14 below.

happen in some dramatic way. It was simply part of the historical-critical ethos that sought more crucial classifications and orderings on the basis of source- and form-critical investigations.³

If there were continuous sources that overlay the canonical book divisions, then it would require some explanation why the practice stops here. One ought to be able to track them into ensuing books and speak of a Hexateuch or Tetrateuch or even an Enneateuch. And so this transpired. The broader conception was also assisted by the recognition that Deuteronomy stood on its own, and its origins were to be sought in a different context of excavation (according to the theory in place, this was the Book of the Law "discovered" during the reign of Josiah, as reported in 2 Kings 22-23). So its place as a "final word" within the logic of a Pentateuch needed to be reconsidered given the conceptual weight occupied by the earlier J and later P continuous sources and the possibility of their extending beyond Numbers and into the Former Prophets.

On the second, form-critical score, the creative reconstruction of Gerhard von Rad was probably the major influence on the idea of a Hexateuchal and not a Pentateuchal conception of significance—and it was for him both a critical and deeply theological significance joined at the hip. He held the view that the earliest traditional recitations by Israel could be identified in what he called the short creeds of (oddly, one might have thought) the book of Deuteronomy (6:20-25 and 26:5-11). These conclude—unsurprisingly given their role in the narrative of Deuteronomy, which anticipates the entry into the land—with explicit reference to occupation of the land. Also, he and his colleague Martin Noth observed these creeds left out any reference to Sinai and the giving of the law—again, unsurprisingly given the attention paid to this otherwise in the book of Deuteronomy, where the entire Sinai

---

³ So Gerhard von Rad produced a compelling account of the origins of the material in question with the German language title *The Form-Critical Problem of the Hexateuch*. He wasn't trying to be provocative but rather felt that his tap-root "small credos" lying at the beginning of the traditioning process pointed to a hexateuchal and not a Pentateuchal end point.

framework is presupposed and extended for the next generation as the main theme of the book. This left the "articles" of the creed as promise to patriarchs, descent into Egypt, and entry into the promised land, corresponding therefore to Genesis, Exodus, Numbers, and Joshua. Though the origins and development of Leviticus and Deuteronomy were to be sought elsewhere, because the theory focused on the salvation-historical movement from Genesis to Joshua, the term "hexateuchal" entered into the lexical domain of serious historical-theological usage for the period.[4]

On both scores—source critical and form critical—the significance of the Pentateuch as a canonical presentation receded in favor of a traditional-historical conception said to appreciate the salvation-historical character of the material as extracted. This happened with no real fanfare. It was simply not the attitude of the period to believe there was any theological significance intended by the final form of the Pentateuch. It was simply there to be probed and rearranged to historical purpose. Its canonical presentation was not a matter for serious reflection as it was considered an arbitrary stopping point on a far more shimmering developmental reconstruction.

The careful reader of the period will also see how deeply this affected the character of the individual books of the Pentateuch as books. Because the idea of continuous sources overlaid the conceptual framework, the fact of books as books, with their own internal development toward that fivefold end, was lost in the wave of enthusiasm for another conception. In some ways this might seem an odd and unexpected development. As would later be acknowledged, Genesis is really its own affair.[5] More recent

---

[4] Noth kept his council on the propriety of the term and preferred to speak of a tetrateuch, anticipating his view of Deuteronomy as associated with the following books in a single History. Still he borrowed the idea of creedal "articles" and worked with them instead as "themes" in his densely written *History of Pentateuchal Traditions*.

[5] Compare the very different conceptions of Moberly (*Old Testament of Old Testament*) and Schmid (*Genesis and the Moses Story*), who otherwise share this perspective.

heirs of the source-critical method, even sharing different models amongst themselves, note that the theme of promise to the patriarchs isn't heavily influenced by the descent into Egypt when one reads Genesis carefully (and noting exceptions of course). The theme anticipates Joshua more than Exodus, would be one way to put it. So Genesis has its own integrity and has only been lightly redacted so as to make it function in a more integrated way with the book of Exodus to follow. This is held to be true even of the Joseph story, which need not be read as anticipating anything like a lengthy stay in Egypt, and nothing remotely anticipatory of Leviticus or Numbers.[6]

We have already noted the exceptional character of the book of Deuteronomy: its origins and singular views of Moses, Levites, cult, and so forth. Many argue its account of the patriarchs is also unique and does not match robustly what we find in Genesis. And Leviticus bears little if any trace of the Yahwist hand said to be so crucial in linking together the articles of Israel's faith and producing its shimmering first salvation-historical narrative record. That leaves Exodus and Numbers. We have already dealt in some detail with the book of Exodus in respect of the criterion of the divine name. There are other ways of understanding the transition from Genesis to Exodus that do not require two continuous sources, the theological origins of which spin out of a disagreement over the first appearance of the name YHWH. This is what energized the theory of continuous sources in their classical expression beyond the basic literary observations of the use of different names for God in Genesis and Exodus. Again, as noted above, in theory the criterion ought to be of little logical use after Exodus 6 anyway. One can see in scholarship at present an interest in associating the older J with D, in part to provide a different rationale for distinguishing what are now called J and non-J or "J/D" and P.[7]

---

[6] One is struck by how many essays in Dozeman and Schmid's *Farewell to the Yahwist?* deal with the end of the Joseph material and the beginning of Exodus for a book purporting to deal with the Yahwist or the adieu to him more widely.

[7] The proper terminology is difficult to find given the older legacy and its

As for Numbers, Martin Noth once famously observed that if we only had the book of Numbers to evaluate, one would never have come to the idea of continuous sources at all. It is simply too *sui generis* as a work. Its contents and composition as a book are the subject more properly of evaluations made at that level.[8] It is not obvious how much its interpretation is assisted by plugging its diverse contents into a source conception, the older one or the more recent alternatives. This also reminds us that in some ways what is true of it is also true of Exodus. Consider how much of the present book is non-narrative/legislative in character and how much in turn of that is focused entirely on the design of and construction of the tabernacle (Exod 25–31; 35–40)—fully a third of the present book. The bulk of the material in the first ten chapters of Numbers involves census material and the arrangement of the camp and sacrificial duties. The final fifteen chapters (21–34) contain the Balak/Balaam cycle, a second detailed census, and a diverse collection of traditions hard to classify as salvation-historical narrative.

With the development of a theory of the existence of a Deuteronomistic History extending from Deuteronomy to Kings, notions of a Hexateuch began to confront a different kind of challenge. Deuteronomy could be conceived of as essentially introducing what follows, and so the interpretation of Joshua and Judges no longer existed in the domain of source criticism of the Pentateuch. If on the other hand its placement was intentionally to close off a Pentateuchal entity, this would in turn ask us to reconsider the questions of the Pentateuch and the Deuteronomistic History in a fresh way altogether quite apart from the source- and form-critical ones as previously.

---

classical account, where the terms functioned differently. This is discussed in *Farewell to the Yahwist?* and kindred recent works. Given that the neo-Wellhausian impulse is to retain them and their reconstructed framework from the prior period, the problem of consensus terms of reference is obvious.

[8] See the careful study of Dennis Olson, *The Death of the Old and the Birth of the New: The Framework of the Book of Numbers and the Pentateuch*, BJS (Atlanta: Scholars, 1985). The original thesis was written under Brevard Childs and represented one of the ongoing challenges for understanding the shape of individual books as set forth in his 1979 introduction.

Deuteronomy has been purposefully set as the final book of the Pentateuch so as to take the new generation of Numbers' conceptual framework seriously and project their life into the promised land as an exemplar for each new generation to come, in every generation returning to Sinai with the chance for life and not death. Rhetorically charged to make its exhortative point clear, Deuteronomy insists that the commandments were not given to the generation at Sinai—even though they were—because they are designed to speak to every generation, and that is their true divine purpose: "The LORD God made a covenant *with us* in Horeb. Not with our fathers did the LORD make this covenant, but *with us, all of us* here today, *all of us* who are alive" (Deut 5:3; emphasis added).

In sum, fresh work on the Pentateuch should recognize and acknowledge the peculiar shape and form each one of the five books presents and see this factor as significant in itself. The Tabernacle presentation of Leviticus exists as a deeply textualized reality, and not one simply to be retrofitted (with difficulty) into a history of religion stretching from an ancient tent shrine to the mature Temple. To assume this character of referentiality as decisive is to miss the significance the presentation of Leviticus, and those long sections of Exodus as well, intends to make as canonical speech from the tabernacle of the text. Origen most notably read the book as an encounter with God occurring in the very act of reading itself. That such may well be the canonical intention of this book must be weighed carefully before assuming as a book it makes its contribution only when it has been correlated to theories of sources or traditions or a history of religion reconstruction of cultic development. The fact that each of the five Pentateuchal witnesses is so very different compared with the others means that the development internal to them as books must remain the more important diachronic and canonical dimension honored in exegesis. Perhaps the fissuring nature of modern Pentateuchal inquiry signals that the wrong questions were being foregrounded as starting points for evaluating the character of the five books that comprise the present Torah of Moses.

10

Prophets

The Prophetic section of the canon comprises what may appear to be an odd combination of substantive narrative chronicle and poetic/oracular material, the latter more instinctively thought of as prophecy: Isaiah, Jeremiah, Ezekiel, and the smaller Twelve prophetic books beginning with Hosea and ending with Malachi. The tradition would in time refer to these two corpuses as "Former Prophets" (the books of Joshua, Judges, Samuel, and Kings) and "Latter Prophets," not highlighting a difference between them—narratives here, poetic oracles there—but collectively referring to them as Nebi'im (Prophets).[1]

---

[1] There are some fascinating portions of overlap, as with Isaiah 36–39 and 2 Kings 18–20. See my discussion in *Zion's Final Destiny: The Development of the Book of Isaiah: A Reassessment of Isaiah 36–39* (Minneapolis: Fortress, 1991) and more recently *Prophecy and Hermeneutics: Toward a New Introduction to the Prophets* (Grand Rapids: Baker Academic, 2007).

In time the "former" section would find a fresh affiliation with kindred chronicle/narrative material, whose books exist otherwise in the Writings: Ezra-Nehemiah, Chronicles, and Esther. This created something like a historical category of books. On my view this occurred due to an instinct to associate like with like in early translational versions of an earlier tradition, in an emerging Greek language version of the Hebrew Bible.[2] The result was to split Former from Latter Prophets, create a fresh category of historical writings, and allow the term "prophets" to more clearly refer to the three Major Prophets, the Twelve, and also a relocated book of Daniel, not now a wisdom writing (Dan 1:4) but one of the prophets. The consequence of this, further, was the collecting of the remaining titles under a rubric of "lyrical books" and with it a dismantling of the tripartite arrangement of Law, Prophets, and Writings. That said, the lists we have in Christian circles do not have a single fourfold alternative form and frequently give evidence of the the Law, Prophets, and Writings conception (that is, with prophetical writings remaining in the center of the list). As noted above, the books that most frequently conclude the Elder Scripture in Christian circles are Daniel and Esther. We will discuss the variations that appear in Jewish lists briefly here and in the chapter to follow. They are more minor in character.

As we have noted above, the scriptures of Israel in Hebrew dress move from the final book of the Pentateuch (Deuteronomy) into a new, second section, called simply Prophets (Nebi'im). English printed Bibles replicate this movement partially but include Ruth between Judges and Samuel and then continue on a more historical timeline with Chronicles, Ezra-Nehemiah, and Esther. Prophets is organized otherwise into a Joshua-Kings portion (called in historical-critical parlance "the Deuteronomistic History") and an Isaiah-Malachi portion. In time the first block could be called "Former" and the

---

[2] The argument is defended in *The Goodly Fellowship of the Prophets: The Achievement of Association in Canon Formation* (Grand Rapids: Baker Academic, 2009).

second "Latter" divisions of Prophets. The present MT presents the familiar Isaiah, Jeremiah, and Ezekiel order followed by a twelve-book collection. As noted above, the Twelve and Isaiah are most often paired in subsequent lists in Christian circles, usually in that order. They are approximately the same length.[3]

The Prophets as former and latter represent narrative and classically prophetic material, respectively. That is, the three Major and twelve Minor prophetic books consist of proclamation in largely poetic form, going back to the oral speech of the prophets in live time, delivered to Israel by major prophetic figures. Sometimes this is called "writing prophecy" to distinguish it from prophetic activity that was not preserved in the same form of literary presentation.[4] So, Elijah and Elisha find a prominent place in 1 and 2 Kings, but their oral speech has not been put in the literary form that we see, for example, in a Hosea or Micah, or any of the other prophetic books. To call these "writing prophets" introduces a possible confusion, however, since none of them produced their own written books. That activity was taken up by others in a manner we will discuss below. The point of the nomenclature was to make a distinction between the prophetic activity recorded in the Deuteronomistic History and what we see in prophetic speech preserved in book form. The distinction is also more keenly felt when Joshua-Kings no longer is followed directly by Isaiah-Malachi but separated and assigned to new locations such as are found in modern English Bibles, for example.

To place the narrative material of Joshua-Kings next to that of the classical prophetic literature creates some important effects. (1) It picks up on the notion of a succession of prophetic activity

---

[3] On the appearance in lists next to each other of Isaiah and the Twelve, see Julio Trebolle-Barrera, "Qumran Evidence for a Biblical Standard Text and for Non-Standard and Parabiblical Texts," in Timothy H. Lim, ed., *The Dead Sea Scrolls in Their Historical Context* (Edinburgh: T&T Clark, 2000), 89–106, esp. 94–95, 98.

[4] A standard classification such as we find in textbooks introducing the prophets. Joseph Blenkinsopp's is a good recent example: *A History of Prophecy in Israel*, rev. and enlarged ed. (Louisville, Ky.: Westminster John Knox, 1996).

to follow after Moses, thus insisting that the entire period represented by Joshua-Kings is governed by divine prophetic oversight, via the Torah of Moses or by specific prophetic figures so called. (2) It serves the purpose of showing us the scope of the historical season during which the prophets to follow can be located. The loose analogy of Acts and the Pauline letter collection comes to mind, though by distinction, the Major and Minor Prophets and the Deuteronomistic History provide very little overlap when it comes to locating the former at specific moments on the timeline of the latter.[5] Only Isaiah and Jonah make an appearance in the history. The superscriptions of the prophetic books function to make clearer from that side of the ledger just when and where the prophets were active. The undated and unlocated books within the Twelve are a special case that needs discussion below.[6] The final three books of the Twelve pick up the timeline after the exile and so move out beyond the ending of 2 Kings in important ways, leaving us with a sense both of continuity and of horizons to come. The introduction to Zechariah does this quite explicitly, for example (Zech 1:1-6), in taking its bearings from the words spoken by prophets previously (see also the references to former prophets in 7:7, 12). The final book, Malachi, is a special case that requires additional comment, as it appears to introduce a name ("my messenger") that carries the book forward into the future beyond that of prophecy in classical form.

The two-part Prophets section of the canon, then, serves to bridge the giving of the law to Moses forward to generations to come, and assisted by specific agents like Moses for their generations, called prophets. Part one is content to focus on the first dimension while not failing to mention specific prophets as such, while part two concentrates on prophetic speech in its classical

---

[5] See my discussion in *Colossians*, Brazos Theological Commentary on the Bible (Grand Rapids: Brazos, 2014), 193–96; *The Character of Christian Scripture: The Significance of a Two-Testament Bible* (Grand Rapids: Baker Academic, 2011), 157–67; *Goodly Fellowship of the Prophets*, 102–3.

[6] See my discussion in *Prophecy and Hermeneutics*, 113–220.

guise. It can be possible to theorize that within part two the term "torah" has a less formal meaning than is suggested in the present deuteronomic depiction. Indeed this aspect had been taken in the source-critical heyday as Exhibit #1, establishing that the prophets really knew nothing of law except in more ad hoc senses of "instruction" appropriate to their inspired genius and insight. In classic Wellhausian terms, the law is later than the prophets and by no means its foundation.[7]

Yet whatever we may reconstruct in respect of the term *torah*, the simple fact of juxtaposition of these two major sections under the one rubric of Prophets implies that the mature Torah of Genesis-Deuteronomy is consistent with law as the prophets refer to this on the occasions when they do. The Deuteronomistic History returns the favor by simply crediting the proclamation of God's law to every generation under a rubric "by all my servants the prophets" without then stipulating which figure now appearing in part two they have in mind more specifically. The effect of the almost word-by-word appearance of Isaiah 36–39 at a critical juncture in 2 Kings 18–20, whatever else it may mean, leaves no doubt that the Deuteronomistic History and the classical prophets are seen to be complementary and working in tandem. Similar moves within the second part itself (the appearance of Isaiah 2 in Micah 4) reinforces the "all the prophets" theme as one of consistency to the point of overlap. Jeremiah's reference to Micah and Hezekiah may also be mentioned here (Jer 26:18).[8] In sum, introductory courses may be useful in speculating about how something like "law" functioned in more occasional uses in the prophets and only later culminated in the monumental Pentateuchal expression of the same, but the later development deserves to be acknowledged for what it is and its effect considered and appreciated on the terms of the present canonical

---

[7] See the preface to the *Prolegomena to the History of Israel* (Edinburgh: Adam & Charles Black, 1885; German original, 1883), where Wellhausen speaks quite personally about having a bad conscience in not seeing evidence of the Law in the Former Prophets and wondering what this might mean.

[8] See Seitz, *Prophecy and Hermeneutics* (128, 197, 212) on this point.

portrayal. This phase of development deserves the label "historical" every bit as much as reconstructed, earlier, theoretical ones.

Our concern in general is with modern approaches, the character of canonical shaping and association, and the sorts of issues that may arise in one's first critical look at the Old Testament. So it will not be my purpose here to engage in detailed, individual treatment of the three Major and twelve Minor Prophets. I have published previous commentaries and monographs on the Prophets of Israel and the Deuteronomistic History.

In one of the (nearly playful) musings of the rabbinic material, the order of the major prophets is declared to be Jeremiah, Ezekiel, and Isaiah, and an explanation for this is given.[9] We are watching an upward curve, from all judgment, to half-judgment and half-salvation, to all salvation. One might say that this is roughly accurate: Jeremiah predominates with judgment oracles at the end of the period of Judah's existence and provides a sober account of the destruction of Jerusalem and termination of the monarchy (another place of substantial overlap with the last chapters of Kings and the Deuteronomistic History). Ezekiel's grim pronouncements focus on the same period, in exile, and conclude with hopeful declarations of a new heart, a new spirit, a new rejoined Israel, and a new temple. Isaiah soars with the language of salvation, contrapuntally in the first chapters and in sustained notes in the latter. We can also see this order in certain Christian lists, with the Twelve preceding Isaiah.

The order with which we are familiar has Isaiah in first position. His is the most historically comprehensive portrayal; if critical theory is correct, stretching over several centuries from seventh to fifth and later. In its present form, traditional exegesis also credited the book with an extraordinary range of coverage and put this down to the marvelous prophetic powers of Isaiah of Jerusalem, who saw into and through the exile and comforted the mourners in Zion (so ben Sira). The shape of Isaiah 66 moves

---

[9] B. Batra 14b.

from denunciations in the reign of Ahaz; a figural linking of the outstretched arm of YHWH to include Assyria and Babylonian agents of judgment both; to their eventual demise, within the larger national landscape; with a deliverance of Jerusalem, which contrasts Hezekiah favorably with Ahaz previously and serves as a sign of Jerusalem's eventual recovery and pilgrimage center for all the nations previously brought under God's sovereign rule. King and servant combine in the larger movement and bring about, through suffering and death, a means of expiation for Israel that in turn awakens the hearts and wills of all peoples.[10] The signal position of Isaiah serves to guide us as we make our way forward, much in the same way the letter to the Romans stands in first position and gives us a comprehensive portrayal of creation, justification, sanctification, election, and adoption as the lens through which to view the twelve letters to follow.

Jeremiah's presentation is far more chronologically narrowed in coverage. This focus also creates a somber portrayal. Hopeful notes that sound in the opening chapters are directed to a northern kingdom and then held up as an object lesson to Judah for not having learned the lesson of her fate in the previous century. Penitential notes also arise, but these appear to be representative of a later audience who watch the disobedience and register their acknowledgements of the righteousness of God's actions with their forefathers and mothers.[11] Jeremiah's own role in the book is crafted to track alongside that of Moses, now as lawgiver of curse and not blessing, given the refusal to heed. I have elsewhere argued that the question of historical Jeremiah's awareness of D ought better to be considered from the angle of his depiction in the book itself, as a

---

[10] I have written in detail on these matters in *Isaiah 1–39* (1993); *Zion's Final Destiny* (1991); "Isaiah 40–66," in *The New Interpreter's Bible* (2001); and several journal articles.

[11] Seitz, "The Place of the Reader in Jeremiah," in Martin Kessler, ed., *Reading the Book of Jeremiah: A Search for Coherence* (Winona Lake, Ind.: Eisenbrauns, 2004), 67–75.

prophet like Moses.[12] Instead of broken tablets we have a burned and reconstituted scroll. Instead of Caleb and Joshua as exempt from death in the wilderness, we have Baruch and Ebed-Melech carrying forward beyond the wholesale judgment over Judah and into a new but uncertain future. Jeremiah must share the fate of Moses and is not exempted, though he sees from afar a new day in the same manner Moses is permitted to look over into the Promised Land before death. The theme of the death of one generation and the birth of a new one, which we see in Numbers, is calibrated so as to be completed within the span of seventy years.[13]

The influence of Deuteronomy on Jeremiah is obvious and penetrating. The book is a combination of (1) poetic oracles such as we find them in Isaiah; (2) deuteronomic sermons of a "choose this day" and "do this or this will befall you," with the latter frequently presupposing a negative response and so culminating in judgment; and (3) biographical episodes and personal lamentations. Much of the material is specifically dated, also in the manner of the DtrH. The book marches inexorably toward its conclusion, first with exile of king and population in 597 and then with more dramatic results in 587.

Ezekiel opens with an even sharper historical focus.[14] He is a prophet who accompanied the exiles of the first deportation. He is able to address them and the concrete situation unfolding back in Jerusalem at one and the same time. He is given a terrible scroll to swallow, but unlike Jeremiah offers no lamentation after being given an antacid of divine comfort. And so he declares the terrible judgment he does. Biographical material also pervades his book, including a series of sign acts whereby in his own flesh he enacts

---

[12] Seitz, "The Prophet Moses and the Canonical Shape of Jeremiah," *Zeitschrift fur die alttestamentliche Wissenschaft* 101 (1989): 1–15.

[13] Olson, *Death of the Old and the Birth of the New*.

[14] Christopher Seitz, *Theology in Conflict: Reactions to the Exile in the Book of Jeremiah*, BZAW 176 (Berlin: de Gruyter, 1986); see especially "The 597 Perspective of Ezekiel Traditions," 121–63. See also Seitz, "The Crisis of Interpretation over the Meaning and Purpose of the Exile," *VT* 35 (1985): 78–97.

the awful fate in store for God's people. Israel has become like Pharaoh or a foreign nation, and even worse. So the "then you will know that I am the LORD" refrains we recall from Exodus in the confrontation between Moses and Egypt here appear in the form of knowing YHWH God in his judgments and not his deliverances. Then the judgment over city, temple, priesthood, king, and false prophet is finally prosecuted, and our prophet can then begin to see a new day. Out of the corpse of a people in a valley of dry bones, Ezekiel is given to see the Spirit of God breathe new life. Israel and Judah are rejoined after centuries of division. Good shepherds rule. Prophecy begins to regather strength. A new temple is to be built and the principalities and powers emptied of their awful might, having evacuated themselves in the role of agents of national judgment over God's people.

The three Major Prophets span the horizon of God's work with Israel and Judah and then see into a new future. Comprehensively, they confront all the institutions and manifestations of authority inside God's purposes with his people and expose the dry rot down to the nails and mortar. Isaiah is bold to say that this act of judgment has an expiatory effect that will cleanse the future generations. It will also be the means by which Israel, brought in contact with the nations of the world, will suffer a fate that enables these same peoples to see God at work, in judgment and in salvation, and so come to the knowledge of him via their fate. The diaspora of God's people will remain a fact into the New Testament and provide the synagogue reality into which the prophet Paul will stride centuries later, opening anew the book of Isaiah and declaring that God's plan and his secret mystery are being shown forth onto a new day of God's action. The former things are giving way to new things, and did not I, the Lord, say it long ago?

The Twelve

The twelve minor prophetic books, which follow Ezekiel, existed on a single scroll of similar length to that of an individual Major

Prophet. The order of the books is as we find it in English Bibles, with some minor exceptions in the history of lists. Some Greek manuscripts place superscripted books together in the first half of the Twelve and create an order of Hosea, Amos, Micah, and then Joel, Obadiah, and Jonah. This tracks with the tendency of the Greek texts to organize like with like, unaware of the significance—if there is such for them—in the Hebrew tradition they have inherited.

Upon inspection it is clear that the movement across the Twelve, if one examines the superscriptions, is roughly chronological. That is, Hosea and Amos are the earliest books and Zechariah and Malachi the latest, with Micah in the middle. Yet half of the books give us no dating reference (Joel, Obadiah, Jonah, Nahum, Habakkuk, and Malachi). The church father Jerome conjectured that undated books were in chronological order due to association with dated neighbors, but the theory is speculative and does not find universal acceptance in the history of interpretation. More recently an alternative notion has found stronger persuasiveness, namely, that undated books are placed where they are for thematic or theological reasons, as they are now found in association with books surrounding them.[15] There is certainly a strong argument to be made for seeing Joel, Obadiah, Jonah, and Malachi as late witnesses and as serving this function. Nahum and Habakkuk certainly fit well within the places we now find them, as we will explain shortly.

The superscription of Hosea closely approximates that of Isaiah, and may be one reason the two collections are often placed next to each other. Though standard textbooks incline to treat Amos as the first prophet historically speaking, the two prophets are clearly contemporaries, and there is good evidence that their respective works were mutually influencing in editorial development.[16]

---

[15] See most recently my discussion in *Joel*, ITC (London: Bloomsbury, 2016).

[16] See the very insightful essay of Jörg Jeremias, "The Interrelationship between Amos and Hosea," in James W. Watts and Paul House, eds., *Forming Prophetic Literature: Essays on Isaiah and the Twelve in Honor of John D.W. Watts*, JSOTS 235 (Sheffield: Sheffield Academic, 1996), 171–86.

Hosea's superscription, moreover, gives him a more comprehensive feel, by speaking of his activity during the reigns of four Judahite kings and two Israelite rulers. Amos by contrast delivers his strong message into the specific context of the northern kingdom during the reign of Jeroboam.

But the stronger argument in favor of Hosea's signal position is the message he delivers. The passionate YHWH must judge his people but cannot give them up. The marriage of the prophet to Gomer mirrors this theological truth in personal and deeply moving terms as the book opens. And at its close it issues an appeal. Return to the LORD, and he will heal and your fruitfulness will again be resplendent (Hos 14:1-8). The book ends on this note and in so doing opens onto the history that will follow. Through every prophetic word to be uttered, this divine appeal stands ready to be heeded and acted upon in Israel's favor and blessing.[17]

To reinforce this point, the book that follows is effectively the words that Hosea said were to be taken so as to approach God in penitence and confession (14:2-4), now scripted in the undated book of Joel that follows. A great locust plague serves as the occasion for lamentation and mourning, and a concrete worship context for approaching the Holy Lord. The locusts are a natural disaster on the one hand, and figures of the national assaults, which we will read about, as YHWH's justice descends upon his people. Joel serves to script the penitential words that, if uttered in full voice, will provide for a remnant through any and all judgment to come. The bounty that will again be Israel's is held out as God's promised response. The nation/locusts will be but for a season and then will be gone. God's word of love and devotion, as we heard it ring forth from Hosea, will be the final word through the changes and chances of the history to follow. Amos repeats word for word the refrain of Joel right at the start of his work so as to

---

[17] Raymond C. Van Leeuwen, "Scribal Wisdom and Theodicy in the Book of the Twelve," in Leo Perdue, Bernard Brandon Scott, and William Johnston Wiseman, eds., *In Search of Wisdom: Essays in Memory of John G. Gammie* (Louisville, Ky.: Westminster John Knox, 1993), 31–49.

alert us to the serial character of the presentation to follow (Joel 3:16 and Amos 1:2).

The opening tableau of nations (Amos 1:3–2:16) serves to establish the LORD of Israel as the God over all nations and over all creation. The sins of Edom mentioned at Joel's close (3:19) are here classified more broadly (1:11-12). But now the judgment of the nations serves as a prelude. It is Israel, "the whole family that I brought up out of Egypt," that the prophet means finally to address. The main theme of Hosea (knowledge of YHWH) is here referred to (3:1), with the intention of making sure we read Hosea's critique of cultic abuses and Amos' focus on social crimes as two sides of one coin.[18] Though both prophets address the sins of the northern kingdom, one can also see clear evidence that the books wish to warn Judah in no less urgent terms (we see the same movement later in Jeremiah, from the standpoint of Judah itself). Though Amos is viewed as the stern and unmoving prophet of doom that so entranced Wellhausen and early twentieth century interpreters—the first great prophet, without antecedent, a shepherd called against his will—the center of the book also shows us a man of great compassion and concern (7:2-3, 5-6). Though he receives visions of utter devastation, he begs for mercy. Mercy is then forthcoming.

But unaware of his saving action of intercession, the authorities can only hear haranguing and interference from a professional "hired gun" of Judah. By silencing him, they cut off the only

---

[18] "I can understand these literary connections . . . only if the pupils of Amos and the pupils of Hosea who handed down the message of the prophets wanted to teach the readers that they could not grasp the central ideas of these prophets by reading their books in complete isolation from one another. By contrast, the readers of the written words of the prophets were supposed to notice the similarity of Amos's and Hosea's message from God . . . The literary connections between these books show that they should be read in relation to each other. I want to show that the traditionists are on their way to discovering something like a common prophetic theology, not by denying that each prophet lived in singular historical circumstances, but by denying that this fact is decisive for their message" (Jeremias, "Interrelationship," 171–72).

lifeline being held out to save them.[19] The final visions of the prophet confirm that "the end has come upon my people Israel," and so it has. Amos ends however in a way that reinforces the message of Joel. God will purge his people as with fire. He will not destroy them utterly. Those who say "evil will not overtake us" will be doomed. Hosea and Joel and now Amos agree on this fundamental point. The wise are those who walk in the ways of the LORD (Hos 14:9), in every generation. As Psalm 25 clarifies, the ways of the LORD consist of his character as revealed at Sinai, merciful and gracious, but by no means clearing the wicked. To walk in the ways of the LORD is to understand his character and to come to him with confession and penitence. Those who do not know these ways ignore their sin and so also avoid coming to learn of his great mercy as well. We see this very drama play itself out with Amos, Amaziah, and Jeroboam.

Edom plays a specific role in the Twelve, as we have seen thus far. On the one hand this role is familiar from Psalm 137 and elsewhere (Lam 4:21-22). Edom stood aloof when Jerusalem fell and even aided Israel's enemies (Obad 10-14). Special retribution therefore awaits her. But Obadiah makes clear that this specific crime has its focal point in one major flaw: Edom rejected her role as twin brother of Jacob and so with a specific vocation in God's plans. She wanted to be a nation (vv. 1-4). She thought to raise herself up above her station, and so God will reduce her and leave her fate in their rapacious hands. So as Jonah opens we are aware of the "nations" as a major agent in wrecking God's judgment and of overreaching and so punished in the end. Yet this is not all that can be said about the nations. They are not simply pawns on a great chessboard of God's ways with his own people.

The book of Jonah rejects that view and resoundingly so—to the point of satire and a humiliating portrait of God's people and

---

[19] Jeremias' close reading of the central panel at 7:1–8:3 is brilliant on this point ("Interrelationship," 32). See my summary in *Prophecy and Hermeneutics*, 206–7. Jeremias writes, "God's patience ends where the state represented by the priest tries to decide when and where God may speak through the prophet" (32).

the prophetic agent Jonah. Jonah wants to flee from the God who made the heavens and the earth, the seas and dry ground. He rejects his role as prophet of judgment. But he becomes a prophet in spite of himself, when by deduction the sailors know the one hiding must be the one with the True God (Jon 1:6-10). They offer sacrifices and become true worshippers in calling on the name of YHWH, as they throw the disobedient one overboard (1:15-16). Yet Jonah is rescued by a great fish, and he takes up his distasteful role. He announces judgment and effects a great wave of penitence. We who have been reading the Twelve know this theme and where it will go, and apparently so does Jonah. He tells God this is why he stayed away from his job. God has ways of mercy and justice both. Having marched but a day into a city three days' journey wide he sulks under a booth he has constructed for the purpose (3:3-4). The question hovers in the air as to whether the sackcloth repentance of man and beast will hold. Is it a hungover oath sworn in haste to quit drinking for good? While waiting for his answer God turns to Jonah instead. He makes the shade cease that he had given him by a great plant. God points out that it is a bit odd to care more for a dead plant than for a dead people, and so Jonah suggests its time then for him to die. Like the parable of the prodigal son when the older brother complains of God's grace, we are left with a question. God reserves the right to have pity and to make merry. So get used to it. Ninevites and prodigals he has come to save.[20]

The ultimate fate of Nineveh—if indeed we are right in how we take the scene outside the city—is not actually given in Jonah. But we know God's mind on the matter. The book of Micah returns us to the landscape of Judah and the history of God's people amongst the nations. He promises a day when nation will not lift up sword against nation but instead will flock to God's holy mountain, asking that they may be taught God's torah (Mic 4:1-4). In this day, God's judgment will cleanse the nations and bring their

---

[20] The resemblance of the older brother in Luke 15 and Jonah is unmistakable. Both stories end with a question as well about the character of God's mercy.

hostility to an end. As it is now, they walk in the ways of their own Gods, but Israel knows the God YHWH is their God, and wills to be Lord over all as well. The book ends with the refrain we are beginning to see functioning like a red thread through the books of the Twelve (7:18-20). In doxology God is praised for the mercy that can throw the sins of a people as deep as the sea that held Jonah in its grip.

The appearance of the book of Nahum tells us that the ceaseless iniquity of Assyria won out in the end, leaving a poignant reminder in our mind of a scene of great heartfelt repentance on their part in the days of Jonah. The book opens with the refrain that closed Micah, but now God is great not in mercy but might (1:3). He will by no means clear the guilt. Where Jonah ended with a question, so does Nahum, about which he asks, "For upon whom has not come your unceasing evil?" Habakkuk picks up the question and turns it toward God. The one who raised up Assyria as agent of judgment has in turn raised up a more ruthless nation to bring that role to an end. Yet it is unclear how this can be a good plan of action. So the prophet takes his stand on the watchtower to see God's answer to his Jeremiah-like lament. The book of Habakkuk is itself to be a vision of justice that others may read to learn the answer God gives. "He who runs" is the one God has given swift feet, and has raised up and strengthened (Isa 40:31).[21] This strengthening comes from reading the vision of Habakkuk, where we learn that God's justice may be slow, but it will not delay long. The woes that follow in the present book show God assuredly judging the nations. The final psalm prayer pays tribute to this God of old, and gives the reader the language needed to stand strong through a time of waiting (3:1-19).[22] What Joel did following

---

[21] See within the larger argument of Francis Watson for the signal role of Habakkuk in the Twelve these important insights on the watchtower scene, in *Paul and the Hermeneutics of Faith* (London: T&T Clark, 2004); my engagement can be seen in *Prophecy and Hermeneutics*, 118.

[22] The "feet like hinds feet" (3:19) show a faithful running àla 2:2, that is,

Hosea, Habakkuk does following Nahum and anticipating the great and terrible day of the Lord of Zephaniah.

With the ninth book of the Twelve we reach a crescendo. The prior references to a Day of YHWH from Joel forward here coalesce and create a dramatic picture of the entire cosmos wracked in judgment (Zeph 1:1-6). The prayer of Habakkuk is indeed a necessary support as the movement from Assyria to Babylon reaches a fever pitch. One may suppose that the events of 597 and 587 are being anticipated on the historical plane but that this entails something yet more penetrating in its cleansing power on the heavenly plane. The final chapter depicts a patient and humble remnant, protected and sustained, and Zion herself rejoicing as all the prior judgments are exhausting their hold. The LORD is in her midst through it all. Her children will be brought home from the places they have been dispersed. Her fortunes will be restored before her very eyes (3:8-20). This is a waiting (" 'Therefore wait for me,' says the LORD," 3:8) that will bear fruit, as Habakkuk has sought to assure us. Haggai then picks up the thread on the other side of judgment and exile as he begins the concrete business of starting anew.

The book of Haggai is short and entirely in narrative form. Its dating structure is carried over into Zechariah, at least in some measure. Dates seem to be important, and they are provided with a fresh kind of precision (Hag 1:1; 2:1, 10, 18, 20). The book poses the central question as to whether Israel's life as before is something that can be restarted, and if so, when, exactly. The oracles Haggai receives say with urgency Yes, but this cannot be a simple thing, given the din and drama of such a total judgment by YHWH. How the house of God could be made clean again, after the assaults of the nations, surely haunted the day. If the reestablishment of the house of God is what assures fertility and spiritual renewal, then surely its place must be restored. But how is this to be done properly, as there is no template for its execution? Temple, priesthood, kingship, wisdom—all lie in ruins. Indeed, Haggai and the ensuing

---

energized by the vision that is the book of Habakkuk (1:1 and 2:2-3). Watson's interpretation of the vision scene (2:1-4) in relation to 1:1 and 3:19 is insightful.

books must themselves be questioned when considered from the perspective of whether prophecy is possible or its vital force spent. Who is this Haggai, and how is God's word in his mouth to be trusted? These would seem to be the challenges his oracles in the form we have them are addressing. Something is about to happen. It will be a dramatic restoration on the order, even, of the preceding judgment, as Zerubbabel picks up where the destroyed monarchy lay before him in tatters.

Zechariah seconds the word of Haggai, and one may wonder whether a "seconding" is now absolutely critical if Israel is to find its way. The book is highly unusual, consisting of a series of eight (the perfect seven plus yet another) night visions. It is as though the fate of Israel is in midair, and seen not in day but in the shadow land of night. Israel's destiny is "up in the air," moving, but unstable.[23] The visions the prophet is given amount to divine reestablishment of Israel's condition: in the face of national forces unleashed by God but now at rest, concerning her religious center, her dispersed peoples, her priesthood and civil authority, her spiritual health and removal of past toxins, and the crowning of king and priest for fresh duty. The words of the prophets preceding are now a kind of category, known to be such: they are former prophets, for now we are in a new age (Zech 1:4-6; 7:7, 12). Their words live on and direct the present life of the community. In some ways, they are also the warrant answering the last question to be resolved: can there be prophecy, and can there be prophets again? The final chapters of the book are replete with quotation and citation from previous prophetic works. The former words of the prohets, which Zecharaiah said outlived the men who spoke them and press on with overtaking power, continue to seek resolution and final fulfillment. Even a reestablished Israel in the aftermath of national destruction and violent upheaval looks to a final day of the Lord, when a final and permanent cult, priesthood, ruler,

---

[23] Baruch Halpern, "The Ritual Background of Zechariah's Temple Song," *CBQ* 40 (1978): 167–90.

and prophet are the lasting standard of God's ways with Israel and the world (14:1-21).

The one crucial thing to note about the strange final book is that its agent of delivery is also at the same time a protagonist active in the work itself (3:1). "My messenger" is sent by God for a great work of preparation, to ready the people with one final prophetic action, so they may stand before the coming final Day of YHWH. Whoever "the prophet Malachi" is within the timeframe and religious context assumed in the opening chapters, he is in that role a figure or type of the messenger to come. His exhortations serve the purpose of modeling what the great messenger to come will be about, yet more dramatically and finally. The final book of the Twelve is then a book in the Twelve and a standard bearer for a future and final encounter with God, unlike anything Israel has experienced and for which there must be a warning bell and a final moment to stop and be ready. Those who heed in Malachi's day are models for the conduct necessary for the future Day (3:16-18). In the time before that day, the law of Moses will serve as guide. Also referred to is a book of remembrance (3:16). A popular interpretation is that this a book into which are registered the names of the faithful who fear the LORD in Malachi's day. This appears to be the meaning given in most translations. But it has also been argued that the book is a memorial established before the LORD that serves on behalf of those who fear him, and that what is being referred to is the prophetic collection of the Twelve as such.[24] Malachi self-consciously closes that collection and points to a future Malachi and a past memorial at one and the same time. Whether such a reading is to be preferred there can be little doubt that in its present form the book of the Twelve serves to guide and direct the faithful remnant of Israel until the great and terrible day spoken of from Joel to Malachi.

---

[24] This is the position of James Nogalski.

Prophetic Inspiration

One of the hallmarks of modern biblical study is attention to an author's intention. Even at the Reformation a general concern to attend to the historical author and the location and specifics of his writing was thought to be critical, and a way to avoid a sense that seemed to float about the human author and that obscured what the Bible wanted to say more efficiently. Yet in this same period appeal to the human author was a far less complicated piece of hermeneutical guidance. Moses and Isaiah and Jeremiah and Solomon and Zechariah were authors whose books were quite directly before us in the canonical form we find them. It might be necessary to think about how Moses wrote Genesis, but this did not amount to positing four sources in the Pentateuch. The rabbis might credit Isaiah's authorship to the men of Hezekiah (B. Batra 14b), but whatever this might mean, it never prevented the history of interpretation of thinking of him as endowed with a tremendous charism that enabled him to see into the future of exile and return. The author Isaiah's intentions were registered in the book that bore his name.

This appeal to a stable intentionality in the literal sense would soon be asked to bear an additional burden. A history that sat alongside the text and to which it was making reference would soon seem far more realistic in character than the world of Isaiah, book and author both. John Calvin had no book on his shelf called "the history of the world" with which he then correlated the Bible in some way. I choose him because of the early modern readers he more than anyone was sensitive to what we would now call "ostensive reference" and the historicality of the Old and New Testaments. But very soon it would no longer be possible to keep the referentiality of the Bible coordinated with the canonical presentation of its literary givenness. Even the term "literal" would soon come to mean "factual" or "historical."

A theory of inspiration that works very hard to determine a human author's intentions will struggle within battle lines set up by the discipline of biblical studies as this would evolve in the eighteenth century and gather force in the twentieth. Under debate was the prophet Isaiah as the author of the book with which he is associated. If he was not the author, then how much of it and in what concrete setting are we to understand him at work, intending to communicate this or that to this or that audience? In the case of Isaiah—though any biblical work could be chosen as an example—chapters 40–55 seemed to address a different time and context, and actually did not appear to present themselves as prediction from afar but rather contemporaneous address to an audience other than that of Isaiah of Jerusalem.[25] It is difficult to understand what intention of communication there would be for Isaiah's audience at the time of Ahaz and Hezekiah. It seems more likely they would scratch their heads and, like Daniel being given a vision not for his day, need some special reassurance that all would be well (Dan 8:17, 27; 10:8-12). How do we move from Zechariah 1–8 into 9–14 and not sense a shift of author and context? Or from Galatians to Colossians? Or from Genesis to Exodus? Or from sections of one book to others within the same book? Who as human author intended Isaiah 2:1-5 and Micah 4:1-4, and why are they so similar? Did Jonah borrow from Joel or the other way around?

But there is an additional problem that arises apart from the matter of historical reference and the way the biblical material gives us quite a challenge when it comes to extracting a human author and his intentions in historical context. It is also belied by some of the examples given thus far. For inspiration can also be that act of provision of speech and vision that the prophet is given to declare *whose final purpose and intention is greater than he or she understands or intends.* If this is what divine inspiration really means, then a prophet or inspired author can communicate meaningfully to an audience in time and space and say more than he can line up with what God intends to do and say with that selfsame speech as time marches on under God's providence.[26] The biblical text can tell

---

[25] Christopher Seitz, "How Is Isaiah Present in the Latter Half of the Book? The Logic of Isaiah 40–55 within the Book of Isaiah," *JBL* 115 (1996): 219–40.

[26] See my final comments on intentionality in the Psalter in Christopher

us this with clarity, as when Isaiah is told to bind up his speaking and preserve it, so it can be opened and then address a new day (Isa 8:16-20; cf. 29:11-12; 30:8). God will superintend the way a former thing will become a new thing. Inspiration entails obedience in speaking what one is given as chosen agent, not crafting an intentional word according to the canons of ordinary communication (themselves not straightforward when it comes to intention and reception!). The word of God accomplishes things (55:11). It doesn't stay put under a single intention—though that intention is divinely time-given—and so whoever we say "intended" Isaiah 2 and Micah 4, it is perhaps better to stand before the challenge of God's accomplishing speech as a fact to be considered as such.[27]

So when it comes to the Book of the Twelve, the standard procedure of determining human authors in time and space gave us a timeline running from Amos to Hosea to Micah, splicing in Isaiah and Jeremiah when able to do so, and moving forward to the latest books as conjectured according to this grid of intentionality (Joel or Jonah or Malachi). The alternative is to deal with intentionality through close reading of the canonical form and seeing if there is another way to understand the communication of God's word. This would be one in which time—accepting there are late works and early works—can double back on itself, seek associations by closer and subsequent reading, offer juxtaposed and inspired speech, as in Joel or Obadiah or Jonah, so as to draw out a meaning that God intends but which becomes available as he accomplishes things in time with a chosen people.

Seitz, "Psalm 2 in the Entry Hall of the Psalter: Extended Sense in the History of Interpretation," in Ephraim Radner, ed., *Church, Society, and the Christian Common Good* (Eugene, Ore.: Cascade, 2017), 95–106.

[27] Christopher Seitz, "Prophetic Associations," in John J. Ahn and Stephen L. Cook, eds., *Thus Says the Lord: Essays on the Former and Latter Prophets in Honor of Robert R. Wilson*, LHBOTS 502 (London: T&T Clark, 2009), 156–66; "Scriptural Author and Canonical Prophet: The Theological Implications of Literary Association in the Canon," in Katharine J. Dell and Paul M. Joyce, eds., *Biblical Method and Interpretation: Essays in Honour of John Barton* (Oxford: Oxford University Press, 2013), 176–88.

The only way to establish the character of divine intentionality seen through associations is by familiarizing ourselves with the variety of ways the canon invites us to appreciate its character. The Book of the Twelve may convey an intention that arises from the individual witnesses themselves on the one hand, that is, there are twelve books, and their beginnings and endings are carefully marked and the idea of an individual realistically confronting an historical audience is firmly in place. Yet one can also appreciate that alongside this there is another level of intentionality equally deserving to be called historical that arises when one carefully attends to associations that are now there to be seen and argued for when one takes the canonical form seriously. Yet the case of the three Major Prophets equally establishes that order and sequence may mean not very much at all; witness the ability of different orders to emerge and not really matter much.

It is important to keep this general observation in place as we move to the third division of the Hebrew Bible. It is also preserved in Jewish and Christin lists in different arrangements, and as we have seen in some places, dissolved altogether so as to give rise to different global arrangements. The Prophets are an amalgam of Deuteronomistic History (Joshua-Kings or Former Prophets) plus the Three plus the Twelve. The major connection of part one (Former) and part two (Latter) keeps prophecy within a field of association that is historical but also figural and affiliated in character. Shifting part one into a single historical timeline, as we find in English printed Bibles, is a move that one can easily understand—put like with like—but that ought not run interference for our thinking carefully about the canonical presentation of Prophets such as we find it in the major Hebrew attestation.

11

Writings

There is more variation in evidence in this third section of the Hebrew Bible than in the Law or Prophets. The category "Writings," moreover, is of such a nature that one might expect even further variation than what we do find. This points to the general principle that for reasons of practicality and use, stabilization of an order of some kind is a natural outcome. We conclude our survey of the shape of the canon by maintaining a concern with understanding what the different orders seek to communicate, more than arguing in strong terms for the priority of one over another. By its very character, the writings contain a variety of works most notable for how they are neither Law or Prophetic, though composed with an awareness of this "core canon." It is for this reason that their number and order are frequently misunderstood in terms of their significance for questions of the "closure" of the Elder Scripture.[1]

By its very name, the final section of the Hebrew Bible indicates several things straightforwardly. (1) What we have is a general miscellany, for which the terms "prophet" and "law" do not apply. (2) We have a plural entity in the form of different writings, which cannot be classified any more specifically because they are diverse in length and character. (3) The order and arrangement of the material, as we shall see, mean less than in Law and Prophets. (4) If this is true, then it is equally an open question as to the significance of scope and number of books.

We have already noted the very different arrangement of these and the other non-Pentateuch books in subsequent Christian lists. The familiar practice of modern printed Bibles in English shouldn't mislead us into thinking that fourfold canonical arrangements are a single meaningful alternative to a threefold arrangement. The matter is far more haphazard when one moves from the Law-Prophets-Writings Hebrew Bible.

When one looks at the arrangement of the Ketuvim in Hebrew orders, three different sequences can be noted. (1) The MT and most witnesses have three sub-divisions: poetical books (*sifre emet*), Psalms, Proverbs, and Job; five festival scrolls (*megilloth*) consisting of shorter books read on Passover (Song of Songs), Weeks (Ruth), Ninth of Av (Lamentations), Booths (Ecclesiastes), Purim (Esther); and three other books (Daniel, Ezra-Nehemiah, and Chronicles) that fall outside the first two subdivisions. (2) The Babylonian Talmud (B. Batra 14b) gives a different order of Ruth, Psalms, Job, Proverbs, Ecclesiastes, Song of Solomon, Lamentations of Jeremiah, Daniel, Scroll of Esther, Ezra, Chronicles. Here we can see that the festival scroll idea is not present. Ruth is in first position, the

---

[1] See my treatment in *The Goodly Fellowship of the Prophets: The Achievement of Association in Canon Formation* (Grand Rapids: Baker Academic, 2009), 99–125. More recently, see "Ketuvim and Canon," in Julius Steinberg and Timothy J. Stone, eds., *The Shape of the Writings* (Winona Lake, Ind.: Eisenbrauns, 2015).

poetical books are together as in the MT but in a different order, and the books associated with Solomon are also associated. (3) In Tiberian Masoretic codices, including the Aleppo Codex and the Leningrad Codex, and often in old Spanish manuscripts as well, the order is Chronicles, Psalms, Job, Proverbs, Ruth, Song of Solomon, Ecclesiastes, Lamentations of Jeremiah, Esther, Daniel, Ezra. Chronicles has been move to first position. The poetical books are together as in (2). Ruth follows Proverbs and so breaks up the Solomon trio. Ezra is the final book.

What we learn from this is that a fixed order never took hold and was probably not necessary to the maintenance of a division, whose total number of books nevertheless stayed the same. This means that the individuality of the witnesses remained more important, even as associations could be sought (poetical books, Solomon books, Ruth following Proverbs). Yet a single set of associations did not win out over others. We can have little trouble seeing why this or that order may have become popular and so is now represented. But this does not detract from the overall sense that in this division we have a miscellany of individual works. Stated differently, in time diverse orders in such a case as this will seek a stable sequence just for purposes of memorization and cataloguing, but that did not happen with the Ketuvim. Different communities present us with orders that have become stable with themselves but not across the board.

I have argued the case in a previous publication that what is characteristic of the Writings as a collection is that the individual works represented there presuppose the existence of stable Law and Prophets sections, which they are not part of and to which they relate to make their communicative sense.[2] Stated differently, though any order will in time find a means of associating a mixed group of writings into patterns like the three above, this level of association is not more important laterally than one assumed to be relevant outside of the Ketuvim. To choose the one in Tiberian

---

[2] Seitz, *Goodly Fellowship*, 99–125.

codices: Chronicles works alongside 1 and 2 Kings; Psalms and 1 and 2 Samuel; Job and Genesis; Proverbs and 1 Kings; Ruth and 1 and 2 Samuel; Song and Ecclesiastes and 1 Kings; Lamentations and Jeremiah. The final three pretty much function on their own, with Ezra picking up from 2 Chronicles and extending the Deuteronomistic History's record. I think that general picture is largely correct, though some internal associations in some lists make lateral sense as well; the Solomon trio is an obvious one.

I stay with this topic here because in my view it also relates to the debated issue of closure of the canon: when this happened, how it happened, what significance it might have for what terms we use ("scripture" and "canon" have been invented to work in strong contrast, for example), and indeed what weight a term like "closure" may be said to have. On my view, if the main distinction to be made is that the writings in the third section function in relation to a stable Law and Prophets, then their total number is not as significant as has been held. Probably some thought has gone into what book will appear last in the collection, at some point in time when the idea of further Hebrew language writing was not occurring. Some hold that a major difference exists between a Chronicles or Ezra-Nehemiah ending. The former seems to see the future unfolding as the nations go up to Jerusalem, where the latter would enclose that hope within the focused attention paid to the temple as such. But these are speculations whose significance is hard to judge.[3]

To give some further thought to associations in the canon, let's take the case of the Solomon trio from the reception history perspective. A Jewish interpretation thought in terms of the ages

---

[3] John H. Sailhamer, "Biblical Theology and the Composition of the Hebrew Bible," in Scott Hafemann, ed., *Biblical Theology: Retrospect and Prospect* (Downers Grove, Ill.: InterVarsity, 2002), 25–37. My discussion is in *Goodly Fellowship*, 115–17. See also Georg Steins, *Die Chronik als kanonisches Abschlußphänomen. Studien zur Entstehung und Theologie von 1/2 Chronik*, Bonner Biblische Beiträge 93 (Weinheim: Beltz Athenäum Verlag, 1995). The issues are the subject of recent review in *Shape of the Writings* (2015).

of Solomon: he wrote Song as a young man in love, Proverbs as an adult, and Ecclesiastes as an old man. The name "Koheleth," it was conjectured, he took for himself after he failed as king and took foreign wives and built idols. He wandered the earth and penned Ecclesiastes in a penitential mode.[4] Early Christian interpreters also thought in terms of stages, as Solomon increased in wisdom. He first wrote Proverbs to catalogue the basic rules of the road of life. Then came Ecclesiastes, which they took as a deeply profound meditation on the limits of human wisdom and the suffering that this age brings, and that the true Ecclesiast Jesus Christ entered to redeem. Song of Songs is next, and it speaks of heavenly life in the mode of discourse appropriate to that: song. The three superscriptions move from Israel, to Jerusalem, to the unstipulated realms of the true man of peace.

The Babylonian Talmud has the order that became familiar to the early church in certain Greek language lists and that invited the stages of divine knowledge reading. The Tiberian list gives the order Song, then Proverbs and Ecclesiastes, but Ruth interrupts the sequence by following Song. Yet it is hard to believe that either reading—Christian or Jewish—required an exact sequence in order to compel the interpreter in this or that direction. The three books all refer in some way to Solomon. The absence of reference to his name in the case of Ecclesiastes is taken to be significant in both traditions. For Christian reading, it points beyond the historical Solomon to his figural counterpart Jesus Christ. For Jewish reading it means that something profound has happened that has turned Solomon into another man, now transmitting the wisdom appropriate to suffering and learning the limits of wealth, wives, wine, and accumulation under the sun. The Ketuvim's order is not so single-minded as to force a reading but rather invites the reader to make associations in the wider canon as these are appropriate, assisted by the narratives pertaining to Solomon in 1 Kings and

---

[4] See references in chapter 14 below. Cf. my "Koheleth and Canon," in S. A. Cummins and Jens Zimmerman, eds., *Acts of Interpretation: Scripture, Theology, and Culture* (Grand Rapids: Eerdmans, forthcoming).

what is and isn't mentioned in the superscriptions of the Solomon trio where it is now found distributed in lists.

The two other big poetic books, apart from Proverbs, are Psalms and Job. The association of Psalms with David is traditional and of course well attested in the superscriptions of the Psalms. These attestations are heaviest at the start of the five-book collection. At the end of book 2 we see a transition to the monarchy and Solomon, along with the introduction of guilds known to us from Chronicles. David all but disappears in book 4 as the suffering associated with David in book 1 becomes emblematic of the people Israel in exile. Book 5 sees Psalms of Ascent and the reemergence of monarchial hopes, now headed toward the endless alleluia of all creation.[5]

There are some longer psalm superscriptions that relate the psalms in some way to specific episodes in the life of David such as we can read these in the narratives of 1–2 Samuel.[6] The superscriptions in this form appear to be a kind of Midrashic effort to think prayerfully through the details of the preexistent psalm so as to illumine episodes in Samuel, open up David to spiritual reflection and imitation, resolve tensions in the Samuel narratives, or make wider associations across the canon. All in all, the frequent association of individual Psalms with David creates the impression that what began on the ground with David as a man of prayer and song formed the basis for an extended use of his name so as to link the narratives of David with the prayers of the Psalter. Equally, we should be open to the possibility that the Psalter is giving us its own very specific account of the

---

[5] The bibliography on the Psalter as a canonical presentation is enormous. I have some reflections in "Royal Promises in the Canonical Books of Isaiah and the Psalms," in *Word without End: The Old Testament as Abiding Theological Witness* (Waco, Tex.: Baylor University Press, 2005), 150–67.

[6] Brevard S. Childs, "Psalm Titles and Midrashic Exegesis," *JSS* 16 (1971): 137–50. I have an evaluation with a focus on Ps 34 ("Psalm 34: Redaction, Inner-Biblical Exegesis and the Longer Psalm Superscriptions") in Christopher R. Seitz and Kent Harold Richards, eds., *The Bible as Christian Scripture: The Work of Brevard S. Childs* (Atlanta: SBL, 2013), 279–98.

significance of David and the monarchy, including an eschatologically driven concern that belongs to the genius of the Psalter in its present canonical form.[7]

Modern interpretation of Job exists within a popular designation of introductory courses called "wisdom literature." This is held to be a distinct body of Old Testament material emerging from the religious world of ancient Israel, beginning with school wisdom in Proverbs. Without getting into the topics that are often held to be critical for understanding this material (reconstructions of education in Israel, wisdom transmission methods, early "clan wisdom," secular and religious wisdom, wisdom in ANE sources), at its most basic level the notion one encounters is of a movement from conservative and optimistic epistemology; to questioning this view; to its final deterioration. In so doing a special "canonical" subdivision emerges in Proverbs, Job, and Qoheleth, departing in strong ways from the present orderings of the Writings. Job is in medial position. Its beginning and ending consist of a folktale that upholds conservative wisdom; the dialogues deconstruct that view, said to be animating the thinking of Job's comforters; Job receives some kind of answer from God that consists of no answer or a power grab; Elihu is differently evaluated as trying to right the ship of conservative wisdom or as a stooge.[8] Ecclesiastes then emerges to put paid to any idea that there is order in God's creation except as a way to put us in mind of the vanity of human wisdom if not creation itself.[9]

On this view of Job, the book is best understood as the container that holds in tension various sides in a debate, carrying us well into postexilic period and authors working at the time. The concept of wisdom literature is a modern invention with no canonical or

---

[7] Christopher Seitz, "Psalm 2 in the Entry Hall of the Psalter: Extended Sense in the History of Interpretation," in Ephraim Radner, ed., *Church, Society, and the Christian Common Good* (Eugene, Ore.: Cascade, 2017), 95–106.

[8] Seitz, "Job: Full Structure, Movement, and Interpretation," *Int* 43 (1989): 5–15.

[9] Fuller discussion follows in chapter 14 below.

history of reception warrant. The three Solomon books do not represent it in Song of Songs. Job circulates as a major poetic collection alongside Psalms and Proverbs in all major listings, including modern English Bibles, and stands on its own two feet. The ending of Ecclesiastes appears to relate it to Proverbs, but more arguably in a complementary than an antagonistic sense. There are the rules of the road and the exceptions to the rules. There are paradigms and conjugations in a basic grammar, but the later chapters introduce the heart of the real language as it lives, with false cognates, rare forms, and strange refusals to exist in declensions.

The canonical presentation of Job is as an ancient, worthy contemporary of Noah and Dan'el, a Canaanite hero of yore. As we have seen, the book keeps the divine name at a strange distance and introduces it much as it might appear in Genesis. Job is not an Israelite at all, and participates in no genuine inner-Israel debate over wisdom. He is a man on his own, from the land of Uz, friend of those from Arabia who come to comfort him. He exists in the canonical presentation as before the call of Abraham, and the presentation keeps that perspective firmly in place without a suggestion he is a cipher for later wisdom squabbles. One medieval interpreter held the friends to be representatives of schools of what will become Islam in time. Job appeals to no torah, prophet, priest, or documentary source. He is the man from Uz undergoing a terrible assault from God. Here is a place where interpretation of the book will go wrong because it makes a reverse move from anachronism by denying the book its right to exist within the logic and constraints of the temporal context in which it chooses to pursue its theme. "Can a man serve God for nought?" (Job 1:9). This is an ancient and a perennial question. Is our life under and before God life for his sake and its sake, or does it consist in the exchanges of blessing and bounty for which we wait? That question has no date, even as within the book of Job it is located meaningfully at a time when no law, prophet, priest, or wise man is there to consult. And the ones who do appear offer only false trails or are passed over in silence.

I have referred in my own essay to the canonical design of Job and how that design carefully distinguishes the reader and what she knows from the man Job and what he undergoes, so that the test is ours and his both, but predicated differently of course. On my reading Job gains in knowledge and insight through his struggles, while in a third round the friends fizzle and find their wisdom silent. Elihu stalls the action and provides what he appears to think is all God can give, via his mouth, since he does not appear in court of human summoning, no matter how grievous the charge. But appear God does. Job proves that a mortal can serve God for naught but staying on the field of play and refusing to take any answer but the one God gives when he decides to give it. In this manner Satan is defeated. But Job will never know this since the gambit is beyond his ken. When he steps forward to pray for the friends, in his terrible condition and still on the ash heap of God's assaults, he becomes all he was before, the man whose prayers made him as renowned as his righteousness and blamelessness. At that moment, God restored his fortunes and blessed him beyond measure.

This is not a book to be ranged on a grid of deteriorating confidence in wisdom. It belongs on its terrible own, towering over domestications of any kind so as to speak its demanding and mouth-stopping truth about God and humanity when shorn of anything except himself and a man like Job.

Let us move next to Ruth as an example of a book that likes neighbors and has attracted several different ones on its canonical journey. The most familiar one is as the stopping point between the grim conclusion of Judges and the grim but about-to-change opening chapters of 1 Samuel. The book has been taken in historical-critical circles to be a late composition whose true neighbor is Ezra-Nehemiah. Intermarriage is condemned in the postexilic period and in the context of its challenges. Ruth was written to counter that xenophobic spirit. It might have been helpful if Naomi had married a Moabite after her husband died, so as to make this point more effectively, and if Ruth had decided that the worship of YHWH could happen just as well alongside Moabite deities in her own land. But the book goes a different direction. Another possibility, along something of the same line, is to claim the book's purpose is to show that King David came from foreign stock, with Ruth as his great-grandmother. This at least tracks more persuasively the actual narrative presentation of the book, which ends with a genealogy. Though it is surely a strange feature that the genealogy goes backwards six generations to Perez before it goes forward to Jesse and David.

In the canonical orders Ruth also follows Proverbs. Striking in this regard is the praise of a virtuous woman with which Proverbs closes, in a single individual poem called "the words of Lemuel, king of Massa, which his mother taught him." It is an acrostic composition that praises the bold woman of virtue and asks where she can be found. This is the same phrase that is used of Ruth, and reading the poem and reading Ruth in the light of it makes for a marvelous surprise like the surprise of the book itself. The third and final location of Ruth is as book 2 of the Megilloth, where following the reading of Song of Songs at Passover, it is read for the Feast of Weeks. The harvest time surprise of Ruth and Boaz makes for a theme of great uplift and hope. That spirit of uplift also helps us transition from Judges' hopeless conclusion. No king in the land. Everyone hacked up concubines as was right in their own eyes. But Ruth and Boaz's offspring will be King David's eventual grandfather, and the hopelessness of Judges reversed. "A son is born to Naomi" the women of the village proclaim, so even her bereft and childless condition is addressed, just as is Ruth's, Boaz's, and the people of Israel's.

All three of these canonical associations are worth pondering. Each has its contribution to make. We are reminded by Ruth not to turn a canonically rich book into one that can only make sense if we determine the correct or original order. Here again a canonical intentionality proves far more resilient and capable of communicative surplus than one based upon discovering a human author in historical time. The final genealogy moves our eye back to Perez and the account found in Genesis. Not just the wily and sturdy foreigner Ruth but also the resolute Canaanite Tamar belong inside the purposes of God, which lead up to the son of Jesse.

Thus far we have been discussing the character of association whereby individual writings make their sense in relation to works already established as such in the Law and the Prophets, and secondarily on that basis with one another in certain cases (compare Ruth and Job, for example). The more significant point emerges when one considers the concept of a canon as a closed and stable collection of writings. It is usually maintained that the Old Testament is an open assembly of diverse works and it becomes a "canon" when external forces make it so. Yet what we are observing is the instinct to defer to a stable and known collection of writings in fixed form (Law and Prophets) within the Old Testament itself. The Writings make their sense in relation to a core canon of "Moses and the Prophets" and what the New Testament itself speaks of in the same way.[10]

The Writings are eleven diverse works that appear in a limited form of three basic sequences. The wise man Daniel's book shows him reading prophecy (Jeremiah) and seeking a further meaning within its literal sense that can be applied to his day and his times. Lamentations orient themselves around the tragic fall of Jerusalem and destruction of the Temple as reported in 2 Kings, and that function is made explicit in the festival use subsequently and to this day. That they can be called "Lamentations of Jeremiah" underscores the point that here we have a work in association with a core canon text. Esther is by all accounts—including the earliest appraisals of the rabbis themselves—an unusual book. It does not contain the divine name, and it may have originated precisely within a festival context as its primary context. This is not the same kind of association, but it does suggest the book's singularity is tied to a situation in life which we now refer to as Purim. Ezra (or Ezra-Nehemiah) is often considered a supplement to Chronicles. But Ezra in particular functions alongside Haggai-Zechariah

---

[10] Seitz, *Goodly Fellowship*, 91–125.

in much the same way as the main section of the Twelve relates to the Deuteronomistic History. The prophetic duo plays an explicit role in the center chapter, and Ezra gives us a sense of the historical situation that obtained at the time of the return, which is the background of those two prophetic works. It tries to explain who Zerubbabel is and what the postexilic community is facing in terms of the challenge of rebuilding the community in all its aspects—which is the content of the oracles to Haggai and night visions of Zechariah. And the Chronicles have their own distinctive purpose beyond just telling the history of the Deuteronomist one more time and from a different, Midrashic angle—though that purpose is clear enough and also establishes the main principle of associative meaning for the Writings as a category in the present Old Testament canon.

For the bulk of their reporting, 1 and 2 Chronicles track the history of Israel from Saul to Zedekiah, with special emphasis on David and Solomon, akin to what we find in the Deuteronomistic History. One can of course spot special tendencies and emphases in the Chronicler's history as he retells this story. Most commentary focuses on helping us understand these distinctive features. It is, however, worth noting that the author is quite content to indicate that he is using sources known to the reader and happily sends us there. So the consciousness of a standard and available account dampens the idea that what we have is chiefly an idealized displacement of the "canonical history" as the main purpose of the Chronicler as such.

For our purposes what is more intriguing is the timeline the Chronicler undertakes to introduce. He begins—without warning—with Adam, Seth, and Enosh, and then in uninterrupted fashion produces a genealogy that takes us to David and the history of the monarchy. Nine chapters open the work, and they are almost entirely genealogy, constructed with materials we know from the core canon, and special sources of some kind. Again, we can see special tendencies and emphases, but the more intriguing question is what the purpose of this arrangement of the "history" is, beginning in this way. Also to be noted is that the genealogies don't just bring us to the starting point of the historical record, which in chapter 10 introduces us to Saul en route to David and Solomon. They indicate that Judah and Jerusalem will in time be destroyed and so move us from the start to the end of the house of David, and then into the time of the Chronicler in Judah after exile (1 Chron 3:1-24). A similar perspective is introduced when the Levites are tallied (1 Chron 6:15). Then at the final chapter we find the entire Levitical lineage for life in Jerusalem after exile and related genealogies for this time. When, then, we come to final chapter of the historical narrating of preexilic Israel (2 Chron 36) and read of the destruction of the temple, and the deportation of the King and people and temple vessels, we know this is not the final horizon on the Chronicler's timeline.

We have already commented on the effect of the final verses of this history. It stands in sharp contrast to the end of the Deuteronomistic History. Cyrus of Persia is under charge from the LORD God of Israel. He issues a formal declaration in his name and with his imprimatur and at his bidding. The LORD has charged him to build a house, and all kingdoms have been placed in his hands. The happy invitation is therefore issued, "Whoever is among you of all his people, may the LORD God be with him. Let him go up."

The opening chapters of the history return us to the table of nations and "all the kingdoms of the earth"—to use the language of the final verses. God's purposes for creation have their focus on Israel to be sure, but the Chronicler places again in the foreground this wider canvas and allows it to govern the way he repeats and retells the story of monarchy, temple, and priesthood, from a worldwide perspective of beginning and final purpose. Cyrus the Persian will have the house built. All kingdoms are in his hands. Let Israel go up. However we are to understand what the Chronicler's final vision is, in detail, and how the world perspective will be central to it, we cannot miss the scale and scope of how he conceives time and space and God's purposes. It is for this reason that many regard the Chronicler as the final book of the canon, which position he occupies in two of the three main listings. His is the ultimate associative effort. He surveys what he regards as the boundaries of time in the core canon and declares for one final time what that means for God's next actions. Although we see clearly a portrait of postexilic life, it is conveyed not concretely as a contemporary affair worthy of reportage, but only via genealogy.

It is a question beyond the scope of our treatment here just how influenced Matthew was by this portrayal. In introducing his own genealogical frame of reference, he too insists that the purposes of God lead up to a point of final significance in Jesus Christ. The *toledot* of Genesis and the genealogical reorientation of the Chronicler conspire to produce a three-times-fourteen grid of historical unfolding that culminates in the birth of Jesus Christ, a new descent to and exodus from Egypt, and the appearance John the Baptist, a reprise of prophecy in one final declarative action.

I am not of the view that Chronicles must occupy the final position of the canon in Hebrew dress in order for it to register an important effect, backwards in time and forwards in time. But the fact that it does have the position is significant all the same. The continuous historical narrative into Ezra-Nehemiah appears such an obvious and logical movement, it is striking to find Chronicles closing off the Ketuvim in two major schemes for ordering the books. In the Tiberian tradition Chronicles is the first book, which corresponds to its interest, one supposes, in the genealogies of Genesis. Perhaps even in this important signal position it was thought capable of registering its canonical point, namely, that history starting in Genesis was now at last oriented toward God's final and wider purposes. This happened without neglecting to credit the history of Israel with its own inner and sustained purpose, worthy of retelling, but linking that history all the same to a wider scope and final divine intention.

The Ketuvim serve the purpose of establishing the centrality of the core canon of the Law and the Prophets. They introduce a rich miscellany of writings whose sense-making is enhanced and enriched by association with works outside, and at times inside, the sequence that it presents. It further gives evidence of a canon-consciousness not within a book of Law-Prophets, but from outside. In so doing, it also is capable of finding a settled and ordered existence alongside and closing off this canonical presentation by means of its own unique character and shape. The New Testament's reference to "law and prophets" as a way to point to the Old Testament scriptures is consistent with this perspective, even as now it most likely reflexively has in view the entire Hebrew canon as we know it. When Luke 24 speaks of "Moses and all the prophets" and then "Moses and the prophets and the psalms," he is simply providing two familiar shorthand expressions that point not to a two-part here and a three-part canon there but one and the same scriptural inheritance.

PART THREE

THEOLOGICAL READINGS IN THE ELDER TESTAMENT

The Emmaus Road story in Luke—Mark also has a notice about the Risen Lord appearing "in another form to two of them, walking into the country" (Mark 16:12)—is one familiar to us, due to its length and its special content (Luke 24:13-34). At its present place it links the fact of an empty tomb and interpretations of that by men in dazzling clothes to the named women and others with them (24:1-11) with an actual appearance to Peter amidst the now more credulous Eleven (24:33-34). Out seven miles to Emmaus and back very late that same day to Jerusalem, two men, one named Cleopas and the other unnamed, have a day quite like no other.

As it stands, the two come in the role of pilgrims to Passover returning home upon its completion. This is made clear in their talk to each other and in their rather impatient response to someone who, approaching from the rear, has come alongside them and asked what they were talking about. The urgent topic concerns the very one asking the question as if he did not know, and so they oblige him (24:19-24). Non-recognition is not an unusual feature of the Risen Lord, whom Mary in John's Gospel believes is the gardener (John 20:15). The Risen Lord is other than he was, even as he will be recognized as he was though now alive after death. In John's Gospel the voice and direct address shatter the grief and death Mary had assumed were permanent (20:16).

Luke's version of recognition on the road to Emmaus has its own character, though the role of scripture is present as well in John's Gospel, as conveyed by the beloved disciple at the tomb (John 20:8). He believes in the Risen Lord not by seeing him, but by seeing his absence as meaning just that. His comment "for as yet they did not know the scripture, that he must rise from the dead" applies to others than himself, an application we may rightly anticipate given his extended testimony at the cross concerning the scriptures' disclosing role (19:32-37). The Holy Spirit opens his eyes to the scriptural testimony, pierced by the water of life springing from a pierced side (Zech 12:10).

How are we to understand the first scripture lesson Luke describes on the road to Emmaus thus, "Beginning with (*apo*) Moses and all the prophets (*apo panton*) he interpreted to them in all the scriptures (*en pasais tais graphais*) the things concerning himself" (Luke 24:27)? As an answer to the question the unknown fellow traveler asks, "Was it not necessary that the Christ should suffer these things and enter into his glory?" in response to their sad summary, we cannot be sure it entails their recognizing him as the Lord Teacher as previously during the exposition "in all the scriptures." Has he indeed "entered into his glory" and as such is now to be known precisely on those terms? "He interpreted to them the things concerning himself" can mean, therefore, the narrator is telling us here, and not them, what only they will later know (v. 32). Fitzmyer comments, "One wonders how the disciples could fail to recognize him 'on the road' if his explanation of Moses and the prophets were actually firing in their hearts," that is, as they later report it

(v. 32).[1] He speaks of Luke subtly, building suspense, for the recognition in the breaking of the bread is the climax. Even then, upon recognizing him, he vanishes. Then it is that they report burning hearts at having been taught by him, and having the scriptures opened onto him, by him. So what is said in 24:27 likely means that the first lesson was one in which the scriptures were opened to them with their proper referent everywhere to the fore, and that was the main point to be grasped.

The emphasis of the phrasing in 24:27 is on totality and comprehensiveness. Twice "all" is repeated. Fitzmyer rightly glosses, "From one end of the Hebrew Scriptures to the other they bear testimony about him and his fate." That this might be hard to imagine in a peregrinating seminar over several hours points to the phrase meaning what it says more globally: it will be the church's apprehension that all the scriptures speak of Christ, because he has said this during his earthly ministry and again as Risen Lord. Fitzmyer rightly therefore rejects a literalism that looks for specific Old Testament passages held to be more relevant to this or that aspect of his vocation in the Emmaus exposition as constitutive of the vocation of scripture as such "from one end to the other." Moreover, the repetition at 24:44 underscores the point: "These are my words which I spoke to you, while I was still with you, that everything written about me in the law and the prophets and the psalms must be fulfilled. Then he opened their minds. . . ." The closest analogy to what is being said in the first words of the phrase is found in John's Gospel, rooted in the notion for John that the scriptures speak clearly but the disciples will not grasp their sense until later (see John 12:16 et passim). And this is the scriptures as a whole and not just a species of proof-text. By emphasizing "all" we are not to think of a specific form of bearing witness to him as selected out on the Road to Emmaus, but of a global application, to take the form the Holy Spirit chooses

---

[1] Joseph A. Fitzmyer, *The Gospel According to Luke X–XXIV*, AB (New Haven: Yale University Press, 2005), 1558.

to disclose. The opening of the scriptures is equally an opening of the mind, as the church learned to think of this, in the light of Luke and John most particularly.

To return to the staging of Luke, the men are about to reach their destination—or what they thought was such when they set out that day. The day is now far spent (Luke 24:29). The traveler-teacher is going on, and they therefore ask that he stay with them due to the late hour, and doubtless in the light of the foregoing. It is in the breaking of bread that from his glory is disclosed who he is. Immediately he is gone, and immediately the scriptures are acknowledged as declaring him as such, and now presumably as they know him to have been their teacher earlier that day: "Did not our hearts burn within us as he talked to us on the road opening to us the scriptures?"

In spite of the late hour they make a return trip to Jerusalem and find the eleven gathered together, along with others. Now they receive the news that the Lord has appeared as well to Peter. And then he appears to them all gathered. But the reaction is not on a higher level of perception, but indeed is one of fear, and being startled, and of questioning in their minds. The Risen Body is continuous but also fearsome and disturbing to them. Knowing it is indeed him, though in a death-defied form, gradually turns fear into joy and wonder. And immediately Jesus turns to scripture and opens their minds in a way that will become paradigmatic in the first apostolic generation. Acts will pick up this thread and allow it full scope for ongoing significance. Representatively, "Paul went in, as was his custom, and for three weeks he argued with them from the scriptures" (17:2). A day on a road will become three weeks and will become a lifetime of exposition for the early church commentators.

The Risen Lord was known to the disciples in Word and Sacrament. The Risen and now Ascended Lord is known to the church in the same way. To be known in "all the scriptures" means as well, as the following examples show, that the Lord was known in figures and under signs for Israel, and these are testimonies to him confirming that what will transpire is in accordance with God's eternal purposes. In that sense, our present "recognition" of the Risen Lord is different and kindred at the same time: via scripture and sacrament and apostolic testimony for the church; via scripture and broken bread and Risen testimony for the elect of God (Acts 10:41), with the prophets all bearing witness; within Israel under signs and sacramental presence of a different kind.

In what follows we make no aim to be comprehensive and by our own understanding accept the manner in which the scriptures make manifold testimony through their literal sense is to be grasped on a road to Emmaus that is our lifelong walk with God in Christ. It would not be my view that Paul would have claimed to have been an exhaustive interpreter of the scriptures, but only a truthful and representative one. His own long road to Emmaus was what it was due to his prior deep immersion in "the way the words go," and so he was an apostle untimely born and timely born both.

Our concern above in tracing the canonical shape of the Elder Scripture is to show that achievements of association rise up in the gradual and surefooted manner in which over generations the scriptures receive their final, stable character. That shaping and pressuring forward in time stops, but only to be opened to a yet further extended-sense elaboration in the light of Christ's advent and in the name of making the significance of that clear. The "in all the scriptures" manifestation of Christ is its own kind of incarnational reality, though distinct in kind from the fullness of time manifestation, itself a sacramental reality "seen" with the eyes of faith.[2]

---

[2] "In the literal meaning of Scripture, the Logos is not, properly speaking, incarnated as he is in the humanity of Jesus, and this is what allows us still to speak of a comparison: he is, nevertheless, already truly incorporated there; he himself dwells there, not just some idea of him, and this is what authorizes us to speak already of his coming, of his hidden presence" (Henri de Lubac, *History and Spirit: The Understanding of Scripture According to Origen* [San Francisco: Ignatius, 2007], 389).

12

The Triune Name

This chapter consists of an exploration into the rich semantics of Hebrew and its extension into Greek and vernacular contexts whereby YHWH and *kurios* are capable of Trinitarian conflation and distinction both. It uses a common liturgical example of how the LORD (YHWH) of the Psalter and the Lord of direct worshipful address can be both the same and yet distinguishable as well. The Holy Spirit's role is to effect this worshipful potential.

This in turn leads into a discussion of how certain modern commentators who wish to think theologically refer to the God of Israel: as the Father of Jesus Christ, as YHWH in se, or as YHWH the triune God.[1] We hold the view that the semantics of Hebrew

---

[1] The concern to cordon off YHWH entirely from any extensional life in respect of traditional Christian theology is not one I address in this book. I have in view the position of Walter Brueggemann and others, which I discuss in *Figured*

offer an important analogy in how the Elder Scripture speaks of Elohim and YHWH, anticipating the God and *kurios* language of the New Testament in speaking of the One Lord Jesus Christ and the God with whom he shares that Lordship.

We conclude with an extended examination of how Martin Luther's later Psalm lectures sought to ground an explicitly Trinitarian declaration in the Hebrew semantics of two royal psalms, in so doing arguing against the doctrine emerging in consequence of the Holy Spirit's special talking through later councils of the church or restricted to the New Testament's nondoctrinal voice.

I was raised in, and continue to inhabit professionally, a Christian worship context in which the offices of morning and evening prayer are central. Typical of them is the recitation of Canticles, derived from the Psalter of the Elder Testament, including the so-called "Venite" and "Jubilate" corresponding to Psalm 95 and Psalm 100. Daily selected readings from the Psalter as such join those from Old and New Testaments. Consequently, if one attends these services regularly one hears again and again the phrases taken from the Psalms serving as fixed Canticles, "let us sing unto the LORD," "the LORD is a great God," "let us kneel before the LORD our Maker," "he is the LORD our God," "worship the LORD in the beauty of holiness," "O be joyful in the LORD," "serve the LORD with gladness," "be sure that the LORD is God," and "for the LORD is gracious, his mercy is everlasting." The

---

Out: *Typology and Providence in Christian Scripture* (Louisville, Ky.: Westminster John Knox, 2001) and elsewhere. For a more recent discussion see now Brent A. Strawn, "And These Three Are One: A Trinitarian Critique of Christological Approaches to the Old Testament," *PRSt* 31 (2004): 191–210. He pushes back against the position of Walter Brueggemann that the "transformative presence of Jesus" energized an "imaginative construal of the Old Testament toward Jesus." See Brueggemann's *Theology of the Old Testament: Testimony, Dispute, Advocacy* (Minneapolis: Augsburg Fortress, 1997), 731–32. Also related, see Christopher Seitz, "Christological Interpretation of Texts and Trinitarian Claims to Truth," *SJT* 52 (1999): 209–26; and C. Clifton Black, "Trinity and Exegesis," *ProEccl* 19 (2010): 151–80.

selection reproduced here is from the Venite and Jubilate only, and it could be augmented with examples from the so-called Benecite omnia opera, Benedictus es, Magnificat, Benedictus, and Nunc Dimitis. The last three of these are hymns of praise found in the New Testament, from the opening chapters of the Gospel of Luke. Yet direct address to the LORD there is continuous with the practice we have in the Psalms, and intentionally so given the purpose of Luke to show pious Israel inspired by the Holy Spirit. In that sense they are New Testament examples of Elder Testament Psalms demonstrating theologically significant continuity as the coming of God in the flesh is anticipated. The LORD being praised is the LORD of the Psalter and of the Elder Testament.[2]

I have followed the convention for rendering the divine name YHWH into English with capitals, the LORD, in the examples just given. That is how the Canticles would read because they are drawn directly from the Psalms and kindred texts, or purposefully carry on that hymnic praise in the bosom of Israel as Luke displays it. The Book of Common Prayer does not however use the convention in the services of morning and evening prayer, but prints rather than the LORD in caps "the Lord" consistently instead. This is true even though the Psalter that the BCP reprints in full in its editions follows the traditional convention of rendering YHWH with all capitals, the LORD. So Psalm 100, the Canticle called the Jubilate in morning prayer, opens in the Psalter section of the BCP, "Be joyful in the LORD, all you lands." In the examples of New Testament Canticles from Luke, the Greek has not tried to reproduce some kind of convention for indicating the divine name but follows the practice that has already arisen in Jewish circles of referring to YHWH by *Adonai*, in Greek *kurios*. "My soul magnifies the Lord, *ton kurios*" (Luke 1:46). When Zechariah is filled with the Holy Spirit and prophesies (Luke 1:68), what the

---

[2] Christopher Seitz, "'Be Ye Sure That the Lord He Is God'—Crisis in Interpretation and the Two Testament Voice of Scripture," in my *The Character of Christian Scripture: The Significance of a Two-Testament Bible* (Grand Rapids: Baker Academic, 2011), 173–90.

BCP has given us to praise with him it calls the Benedictus, which opens, "Blessed be the Lord God of Israel, for he has visited and redeemed his people." The unmistakable Lord God of Zechariah's address is YHWH, and we would not be wrong to recall the many psalms which open in this same way, "Bless the LORD" (Pss 103, 104, 134, 144 et passim).

One can see amongst theologically interested exegetes of the Christian Old Testament some variability about the divine name YHWH and the God to which that names refers. In the section of his *Biblical Theology of the Old and New Testaments* where Childs is concerned with the *res* of the Old Testament he quite appropriately speaks of "the full divine reality in its triunity," as we noted in chapter 3 above. Yet here and elsewhere he also reflexively speaks of the God of Israel as "the Father of Jesus Christ." Further in the same section, he warns about reading "the second person of the trinity" back into the Old Testament, which appears to be a correlate of the first statement. This is why he writes "the second person of the Trinity" presumably rather than "earthly Jesus" or the "incarnate Christ." Kendall Soulen heads in the opposite direction and wants to insist on "YHWH the Triune God"—even to the extent of warning Christians about what he judges are the very bad consequences of referring to the name in traditional Trinitarian fashion as "God the Father, God the Son, and God the Holy Spirit." Christians should avoid this and refer instead to YHWH as the triune God of our worship—though how exactly one does that practically speaking, given that the name is unpronounceable and properly so, is unclear.[3] The practice of referring to the divine name YHWH through the convention "the Lord" is one that rises up from within the logic of the scriptures of Israel and the people who preserved it. It is not a Christian imposition.

Where strictly speaking Childs does not reference the tetragrammaton YHWH in making his remarks about the "God of

---

[3] See Seitz, *Figured Out*, 187–90; and R. Kendall Soulen, *The God of Israel and Christian Theology* (Minneapolis: Fortress, 1996).

Israel," John Behr can write in his section on "The Scriptural Christ" that the sacred name YHWH refers to the Father of Jesus Christ. It is worth quoting him in full to be clear what he is insisting on. Though not citing Yeago or Bauckham or others who have made the point, he wants to be clear that the "name above every name" to which Paul refers in Philippians 2:11 is the divine name.[4] This has been noted by myself and others due to the "pressure" being exerted by Isaiah 45:20-25 on the confession of Philippians 2:5-11. The prophet Isaiah solemnly declares the LORD as God alone. "There is no God besides me" (Isa 45:21) is consistent with the prophet's strong rhetoric in defense of Israel and in defiance of rival claims in these central chapters. YHWH can only swear by himself, which he happily does, "to me every knee shall bow, every tongue swear." "Only in YHWH, it shall be said of me, are righteousness and strength." Philippians says that by virtue of the work of the Son in condescension and in death on a cross, the one God has highly exalted him and given him the name above every name so that now, as a result, the name of Jesus will be the name before which the knees of all bow, by God's solemn oath by himself, solemnized and fulfilled in Jesus Christ, "to the glory of God the Father" (Phil 2:11). YHWH is that eternal bestowal in God, Father and the Son, by the Spirit, that in the economy of condescension, death, rising, and ascension is declared for all to see.

Behr states his own view in this way:

> The name above every name, the Divine Name, is bestowed upon the crucified, risen and exalted one, emphasizing again the Passion. However, it is necessary also to remember that even if Paul consistently applies the title "Lord" to Jesus Christ, transferring ideas and quotations which belong to YHWH alone, this is not a direct identification of YHWH and Jesus Christ: Jesus

---

[4] Richard Bauckham, *God Crucified: Monotheism and Christology in the New Testament* (Grand Rapids: Eerdmans, 1998); David Yeago, "The New Testament and the Nicene Dogma: A Contribution to the Recovery of Theological Exegesis," *ProEccl* 3 (1994): 152–64.

is all that YHWH himself is, that is, fully divine, yet without being YHWH himself, for YHWH is his Father.

One might supposedly agree with Behr if it were in fact the case that YHWH refers quite specifically to the first person of the Trinity and that alone. This is obviously the view he represents. "God the Father," however, presumes a Trinitarian context known in the economy of God's actions, and Philippians makes this clear when, after the giving of the name YHWH, the reference is *then* to the name of "Jesus as Lord" and the glory to "God the Father." The giver of the name in the hymn of Philippians is simply the underdetermined "God" and not the overdetermined YHWH or "God the Father." So when he goes on to explain his position, it is not clear he has succeeded on the same plane. He cites 1 Corinthians 8:6, "We have one God the Father . . . and one Lord Jesus Christ." Quite so. One Elohim (God Almighty) and One Lord Jesus Christ. The name YHWH as such is not under discussion here. So when he concludes it looks rather like an opposite point than where he started, for example, YHWH is Father. He writes thus:

> The double barreled name of God in the Scriptures ("the Lord God") is separated. The Lord, as a proper name, is reserved for the Son, while God (ὁ θεός), as a proper name, usually stands for the Father; while as common nouns, rather than names, both are applied to the Father and the Son.[5]

Now Behr would appear to want to stop referring to YHWH as such, and instead speaks of "the proper name" of "the Lord." And now that proper name in Greek (*kurios*) refers to not the Father as above ("YHWH is his Father") but to the Son. Then he introduces the correlate idea of "God" as here "a proper name" that "usually stands for the Father." And then to free up the space

---

[5] John Behr, *The Way to Nicaea*, vol. 1 in *The Formation of Christian Theology* (Crestwood, N.Y.: St Vladimir's Seminary Press, 2001), 64.

to have "God" available to refer to Christ and the Father both, he speaks of "common nouns rather than names."

The far simpler and less internally confused approach—first YHWH is the Father, and then "the Lord" is the Son, and finally both are God the common noun but not name—is to stay with Philippians on the one hand and the practice of the Elder Scripture on the other. God (Elohim) is not a proper name but the general term of reference for God, known by Israel by his personal name alongside it (the LORD God), to clarify how Elohim is God within the covenant people and not as the term otherwise functions more generally. YHWH is the Only Elohim, as Isaiah and the Old Testament insists, whatever may be held by others using the word to refer to "God," "gods," or "the god X." God is YHWH. God gives the name above every name to the Son, that his name might be praised to the glory of God the Father. Now we have the distinction of YHWH as God Almighty the Father and the God the Son "the Lord Jesus." The Greek word *kurios* can continue to refer to God Almighty or the Son and in the New Testament does just that. It further can refer to the LORD of the Elder Testament and does, as in Luke's hymns prior to the condescension of birth described in Philippians.

Thus far we have sought to avoid overdetermination of the kind that may inhabit (the otherwise different accounts of) Soulen or Childs or Behr in favor of a more underdetermined account. This is enabled by allowing the term Elohim to retain its reference to God Almighty, and YHWH as being that God in personal disclosure to Israel and in the son, *kurios* Lord Jesus, to the world. The point is further that the particular structure of personal disclosure and divine transcendence commended by the Old Testament's use of Elohim and YHWH forms a significant analogy to how transcendence and personal disclosure—even death on a cross—are expressed in Christian theological talk and worship.

To return to the services of morning and evening prayer, there is in these services an oscillation that cannot be cordoned off between how the word "Lord" may be thought to function in

Christian worship expressed in prayer and praise. Is the Lord of the Psalms the LORD of the Psalms, Israel's praised God? Yes. The Psalms' use shows unbroken continuity between Israel of the Elder Testament and the church. Without footnotes or clarifications, the assembled church sings forth the praises of Israel from the Psalms, as they exist and have existed and continue to exist within the praises of the people of God the Jews.

When the people of God are addressed with the words at the opening of the service, "O Lord, open thou our lips," are we to think of "the Lord" as the same LORD of the Psalms; or the Lord Jesus; or the Lord God, the Father Almighty; or the Lord God the Holy Ghost? Surely the answer must be an underdetermined, but all the more enthusiastic for being so, "Yes." All are correct. The same effect is being registered when at the close of each and every Psalm reading we are to respond, "Glory to the Father, and to the Son, and to the Holy Spirit" in reference to the LORD God being there praised, lamented, remembered, longed for, thanked, and put on various kinds of notice by Israel, and the church in its wake and in its light, as well. The fact that the same word "Lord" is used consistently and without predication for LORD, Lord Jesus, the Lord of the Spirit is not a matter to be sorted out but a cause for praise as such.

With this opening discussion in place, I want now to turn to the example of Luther's later psalm exegesis. This will allow us to widen the lens on the matter of divine name and Trinity from the context of the Elder Scripture's literal sense pressure.

"Who spake by the Prophets": Holy Spirit and Doctrine in the Elder Testament

It was the lifetime preoccupation of Martin Luther to find in the literal sense of Scripture the solid ground floor of true doctrine and confident faith. In his serial lectures on the Psalms, undertaken over decades, we can see him wrestling with just how the literal sense is what he wished to call the christological sense. The literal and historical were so designed as to speak forth the dogmatic reality of the Son. Allegory in certain of its forms stood in the way of this due to its complexity. Luther wanted something plain and secure because he also believed this was the providential role the scriptures had been given by God. That said, he would return to the Psalms on several occasions and adjust what had gone before in his own presentations. So he was on a quest.

It is not our goal here to lay out the changes and chances of Luther's search for the literal sense over a lifetime. I have written elsewhere about one prominent change in how he viewed the relationship between Christ and the mortal David, but that concern is not the subject of the present reflection.[6]

In the public disputations that marked the era and were signature features of Luther's personal role as a Reforming theologian, toward the latter part of his life he found himself trying to articulate the relationship between the doctrine of the Trinity and its secure scriptural foundation. As Christine Helmer has pointed out, the disputational coal-face of this struggle for an accurate account had two distinct representations.[7] One view held that the articulation of the truthful Trinity confession was the consequence of the Holy Spirit's special work in the councils of the Catholic Church, well after the canon's stabilization. The other view held that precisely because this idea was manifestly "unscriptural" it was not to be followed in any case. That is, the "Trinity" was an ecclesiastical invention that obscured the simple faith in Jesus that the New Testament more properly foregrounded. Alongside this came the view that to speak of the work of the Holy Spirit centuries after the New Testament was to arrogate to the Catholic Church a Holy Spirit locus that the New Testament itself insisted was for the

---

[6] In Christopher R. Seitz and Kent Harold Richards, eds., *The Bible as Christian Scripture: The Work of Brevard S. Childs* (Atlanta: SBL, 2013).

[7] Christine Helmer, "Luther's Trinitarian Hermeneutic and the Old Testament," *Modern Theology* 18 (2002): 49–70. In what follows I am very much indebted to her formulation and acknowledge with gratitude her stimulating historical and theological appraisal.

individual believer in Jesus Christ. Just to claim the Holy Spirit as articulating the church's doctrine of the Trinity was wrong on two fronts at once: doctrinal overreach and unscripturalism (this meaning the presentation of the simple Jesus of the New Testament).

Luther more specifically noted the error of the anti-trinitarian position as insisting that no such doctrine could be inferred before John the Baptist.[8] When the "orthodox" response took the form of insisting the doctrine was explicated by the church, Luther took issue with the "orthodox" failure to defend the scripture's own articulation of this article of faith. Again for him this stemmed from both the conviction that scripture had an authority that the church followed, and not one given to it by the church *ad extra*, and further that God had given scripture so as to assure certainty in the faithful by means of its literal sense deliverances. Consistent with arguments in the present book about the critical role played by an Elder Scripture preceding the New Testament and the church both, Luther asserted that the creed itself insisted the Holy Spirit had "spoken by the prophets." Only the Holy Spirit declares truthful doctrine. As Helmer notes, in a late treatise from 1543 Luther crossreferences the declaration of 2 Samuel 23:2 with the doctrinally strong insistence of 2 Peter 1:21 that "no prophecy ever came by the impulse of man, but men moved by the Holy Spirit spoke from God." The Samuel text declared, "The Spirit of the LORD spoke to me," that is, to David (2 Sam 23:2). To these texts was then added the Article of the Creed noted just above. The Holy Spirit declares doctrine, which the church testifies to but does not create, and this fact is testified to in the scriptures of Israel before the New Testament and the church both. On this New Testament (2 Pet 1:21 et passim) and Elder Testament agree. Because the New Testament asserts that the Holy Spirit searches out everything, including "the depths of God" (1 Cor 2:10), and because it is self-evident for Luther that God is the God of Israel as disclosed in the scriptures of Israel, we are right to suppose his

---

[8] Helmer, "Luther's Trinitarian Hermeneutic," 54.

doctrinal articulation of the Trinity cannot be restricted to the New Testament alone.[9]

The reference to the Spirit of the LORD speaking to David sets the direction Luther heads as the Psalms of his repeated formal explication during the years preceding. Luther further holds the view, with Jerome, that the dignity of the Hebrew text must be respected and not placed lower than what is a translation into a subsequent language (Greek or Latin), the first occasioned by the people of Israel themselves who did not mean thereby to supplant the *Mater*.[10] The matter was close to Luther's own concerns as a translator of a vernacular German language Bible to which he was constantly returning and making revisions. In translating the text of Psalm 110 (109), the first line "the LORD says to my lord" (RSV) was rendered into Greek using the same word for both referents (*kurios*), and the practice was followed in the Latin known to Luther (*dominus*). Spoken aloud or read, the identity of the terms would be clear. In 1535 Luther explains his own divergence from these precedents by virtue of his concern to capture the Hebrew in German and also animated by the doctrinal issues at stake in the psalms, where the spirit of the LORD spoke to David. He renders into German Psalm 110:1 in this way:

> Der HERR sprach zu meinem HErr: Setze dich zu meiner rechten.

The all-capitals HERR is the equivalent of the English language convention of rendering the tetragrammaton YHWH as "the LORD," consistent with the Hebrew *qere perpetuum* Lord (*'adonai*). Yet Psalm 110:1 uses just this word in the direct object "my lord"

---

[9] The Holy Spirit is "the trinitarian person who facilitates access to the inner-trinitarian mystery. . . . The literal speech of the prophets, apostles and church is valorized because the Spirit is responsible for creating these tangible means to access the mystery" (Helmer, "Luther's Trinitarian Hermeneutic," 55).

[10] "Hebrew is the language the Spirit uses to refer to a theological subject matter" (Helmer, "Luther's Trinitarian Hermeneutic," 55; subject matter here being Luther's *res*).

(*'adonai*) in the same line. Now of course we are entering the terrain of exegesis as well as translation. To whom is the LORD YHWH speaking? And who is represented by the possessive pronoun "my"? Rashi, to choose one example, thinks of Abraham. But this is also the only psalm in the entire Psalter for which he gives two different interpretations, signaling that even for him the matter is not very clear.[11] The rest, as they say, is history. Luther is of course guided by the same obscurity finding its resolution in the New Testament. What puzzles the scribes of Christ's own day admits of at least this much, according to the answer Matthew 22:45 gives: if David speaks of him as his own Lord, he cannot also be his son. Luther follows the Christian tradition of assuming the referent is to Christ, the space left open by the non-answer of the Gospels, and provided clearly elsewhere (Acts 2:34-35; Heb 1:13; 10:12-13). So he renders the second, direct-object referent with the curious printing practice we see above, as HErr.

Yet it is important, given the doctrinal parameters he has set for himself, that the proper rendering into German of *adonia* be pressured by the Hebrew text and the Holy Spirit's doctrinal address to David and not a second-testament backdraft or an ecclesiastical decision from the fourth century. HERR and HErr represent a colloquy, "an inner-trinitarian conversation," in the manner of Luther's rendering. Critical to grasp here is the force of the possessive pronoun. Helmer correctly sees the influence—quite basic though it is—of the catechetical form on Luther's thinking.[12] The confession of the Large Catechism is "I believe that Jesus Christ, truly Son of God, is my Lord (HErr)." The Holy Spirit alone gives rise to the confession of the Christian: no one calls Jesus "Lord" except by the Spirit. If David calls the Lord addressed by the LORD "my Lord," it is the Holy Spirit directing what is declared. And the testimony to us made public in Psalm 110 is that the David of faithful Israel has access to the speech of Father to Son by gift of

---

[11] Mayer I. Gruber, *Rashi's Commentary on the Psalms* (Leiden: Brill, 2003).
[12] Helmer, "Luther's Trinitarian Hermeneutic," 57.

the Holy Spirit, "an inner Trinitarian conversation," to which he bears witness.

That Luther believes he is establishing a firm Trinitarian base in the Hebrew semantics of the Elder Scripture that enables certainty in the believer can be shown by the caution he exhibits in respect of the classic interpretation of Genesis 18. The text lacks these distinctive grammatical markers of inner Trinitarian colloquy, and so Luther only grudgingly allows scope for a sort of homiletical sense.[13] This is permissible only because elsewhere we are on firmer ground. Genesis 1 can be brought within the proper orbit of Hebrew trinitarianism because the speech aspect is present in the verb *'amar*, so the tradition and John 1:1 are allowed to function alongside the royal psalms as perspicuous indications of the divine subject and the speech that is his eternal word.

The second royal psalm to which Luther turns is Psalm 2. The psalm had traditionally been taken as conveying a christological significance, not least because of the interpretation given to it in the New Testament. Difference of opinion, however, existed over the temporality intimated by the generation of "today." The Antiochenes, Augustine, and, later, Calvin disagreed amongst themselves. The Augustinian position ("today" is eternal generation) is the one Luther broadly adopts. Calvin argues for the "today" of resurrection, based upon Acts, and he pushed back from the temporal categories of Augustine's reading because it was insufficiently scriptural, as he saw it. The details of this debate need not detain us here. I have discussed the issue elsewhere.[14]

Luther's contribution is to see the significance of the Psalm's dialogical features as tracking with Psalm 110. YHWH is the speaker of verse 6. The LXX passive "I have been set" is rejected

---

[13] "Luther passionately argues at great length for the text's exhortation of Christian hospitality, not for a trinitarian interpretation" (Helmer, "Luther's Trinitarian Hermeneutic," 59).

[14] See Christopher Seitz, "Psalm 2 in the Entry Hall of the Psalter: Extended Sense in the History of Interpretation," in Ephraim Radner, ed., *Church, Society, and the Christian Common Good* (Eugene, Ore.: Cascade, 2017).

on the basis of the Hebrew (so too Calvin and Bellarmine both). The difficult *nasaku bar* of verse 11 Luther reads along the lines of the love between Father and Son, following Jerome but extrapolating so as to capture the constant love of Son and Father. The Father speaks of His Son. The Son responds in the first person. As Helmer puts it, "The fact that the Father speaks has, for Luther, the Trinitarian significance of identifying the Father as the active source of the Son" (62) and "the mutual introduction signifies the transparency of the divine essence held in common between Father and Son" (63). It is on this basis that the traditional idea of eternal generation represented by "today" gains traction—that is, as subsisting in the specific Hebrew design of colloquy—and not by recourse to a theory of eternal generation already in place and guiding the reading. "For Luther, the text's immediacy of direct speech signals the deep mystery of inner-trinitarian reciprocity. The Son is perpetually attuned to the Father; he cannot for a moment look away and refer to the origin of his being in the third person. Conversely the Father's gaze is fixed solely on the Son, his delight and love" (63). The Holy Spirit is the author of the Psalm and publisher-abroad of this eternal reality. The "inner address" from Father to Son and the "outer address" from Son to Father "are brought to literary life by the Holy Spirit" (64). One rightly suspects this is a further reason why Luther distrusts searches for threesomes such as marked the interpretation of the three men in Genesis 18. The Holy Spirit's role is to be transparent to the divine life and love between Father and Son. He blows where he wills and plumbs the depths of God himself, and not his own role or status.[15]

Because Luther is grounding his Trinitarian reading concretely in the semantics of the Hebrew language, he focuses on those texts where this aspect is in the forefront. To be recalled is his concern to defeat the claims of two opposing positions: one that sees the

---

[15] I discuss the matter in more detail in my "The Trinity in the Old Testament," in Gilles Emery and Matthew Levering, eds., *The Oxford Handbook of the Trinity* (Oxford: Oxford University Press, 2011), 28–40.

Trinity as a confession given in the church where the Holy Spirit is instructing centuries later, and the other that denies the existence of the confession as scriptural *tout court*. He collates these positions and then goes to the Elder Scripture on the basis of the creedal confession that the Holy Spirit spake by the prophets. The Elder Scripture obviously predates the New Testament and church both. His concern to diminish reliance on allegory and the forms this takes in the history of interpretation is shared by all humanist interpreters of the period, but by Luther specifically because he believes a better way exists to allow the literal sense scope to do its Christian articulations grounded in the historical revelation to Israel.

One might conclude this consists in a considerable narrowing of resources to ground the theological claims of the Christian church. One must find those places where direct speech and colloquies are in evidence, and not surprisingly Luther's focus stays on basically two psalms (2 and 110). Yet on the other side, his focus on David as vehicle for the Holy Spirit's dogmatic disclosures means the colloquies are not heavenly dramas whose significance no one present at the time of their alleged declarations knew anything about, and that properly so.[16] Luther's concern is for genuine Hebrew articulations of Christian doctrine. YHWH is speaking and his Son is being addressed and David is conveying this mystery because the Holy Spirit is working through him. They are not colloquies "above" the people of Israel whose literal sense record gives access to them, and whose significance can only be grasped long after the fact by means of bringing an ad extra set of reading glasses. This is precisely the position Luther is fighting against. The literal sense of the Elder Scripture certainly and securely speaks forth the Trinitarian truth prospectively, and not as perceived retrospectively by moving the material into a different plane of epistemological significance (prosopological reading). "Luther's particular contribution consists

---

[16] Matthew Bates' work on what he calls "prosopological exegesis" moves in this direction. See my review of Bates' *The Birth of the Trinity* (2015) in *CBQ* 2016.

in his recovery of the Old Testament for Trinitarian theology, specifically Hebrew terms, grammar, and the royal psalms."[17]

Motivating Luther is the concern for certainty and secure interpretation of Holy Scripture, as over against reliance on species of allegory or the church's inspired claims not arising directly from scripture but from claims of spiritual insight subsequently. His work in this regard came late in his life and could be viewed as insufficiently extended and developed given that fact. Certainly various claims about the figural pressure of the literal sense in articulating Christian theology, some of which we explore below, continue their persuasive hold. This is due to the fact that the "monotheism" of the Elder Scripture is inherently dynamic and relational. Having One God and not many means a far more ambitious canonical presentation preserving the sovereignty and transcendence of the One God but also giving scope for relational agency. Unsurprising in Mark's use of Psalm 110 in chapter 12 is the extremely robust defense of the first commandment: "Hear O Israel, The Lord our God, the Lord is One." At issue for Christian theology is how Psalm 110 and Deuteronomy 6:4 in fact rhyme.

Luther uses the convention of the One God's personal naming YHWH as the means by which to explore the inner life of God, especially in Psalm 110 with his use of HERR and HErr to capture the inner-trinitarian colloquy vouchsafed by the Holy Spirit. Helmer rightly speaks of the "trinitarian underdetermination" of YHWH as speaker. By this is meant that only in situations where a distinction in persons of the Trinity is evidenced would Luther find it proper to declare YWHW as "Father," as in Psalm 110:1. This amounts to an "overdetermination" due to the context. Otherwise YHWH "deutest auff unsern HERR, Jhesum Christum, Gottes Son."[18] Helmer concludes that in Psalm 110:2, where no colloquy is envisioned, Luther does not think of YHWH as the first person of the Trinity but instead, as evidenced elsewhere, as "God, the

---

[17] Helmer, "Luther's Trinitarian Hermeneutic," 60.
[18] *Weimar Aufgabe* 54, 85, 29–31, 20–23.

God of Israel, or with the pronoun 'Er.'"[19] Consistently to refer to YHWH as the "Father" only would "overdetermine" the matter. This is especially true, as Luther hints, given the flexibility by which the *qere perpetuum* "Lord" helpfully extends to direct address to Lord Christ in the New Testament.

As noted at the start of this section, in the Christian worship context such as the daily Offices, the flexibility of the word "Lord" is such that it may extend to praise of the God of Israel in the Psalms, to Jesus Christ the Lord, and to the Holy Spirit. And the reverse movement is also true. Who is "the LORD is my shepherd" of Psalm 23 if not YHWH the triune God, the Lord Jesus, and the Holy Spirit who has given rise to the Psalm in the first place. "O Lord, open thou our lips" is address to God: the Father, the Son and the Holy Spirit.

---

[19] Helmer, "Luther's Trinitarian Hermeneutic," 57.

13

Proverbs 8:22-31 and the Mind of Scripture

Our concern in this third part of the book is to provide a range of examples of how the Elder Scripture may be said to pressure forth and open onto a dimension of ontology that finds more explicit articulation in the early church's confession of One LORD God: the Father, the Son, and the Holy Spirit. We have explored the semantics of Hebrew and the way YHWH-*kurios* functions to adumbrate a later creedal "God of God, Light of Light, Very God of Very God" pressured forth by the Elder Testament's own literal sense witness. Luther's handling of the royal psalms helped illustrate the divine name's capacity in this regard.

In this chapter the focus is on the text most often turned to in the debates over the *homoousia* in Christian circles, where it already had a rich history of usage in this light. Surprisingly the text is not from the New Testament but from the Elder Scripture, found in Proverbs 8:22-31. We will rehearse the debate as it finds focus in

Athanasius. The idea that one started with a dogmatic conviction and sought to proof-text its articulation is belied by the sheer volume and intensity of the discussion at the level of basic exegesis. The debate is as much a scriptural debate as a theological one. There is simply no doctrinal truth that exists apart from scriptural pressure and recourse to arguments to that effect that must win assent.

In this particular instance it is the substance of what Proverbs 8:22-31 urges on the exegete by its own literal sense as well as other Old Testament texts that share its particular horizon of concern to speak of a divine agency and identity begotten of the One God of Israel. The phrase "the mind of scripture" has reference to a patristic index having to do with the larger point of the scriptures when various kindred texts are coordinated and heard in their fuller, collaborative voice.[1]

One of the most important rediscoveries of recent times is how there was absolutely no dogmatic discussion in the early church that was not root-and-branch exegetical, a tracking of the way the words go.[2] The church fathers—whatever their philosophical presuppositions—thought the scriptures of prophet and apostle did first-order theological work and that close reading them formed the arena in which—like hammer and anvil—one learned to speak Christianly. We have separate departments of Old Testament and New Testament and Theology and Homiletics in the modern period. They had only one: Christian biblical theology. Many thought that the philosophical schools themselves, once they

---

[1] Just appearing, see the insightful essay of Don Collett, "A Place to Stand: Proverbs 8 and the Construction of Ecclesial Space," *SJT* 70 (2017): 166–83.

[2] See for example the recent contribution of Robert Louis Wilken, *The Spirit of Early Christian Thought: Seeking the Face of God* (New Haven: Yale University Press, 2003). His is but one of many such treatments. The excellent study of Frances Young also comes to mind, *Biblical Exegesis and the Formation of Christian Culture* (Cambridge: Cambridge University Press, 1997). On the properly, ineluctably scriptural character of God-talk, see John Behr, *The Way to Nicaea*, vol. 1 in *The Formation of Christian Theology* (Crestwood, N.Y.: St. Vladimir's Seminary Press, 2001), 19.

became acquainted with Moses and the Prophets, at best cribbed from them, because the Elder Scripture preceded them by ages. Origen famously contrasts the sophistry and sophistication of the philosophical schools with the strange but direct, even confrontational, truth of the Laws, Wisdom, Prophecy, and Hymns that make up scripture's peculiar tongue. Augustine had to wean himself off the soothing and familiar rhythms of the philosophers in order to finally grasp a different medium of truth.

As noted in chapter 3 above, Childs was reluctant to pursue how the *res* to which the letters of scripture referred ought to be brought into the exegetical reading of the Old Testament's *per se* voice. My question is whether we have stayed long enough now with the specifics of the historical sense that it is time to reintroduce a conceptuality capable of thinking creatively about scripture's ontological referent, YHWH and Elohim, God Almighty and the Logos as his living word in creation, patriarch, law, and prophet.

The Surprising Centrality of Proverbs 8 in Doctrinal Debates

Some fifteen years ago I joined colleagues in Theology and Early Church at the University of St. Andrews to teach the exegesis of the church fathers. This led in time to a series of graduate seminars on the history of interpretation.

I still have a very clear memory of that first experience. I decided to look at Athanasius and went to the copy machine to produce a page or two of his exegesis for handouts. I assumed he would be dealing with the New Testament and was surprised to find something I now know well: the predilection of the early church for doctrinal Christian exegesis based upon the Old Testament. In *The Demonstration of the Apostolic Preaching*, Irenaeus is relentless in his preference for the Old Testament in establishing core Christian confession.³ I will return to him at the close. But the thing that surprised me was the impossibility of extracting a page or two, for the text in question was Proverbs 8:22, and the discussion went on for over fifty single-spaced pages.

So the obvious question to begin with is why texts from the Old Testament, and indeed from the eighth chapter of the book of Proverbs become so crucial for Athanasius and Christian dogmatics. Reading his *Contra Arianos* and *de Decretis*, three things seem clear.

First, it was the place where the battle was already being fought, and had been for some time. That is, Athanasius did not enthusiastically go to Proverbs because he thought he could more easily resolve a problem there that was unresolved somewhere else in some other place of scripture. A long list of interpreters preceded him who had argued for the significance of Proverbs 8, often in conjunction with other Old Testament texts (Justin, Irenaeus, Origen, Theophilus, Tertullian, Athenagoras, Origen, Eusebius, Basil, Jerome, Epiphanius, Marcellus). In time it would therefore be a text that the orthodox and their opponents could not avoid. It was at the dead center of the playing field in the discussion.

Second, it was a place, indeed, where the opponents appeared to have the strongest case to answer. That is also why, presumably, the discussion in *contra Arianos* is so long: the length is in proportion to the challenge that this particular text posed. Proverbs speaks of Wisdom in an exalted position vis-à-vis the creation. That was not argued against by Arians but enthusiastically embraced.⁴ Christ is indeed in an exalted place vis-à-vis creation and exists prior

---

³ See now Irenaeus, *On the Apostolic Preaching*, trans. and intro. John Behr (Crestwood, N.Y.: St. Vladimir's Seminary Press, 1997).

⁴ See the comment of Frances Young, "No one in the fourth century challenged the fundamental approach to this text which we can already trace in the work of second-century apologists. The christological referent of personified wisdom was never questioned," and that included Arius (111); Frances Young, "Proverbs 8 in Interpretation," in David F. Ford and Graham Stanton, eds., *Reading Texts, Seeking Wisdom* (Grand Rapids: Eerdmans, 2004), 102–15.

to it. But what Proverbs does not establish, so it was held, was that Christ was of one substance with God, eternally begotten, and other descriptors that establish Christ as both before creation and generated from within God's own self: "From the secret substance of divinity before every creature, even the first, I have begotten you in eternity" (as Augustine wrote in his exegesis of Psalm 110:3).

And finally, it was a place where the Greek verbs focused the question of "was there a time before which Christ was not," due to the potential range of "create" (*ektisen*). If one is creating something, there was a time when it was not. Stated negatively, because Athanasius did not have access to the Hebrew text (where neither *bara* nor *'asah* appeared but instead the more unusual verb *qanah*) he could not appeal to it against his opponents in their arguments over the range of the word in translation they and he shared in debate. One can hold up the use of Psalm 110 by contrast. Verse 3 occupied a significant place in dogmatic exegesis among the various Old Testament texts in the discussion, with its apparent reference, so the Greek and Old Latin, "I birthed you from the womb before the morning star." Cassiodorus will gloss this "From the secret depth of my substance, from the Godhead itself, Entirety from Entirety, Light from Light, Highest from Highest." Jerome, working originally on the basis of the shared LXX, agrees with this reading. "With you is beginning, from the womb before the dawn I begot you." When later he probes behind the Greek versions as part of his larger concern for the Hebrew Verity he will render his Latin translation in such a way that the original, dogmatically charged context disappears. "Your people were eager" instead of "with you is beginning" indicates the start of a very different translation route. Gone is the discussion of whether *archē* means the Father, or the Spirit, as had been true previously, and as he had argued against the Arian interpretation of Eunomius.

Picking up on this last point, one way of framing our inquiry would be to say that Proverbs became a test case for all the reasons mentioned, but that it really ought not to have been.[5] Yet this is where the example of Psalm 110 is useful for comparison.

Jerome wrestles with the translation equivalents in Proverbs 8 as well, and his interpretation will shift accordingly, but with a different end result. Initially he enters the discussion only with knowledge of the Greek *ektisen*. Accepting then that it must refer to an act of creation, he applies the rendering to the Incarnation. This was a move already adopted by Marcellus, and we shall see it classically in Athanasius, though it required for him a difficult maneuver because of the sequence of verses in Proverbs 8 (*ektisen*—incarnation—appearing before *genna*—eternal generation, as he held).[6] When later Jerome acquires sufficient Hebrew to note that behind *ektisen* is neither *'asah* nor *bara* but *qanah*, he rejects the translation earlier intimated in favor of the one we now see in his Latin Bible, *Dominus possedit me*—itself not without problems as a precise rendering of *YHWH qanani*. The issue may be set aside for a moment. The point is that the knowledge of Hebrew did not lead, as with Psalm 110, to so different a rendering that the proof text at verse 3 lost its grip on the doctrinal debate. Instead, knowledge of Hebrew *qanah* returned Jerome to the discussion convinced now that the verbs in both verse 22 and verse 25 substantiated the interpretation of eternal generation.

In some ways this returned Jerome to a position held prior to Athanasius and one that Frances Young conjectures the latter could have adverted to in his debate but chose not to. Instead Athanasius

---

[5] See Collett's evaluation of the modern position that reflexively agrees with such a judgment. He focuses on Bruce Waltke, *The Book of Proverbs: Chapters 1–15* (Grand Rapids: Eerdmans, 2004); Alan Lenzi, "Proverbs 8:22–31: Three Perspectives on Its Composition," *JBL* 125 (2006); Stuart Weeks, "The Context and Meaning of Proverbs 8:30a," *JBL* 125 (2006); Tremper Longman, *Proverbs* (Grand Rapids: Baker, 2006) and *How to Read Proverbs* (Downers Grove, Ill.: InterVarsity, 2002); Roland Murphy, *Proverbs*, WBC 22 (Waco, Tex.: Word, 1998).

[6] The discussion can be seen in Frances Young, "Proverbs 8," 108; and "Exegetical Method and Scriptural Proof: The Bible in Doctrinal Debate," StPatr 19 (Leuven: Peeters, 1989), 301.

opted for a combination of incarnation and eternal generation. It is at this point that Young introduces the idea that there was really no good way to adjudicate the problem, and so Athanasius "won" simply by deductive argument and what she calls, "employing inter-textuality to determine the overall mind (dianoia) of scripture."[7] This may sound like a solid way of proceeding, and at times in Young's writings the appeal to the *dianoia* of scripture may sound both probative and exegetically responsible.[8] Yet that there is something less salutary about this is revealed both in the questions she leaves hanging over Athanasius' juxtaposition of incarnation and eternal generation in Proverbs 8 and its ingenuity, and the conclusion she draws that appeal to the mind of scripture "determines the sense of particular passages, no matter how implausible!"[9] She continues by referring to the appeal to scripture, whose very character is such that "it can be moulded into a meaning that, it is claimed, coheres with the mind of Scripture." The particular reading horizon evoked is what will determine what the words will end up meaning.

---

[7] Young, "Proverbs 8," 111.

[8] The earlier discussion and conclusion in Young's "Exegetical Method" (1989) did not have the same postmodern overtone. "We may not always find the conclusions of patristic exegesis satisfactory or plausible, but this is more often because of a different estimate of what constitutes a valid cross-reference than anything else. From their methods and their endeavor we might learn much. The fundamental exegetical question is: what does this mean, The answer may be obvious, or it may be arrived at by a complex process of rational enquiry about word usage, about signification and metaphor, about syntax, about reference and about truth. There is no escape from that complexity" (304). See Collett on metaphor and theological truth, in "Place to Stand," 179–81. He writes, "The text's literary referent depends upon a particular ontological referent in order to do its sense-making. In this sense, metaphor as a verbal or literary phenomenon is akin to the referential account of sense-making we find at work in allegory. It is therefore a *species* of allegory, or 'ontological' other-speaking, in that it depends upon an ontological reality or non-textual referent *outside* of the text to render its sense" (180; emphasis original).

[9] Exclamation point in the text, Young, "Proverbs 8," 111.

The postmodern feel of this conclusion can only be judged unsatisfactory, one supposes, if Young believes there is an alternative to it. It is by no means clear that she does. She concludes one essay on this note. "For the Fathers were convinced they were uncovering the true, eternal meaning, not permitting their own concerns to determine how the text was read, or self-consciously recognizing the text only comes alive when a reader realizes it, inevitably bringing their own horizon to the process of interpretation. Yet from our perspective that would seem to be exactly what the Fathers were doing."[10] We will return to this and kindred observations from Young below.

But one can read the history of interpretation differently than she has, and also render a different verdict about what Athanasius has done. Let us begin by reviewing the various positions held by interpreters of Proverbs 8 in the run-up to Athanasius.

Athanasius had himself claimed that the verb *ektisen* is required to be taken by the Arians as "creation out of nothing" and that this is questionable. It is an *a priori* narrowing of a verb that elsewhere cannot be so restricted. It is an isolated literalism.[11] Hilary took it as referring to a mode of generation without change of passion in the Godhead, and he did this simply by refusing to allow the word "create" so little range of potential meaning.[12]

Others had simply assumed that the two verbs in Proverbs were synonyms. Dionysius of Rome argued that if one is looking for a distinction, the verb wanted is *poiein* (to make; the verb used in Genesis 1 for Hebrew *bara*). But as for *ktizein* and *genna*, they mutually inform one another and establish the proper context for the interpretation of each. What Arius needs is reference to Christ as a creature (*poiema*), and he does not have this.

Prior to the work of Jerome, earlier Fathers had others ways to go behind the LXX rendering of *ektisen*. The rival Greek renderings

---

[10] Young, "Proverbs 8," 113.
[11] Athanasius, *de Decretis Nicaenae Synodi* 13.
[12] Athanasius, *de Synodis* 16, 17.

of Aquila, Symmachus, and Theodotion all offered *ektēsato* (buy, aquire, get, beget).[13] Eusebius, Basil, Gregory of Nyssa, and Epiphanius all mention this. Basil speaks of a more apt rendering of the underlying Hebrew revealed by these translations. Genesis 4 is invoked: "For he who said, 'I have gotten a man through God,' manifestly used the expression not as the creator of Cain, but as his generator."[14] Epiphanius also knows that behind the alternative to *ektisen*, *ektēsato*, lies Hebrew *qanah* (to get or beget). He goes on to posit another root, "to nest" (*qn*), and speaks of wisdom being hatched like a nestling. In this case, then, we have appeal to an equivalence between the verbs in verse 22 and verse 25 based upon a deeper penetration into the language of translation via access to the Hebrew Verity.[15]

And finally, another position is represented that must be accounted for. It emerges in both Theophilus and Tertullian, and in Athenagoras. They do not focus on a single word and its relationship to a less ambiguous verb in verse 25. Rather, they are attentive to the precise collocation, "first of his ways for his works." They take *arche* as a second direct object and not as an adverbial ("at the first"). *Arche* bespeaks the power or authority over creation for which wisdom has been created. The text is not telling us anything about the precise origins of the logos, and eternal generation is simply inferred on the basis of other texts. Theophilus assumes that wisdom or logos are always present with God; verses 27-31 reflect this basic stance. Eusebius holds a similar view. Wisdom preexists and assists with creation. As Young puts it in the summary of his position: "There is no description of how the Logos came into being. The passage is about his preceding the creation of the whole world and his ruling over all things because set over them by the Lord, his Father."[16] He is the principal agent creating. That is what

---

[13] A useful catalog can be found in C. F. Burney, "Christ as the APXH of Creation (Prov. viii 22, Col. I 15–18, Rev. iii 14)," *JTS* 27 (1926): 169.
[14] Greek text in Burney, "APXH," 172.
[15] Burney, "APXH," 172.
[16] Young, "Proverbs 8," 107.

verse 22 more narrowly seeks to say, and this is complementary to the notion asserted concerning begetting in verse 25. Verse 22 describes Christ as *arche* in relation to the creation that follows; verse 25 claims the relationship in the language of generation. The same idea will be held in respect of Genesis 1:1. *En arche*, in and through the logos, God created the heavens and the earth. Neither Genesis 1 nor Proverbs 8 tell us of the origin of the Son, because that cannot be described; it is presupposed both on the basis of what is said and not said. Arius seeks to undo that careful synthesis. He offends against the "mind of scripture," which speaks of a Father and a Son but does not allow space to grow up between them temporally on analogy with human creating.

Seen in this way, three responses were to hand that clarified as faulty the rationalist literalism of Arius and his followers. One appealed to a false contradistinction in the verbs at verses 22 and 25; one to the translational dimension and the underlying Hebrew; one to the failure to track closely what verse 22 was saying and what it was not saying.

The Mind of Scripture

Thus far I have been testing what might be an appeal to the mind of scripture (including proper attention to "the ways the words go"; the hypothesis and scope of a text). It has been suggested that this "mind" is in fact a postmodern reader-response approach or a false search for objective sense-making, even when one believes that is what one is actually doing. Ironically, in this postmodern assessment of precritical reading what ends up being strongly objective is the verdict that they were deceiving themselves, and we can know that with confidence.[17]

---

[17] "Yet from our perspective that would seem exactly what the Fathers were doing" (Young, "Proverbs 8," 113). Later, "There will be a justifiable critique of the dubious linguistic and contextual moves Athanasius and others may have made" (115). Compare the less postmodern evaluation of Burney.

In order to get some needed perspective on Proverbs 8 I want now to widen the lens and look at a second Old Testament text regularly used for dogmatic exegesis. In one of those rare convergences across the schools of Antioch and Alexandria, interpreters saw in Psalm 2 a key text for articulating basic Christian doctrine. It was not simply that the Antiochenes let a psalm escape its Old Testament frame of reference because it was already located in a doctrinal struggle, though that certainly was a factor.[18] Other texts that functioned in this way—like Psalm 1, 3, or 22—they limited to the period of Old Testament *historia*. Psalm 2's citation in Acts certainly assisted in urging a christological evaluation instead of one focused on David's enthronement or some other setting derived from 1 and 2 Samuel. It was also the dogmatically pregnant "you are my Son, today I have begotten you" and the hyperbolic character of the description of God's anointed one that conspired to make Psalm 2 escape its ancient setting and speak in a single sense-making of Christ—on one of the rare occasions Diodore and Theodore permit this.[19]

One must still address the claim of the Arians that "today" clearly marked a moment in time and so disproved the claim of eternal generation. They responded that "today" referred to the incarnation. Theodore speaks of a "Hymn of Praise uttered by blessed David under the influence of the Spirit for God the word made Man. It refers to the birth of Christ in time. But this is the assumed man's birth." Regarding the verse in which God promises to give authority over nations and the ends of the earth, Diodore counters the Arians: "I mean, if before creation, how could he ask for what did not exist . . . The claim is ridiculous. If, on the other hand, it was after creation . . . how did the Son not have lordship of them when he was by nature lord of their making and creator?"

---

[18] Regarding verse 8, Diodore explicitly mentions the Arian position.

[19] Christopher Seitz, "Psalm 2 in the Entry Hall of the Psalter: Extended Sense in the History of Interpretation," in Ephraim Radner, ed., *Church, Society, and the Christian Common Good* (Eugene, Ore.: Cascade, 2017), 95–106. One can find the bibliography for the ancient sources in this essay.

Augustine represents the alternative that the tradition will lean toward. "Today" refers to time in eternity, and so God is speaking of his eternal generation of the beloved son. Luther will refer to both incarnation and eternal generation and say both are possible.

At this point the interpretation of Calvin is an important alternative, and it may help us make the appeal to the mind of scripture a bit more precise. Calvin does not want the meaning of the Old Testament text to simply be a dogmatic reading supplied by reference to various New Testament texts. Psalm 2 is about David; the Psalter is about David and the choral guilds and Moses and Ethan and Heman. The psalms emerge from the covenantal life of God with his people. So how do the key phrases refer to David? They speak of the "today" of his manifestation to Israel. David was begotten of God and by solemn anointing in accordance with God's plan for the kingdom this today is made known. God manifests this truth to Israel by Saul stepping forward from the baggage and being anointed by Samuel. "He said to me, you are my son, today I have begotten you."

But in these divine actions and in David's speech about them, he is also prophesying. For what David knows of his own kingdom in his own time does not match with what God promises, so in David's words there is a token or figure of a later divine fulfillment. The New Testament will in its time speak of this fulfillment in Christ the beloved Son. But it is still unclear what is the "today" in this later context. Calvin turns to Acts 13. It is the day, again as with David, when the manifestation of God's plan is revealed. For Paul this is the resurrection today. David is a type, with full dignity and integrity in God's economy. Christ is great David's greater Son. The today of his resurrection is the manifestation of what was and is his eternal Lordship.

One thing in particular to note is that Calvin rejects a simple or straightforward appeal *ad litteram* to eternal generation or incarnation as the single sense-making thrust of Psalm 2. He does not start with this because he believes David is the text's referent, and neither eternal generation nor incarnation is consonant with that. They are consonant with the type's final referent, but only on the terms related to that economic fulfillment and manifestation. The today of Psalm 2 will become the today of resurrection in Paul's truthful interpretation of the original type as fulfilled in Christ.

In the case of Proverbs the place held by David in the Psalms is held by Wisdom, who speaks of herself as does David in Psalm 2 (in Prov 1, 8, and 9). All three versions that hold out for the special place of the logos—either in eternal generation or in exalted role in creation—do so on the basis of what is said about Wisdom in attending to the "way the words go" in Proverbs 8:22-31. They do not use the language of typology or prophesying as does Calvin. But like him they do not move to the incarnation as the way to resolve what seems to be a problem in the eyes of the Arians. Neither do they lift the language of Proverbs immediately into a mode of eternality. Rather, they probe what the verbs in question mean by seeking their underlying Hebrew sense or by arguing from the wider use of the terms. They also believe that the position of Wisdom vis-à-vis creation warrants an extension to the logos. To be sure the New Testament supplied the linkage of logos and Sophia, but the latter does so mindful of the use of the term in the former testament, so there is a mutual enrichment grounded in the original scripture—much as with David and Christ in Calvin's reading. The selfsame divine providence holds the types in proper relationship.

In many ways, then, to speak of the "mind of scripture" is not to open onto a general arena of intertextuality and fecundity of meaning, which in turn requires some prior theological or communal framework to put the pieces together into a molded meaning—the molding being of such a nature that we can identify that while they thought they were doing something like honoring the text's coercion or pressure, they were in fact creating meaning. To speak of the mind of scripture will mean above all a grappling with the two-testament character of its presentation. The Bible is not a flat surface of associative potential precisely because the first part gets recycled in the second in a particular kind of way. What is said of David man and king is said again, and finally, of Christ. What is said of Sophia is said again of Christ. The challenge for Christian interpretation is figuring out, or figuring in, how that "saying again" amalgamates and enriches for a clear sense-making: clear because competent to be defended as truly given *ad litteram* and also competent to defeat alternative readings in public testimony.

Psalm 110 and the Associative Reality of *Arche*

In the case of Proverbs 8, there is one further piece of the associative mind of scripture that requires to be considered.

It was noted in passing that alongside Proverbs 8, Psalm 2, 8, and others, Psalm 110 also served a prominent role in dogmatic exegesis. This was for two reasons that are by now familiar. It was quoted in the New Testament as showing that David had a LORD who addressed his Lord. Because the third verse was thought to be consistent with this christological emphasis, and because its rendering in the original Hebrew was difficult, the first lines were translated into Greek "with you (Christ) is *arche*." This created a slight difficulty because the interpretation then offered was that *arche* was the Father. When in the second rendering of Jerome this christological potential was eliminated, due to attention to the Hebrew, it nevertheless persisted in the history of interpretation. Luther therefore judged *arche* as a reference, not to the Father but to the Spirit.

It is clear that *arche* became a significant associative link in the effort to make sense of Proverbs 8 and other texts, because it gives indication of both prominence and rule. But it also opened up the possibility that as *arche*, Christ was the first in a series of created things, even if distinguishable from them on the basis of Arias' conceptuality.

C. F. Burney has helpfully analyzed the references to *arche* and has shown what a key term the phrase was in dogmatic exegesis.[20] Within the context of Jewish interpretation, Philo had judged the *reshith* of Genesis 1:1 as having the potential for agency, and he concluded, with crossreference to Proverbs 8, that it was by torah—the ontology to which *reshith* pointed—that God created the heavens and the earth. Not only did Proverbs speak of *arche/reshith* as wisdom, it also set forth the idea of a master plan by which God created (v. 30).[21] Philo both spoke of *reshith* not as temporality but as agency, and he also identified this agent as the wisdom that is torah.

John 1:1 did a similar thing. *En arche ēn ho logos* was exegesis of Genesis 1. In *reshith* was God's agent in creation, the *arche* who is Christ.[22] Colossians 1:15 spoke of Christ as *prototokos*, and Burney saw in this Paul's creative rendering of *arche* (proto) and *genna* (tokos) as he sought to understand the implication of Genesis 1 in association with Proverbs 8. Epiphanius had adduced an argument along similar lines long ago, though he was somewhat encumbered by his odd understanding of the verb given in Hebrew as *qanani*, which he rendered differently ("to nest").[23]

At issue then is not whether the Old Testament speaks the idiom of Father, Son, and Holy Spirit, such as we see this in New Testament formulation. It does not. The question is rather whether its peculiar form of monotheism is marked by the refusal to countenance anything but one God, but at the same time, and perhaps precisely because of this claim, to understand the one God's personal relating to creation and his Son, Israel, as a uniquely prepared adumbration

---

[20] Burney, "Christ as the APXH."

[21] See also Bereshit Rabba 1.1: "There is no *reshith* except the Law."

[22] Origen, Ambrose, and Augustine all read Gen 1:1 as speaking of Christ as *arche*.

[23] Burney, "Christ as the APXH," 172. Christopher Seitz, *Colossians*, Brazos Theological Commentary on the Bible (Grand Rapids: Brazos, 2014), 86–101.

and anticipation of what Christian confession will call Trinity.[24] The Old Testament bespeaks the figure of the triune God under the verbal icon YHWH, with all that that name means. It is the distinctive character of the God of Israel in relation to his people and the world he has made, as disclosed by the oracles of God entrusted to the Jews, that both enables and pressures a Trinitarian grammar and syntax to emerge.

Yeago has described this well in his essay on the distinction between judgments and conceptions in Philippians 2.[25] The name above every name, the verbal icon YHWH, is given to the Son, so that at his name, every knee shall bow, to the glory of God the Father. The Spirit gives rise to this confession. The same Spirit disclosed the ground for its logic in Isaiah 45, where the figure was set forth in the Old Testament that Paul accesses by the same Spirit in order to speak of Christ in relation to the One God YHWH who has sworn by himself, "to me every knee will bow, only in the LORD are righteousness and strength" (Isa 45:23-24). The *judgment* rendered by Proverbs 8 in conjunction with Genesis 1, Psalm 2, John 1, and Colossians 1 indicates the mind of scripture that the Fathers were seeking. In my view the conclusion of Young leans toward turning this into a piece of post-modern hermeneutics.[26] "The text comes alive in the lives of people who respond to it" may or may not be a true account of affairs. Surely one can hope for that. When she proceeds to say that "this means that there

---

[24] Christopher Seitz, "The Trinity in the Old Testament," in Gilles Emery and Matthew Levering, eds., *The Oxford Handbook of the Trinity* (Oxford: Oxford University Press, 2011), 28–40.

[25] David Yeago, "The New Testament and the Nicene Dogma: A Contribution to the Recovery of Theological Exegesis," *ProEccl* 3 (1994): 152–64.

[26] Compare her salutary cautions about reading postmodern hermeneutics into Augustine's exegesis; Frances Young, "Augustine's Hermeneutics and Postmodern Criticism," *Int* 58 (2004): 42–55. See also my discussion in "Psalm 34: Redaction, Inner-Biblical Exegesis and the Longer Psalm Superscriptions—'Mistake' Making and Theological Significance," in Christopher R. Seitz and Kent Harold Richards, eds., *The Bible as Christian Scripture: The Work of Brevard S. Childs* (Atlanta: SBL, 2013), 287–94.

will be multiple meanings, multiple insights, as multiple readers engage with the text" she is again stating a "good post-modern observation" (as she herself puts it).

What she has failed to show is that the quest for the mind of scripture in the early church operated with the same hermeneutical stance—something she goes so far as to allege they are doing even if they do not know they are doing it. This leads her to a conclusion that seems far from the actual world of the texts she has been reading: "undergirding these multiple meanings is the 'mind' of the Holy Spirit—the intent that each and every reader should be taken up into the divine project of renewal and recreation." This is a homiletical gloss indicating that she is the one who has a clear idea of what the mind of scripture is about—the divine project of renewal and recreation—and has so projected this same conviction onto early Christian exegesis and declared it there as related to what Athanasius and others called *dianoia*. Her project is "transformation and growth to maturity—in other words, spirituality and ethics," and that is fine. But to declare this the "intent of scripture" and speak of it as what the Fathers meant by *dianoia* is a claim being asserted but not substantiated.

As noted, a significant lacuna in her overview is any effort to discuss the "mind of scripture" with attention to Scripture's two-testament character. This is one of the reasons the place occupied by her "rule of faith" takes the form of a creedal summary.[27] The fact that in Scripture a narrative begins and detours and backs up and covers old ground again and moves sideways and stops and starts and in time approximates a closing, and a new one begins again yet purports to uncover something that was ingredient in the first, lies at the heart of how the church searches for and discovers the "mind" of Scripture. The Rule declares One God at work in

---

[27] Young, "Proverbs 8," 115: "For the Fathers, the Rule of Faith provided the crucial criteria, and the creeds were regarded as a summary of the truth of the Bible." See Leonard G. Finn, "Reflections on the Rule of Faith," in Seitz and Richards, *Bible as Christian Scripture*, 221–42; Mark W. Elliott, *The Heart of Biblical Theology: Providence Experienced* (Surrey, UK: Ashgate, 2013), 6–7.

two testaments and correlates exegesis of the Elder Scripture along these non-postmodern lines.

Irenaeus sees this disclosive depth dimension in the Old Testament as profoundly theological. Note the different account of the work of the Spirit in him as compared with Young.

> That all those things would come to pass was foretold by the Spirit of God through the prophets—by this means the OT as such—that the faith of those who truly worship God might be certain in these things, for whatever was impossible for our nature, and because of this would bring disbelief to mankind, these things God made known beforehand by the prophets, that, by foretelling them a long time beforehand, when they were fully accomplished in this way, just as they were foretold, we might know that it was God who previously proclaimed to us our salvation. (Irenaeus, *On the Apostolic Preaching* 42)

As is typical, Chrysostom puts it a bit more brusquely.

> The fact that he has a Son, however, the inspired authors registered ahead of time in the Bible, neither speaking with complete clarity lest they fail to respect your limitations, nor concealing the truth so as to give you a chance later to come to your senses and to glean from your own Bible the teachings of truth.[28]

To speak of the mind of scripture in the case of Proverbs 8 means respecting the "neither speaking with complete clarity" that pertains to apperceptions of old, but also the unconcealed truth that is genuinely there but requires a larger sense of the mind of scripture truly to grasp. This is what is borne witness to in the exegesis of the early church in its reading of Proverbs 8:22-31.

I have mentioned at numerous points the very careful, illuminating study of C. F. Burney, who sought to track what one might call the "gravitational pull" of the Hebrew language reference to

---

[28] Robert Charles Hill, trans. with intro., *St. John Chrysostom Commentary on the Psalms*, vol. 2 (Brookline, Mass.: Holy Cross Orthodox Press, 1998), 114.

"beginning" in the Elder Testament and its reception into the New Testament as a way to understand Christ's relationship to God and his work in creation. At the end of his essay he provides a "running paraphrase of St. Paul's words" in order to show how his mind was working in respect of the "mind of scripture." I will quote it in full as this section closes. He has in view the hymn of Colossians 1:15-18.

> Christ is *the First-begotten of all creation*, for it is written (Prov. viii 22 ff), "The Lord begat me as *reshith* of His way, the antecedent of His works, from of old. From eternity was I wrought . . . when there were deeps was I brought forth." This passage has obvious connexion with Gen. i 1, where it is written "*Bereshith* God created the heavens and the earth." Now the force of the preposition *be* attached to *reshith* may be interpreted as "IN" ("In *reshith* God created"); hence in Him *were created all things in the heavens and upon the earth, seen and unseen, whether thrones, or dominions, or principalities, or powers*. But again, the preposition may bear the sense "BY" ("By the agency of *reshith*"); hence *all things were created through Him*. Yet again it may be interpreted "INTO" ("INTO *reshith*"); from which it follows that creation tends into Him as its goal. Passing on to the substantive *reshith*, we note that it ordinarily bears the sense "BEGINNING"; hence Christ is BEFORE *all things*. It may also have the meaning "SUM-TOTAL"; so that *all things are summed up in Him*. Yet another meaning is "HEAD," i.e. *He is the Head of the Body, namely, the Church*. Lastly, it means "FIRST-FRUITS"; *He is first-fruits, first-begotten of the dead*. Hence it follows that *in all senses He is the fulfiller of the meaning of reshith* (*proteuon*).[29]

We pick up this discussion in more detail in the next chapter, with a second example from Ecclesiastes with special reference to Genesis 1–11.

---

[29] Burney, "Christ as the APXH," 175.

14

The Sun Also Rises
Time and Creation in Ecclesiastes and Genesis 1–11

But if any one, yearning for greater possessions, and letting his desire become as boundless as the sea, has an insatiable greed for the streams of gain flowing in from every side, let him treat his disease by looking at the real sea. For as the sea does not exceed its boundary with the innumerable streams of water flowing into it, but remains at the same volume just as if it were receiving no new water from the streams, in the same way human nature too, restricted by specific limits in the enjoyment of what comes to it, cannot enlarge its appetite to match the extent of its acquisitions; while the intake is endless, the capacity for enjoyment is kept within its set limit. If therefore enjoyment cannot exceed the amount fixed by nature, for what reason do we attract in the flood of

acquisitions, never overflowing for the benefit of others from
our additional income?

Gregory of Nyssa, Homily 1 on Ecclesiastes[1]

Because of its quasipenitential and sober acknowledgment of the limits of human striving, amassing, and the mortal faculties themselves—which entropy into death—the book of Ecclesiastes was one of the most well-thumbed of all of scriptural texts in the Christian Bible in the history of interpretation. The modern period for the most part has seen the book in a different, more cynical light. Its opening and closing poems are critical for a proper appraisal of the book's larger message. We will argue they operate within the same broader environment as Genesis 1–11, which speak of creational stability and seasonal and natural order, threatened but divinely maintained after the flood. Human life and human faculties are comprehended against this backdrop.

For our purposes here the exegetical discussion of Koheleth leads into a theological reflection on ontology and history/temporality as the opening chapters of the Bible carefully calibrate that, by means of *toledoth* formulations, especially the signal appearance at Genesis 2:4. Life East of Eden is the world of Koheleth, as he comes at last to accept that.

This chapter will examine two distinct areas of exegesis and interpretation. One is concerned with the depiction of divinely structured time and creation in Ecclesiastes 1. Some very basic questions of exegesis have produced in modern commentary very different, even opposing appraisals. First, do creation and time mirror the same futility more clearly in place in the realm of human cognition? Second, does the fact that "the sun also rises" point to repetition

[1] *Gregory of Nyssa: Homilies on Ecclesiastes: An English Version with Supporting Studies*, ed. Stuart George Hall, Proceedings of the Seventh International Colloquium on Gregory of Nyssa (St. Andrews, 5–10 September 1990) (Berlin: Walter de Gruyter, 1993), 40–41.

and pointless movement, to be lodged under the same rubric of *hebel hebelim* as human seeing, hearing, speaking, and remembering? Relatedly, does the author mean to describe a contrast, intended to underscore the frailty and limits of human cognition not alongside but "under the sun"?

The other domain to be considered is how the opening chapters of Genesis depict the relationship between creation and history. Gerhard von Rad produced a shimmering account of the achievement of the Yahwist, which marked the apogee of the theory of Pentateuchal sources in their most uncomplicated and most theologically compelling—as he saw it—form. All that has collapsed in the light of newer Pentateuchal criticism, where the terms "Yahwist" and "Priestly" writer point to very different phenomena, extremely complicated and theologically far less compelling for all that. But his work marked an era. By extracting the texts of the Yahwist from the canonical narrative line of the opening eleven chapters of Genesis, the result was a powerful emphasis on salvation history. The Yahwist invented history, on his view. Primeval episodes of sin and mitigation—Adam, Cain, Noah—stopped with the tower of Babel, and what emerged then from the Yahwist was history in the genuine sense of that term, and that was what the point of primeval time was all about: giving rise to salvation history focused on the descendants of Abraham.[2]

The unsurprising effect of this, registered in von Rad's own published work, was the isolation of the wisdom literature of the Old Testament.[3] He struggled to fit this literature into his theological reading of the Old Testament as a total work given the

---

[2] "Von Rad developed an interpretation of the primal history which sees it as intentionally leading up to the election of Abraham; for him, this is connected with a theological subordination of creation faith to a faith in salvation grounded in history" (Rendtorff, *The Old Testament: An Introduction* [Philadelphia: Fortress, 1991], 133).

[3] *Weisheit in Israel* (Neukirchen-Vluyn: Neukirchener, 1970) was his last major work. English translation by James D. Martin, *Wisdom in Israel* (Harrisville, Penn.: Trinity Press International, 1972).

focus on salvation history and recitations about God's acts in time with Israel. The diminution of the Priestly Writer, because of the attention paid to the J extraction in von Rad's reconstruction, is something he would note later and indicate concern about. Perhaps the effect of J would be better appreciated in a conjoined work. But one notes the attention still remains on J and on his achievement as historian, enhanced by P's addition. P, like wisdom literature, sits in isolation and asks us to come to terms with it as something of an outlier. The lure of "things early" hung over the J extraction of course, as over against later developments like P or wisdom. Today the Pentateuchal traditions are dated late, but the job of relating disparate streams like J and P or D or wisdom remains. Indeed, does the term "wisdom literature" itself point up the problem (see Sneed)? It exists as a way to speak of material that has been extracted from an account prioritizing history.

Numerous voices were raised at the time in opposition to this view of things, in which creation theology was subordinated to salvation history, including those of H. H. Schmid, H. Reventlow, R. Rendtorff, H. Spieckermann, and R. Knierim. Some wanted to put creation theology at the center of any wider theological reading, and others simply noted that an extraction of sources has its own methodological problems: including whether there are sources at all, and whether they are wrongly viewed as distinctive or discrete.[4] Rather than identifying the call of Abraham as the focal point due to the extraction of J episodes, when one attends to the coordinating voice of P, the centrality of the Noah material emerges.[5] Creation and its collapse into the chaos from which

---

[4] "It is impossible to reconstruct two independent narratives, so it seems more likely that we have an original narrative with additions" (Rendtorff, *Old Testament*, 133). This is the view of his student E. Blum as well. See the major FAT volume on recent Pentateuchal work.

[5] "After a series of ten generations each of which lives to an extreme old age, the flood brings a profound break" (Rendtorff, *Old Testament*, 133). Also, "Genesis 8,21 und die urgeschichte des Jahwisten," *KuD* 7 (1961): 69–78 (= GS, 188–97).

Genesis 1 declared its grand emergence is, after Noah, permanently closed off. The rainbow belongs to our time and shows that history cannot make sense without a creational foundation.

Brevard Childs had begun to think along similar lines when in 1979's *Introduction to the Old Testament as Scripture* he questioned the assignment of the first *toledoth* formula to the narrative that preceded it, when at every other point in Genesis it introduced the material to follow.[6] Strictly speaking, it would be impossible merely to declare the first three chapters of Genesis as consisting of two different or rival accounts, the first assigned to a P source and the second to J. The effect of the intriguing signal use of the *toledoth* was precisely to introduce the story of Adam and Eve through the lens of the account of creation. Time is generated by means of creation. The heavens and earth have their own actual generating potential, as the terse and underdetermined note at 2:4 seems to suggest. What becomes more transparently generational in the ten formula that follow (thus reinforcing Gen 1's exhortation to be fruitful and multiply in the realm of human expansion throughout the world) is used more specifically in the first example to move us from creation to what we may call "historical time" or temporality as such. I will speak more on this first *toledoth* below, in relation to Koheleth's frame of reference.

In a later work (1992) Childs would note the ontological priority given to P by the simple fact of his being given the first word, through which all that follows under the rubric of temporality will have its foundation.[7] The existence of sources or levels of tradition is not here being questioned, but it is rather their sequence and conjunction that needs proper evaluation. Von Rad had begun to think along these lines in the final edition of his Genesis commentary.[8] It would have taken more years of his life to have processed

---

[6] Childs, *Introduction to the Old Testament as Scripture*, 145.

[7] See the engaging theological proposal of Neil MacDonald, developed from this point (the canonical priority of P) in *Metaphysics and the God of Israel: Systematic Theology of the Old and New Testaments* (Grand Rapids: Baker, 2006).

[8] Christopher Seitz, "Prophecy and Tradition-History: The Achievement

more carefully about how this would affect his account of not just P but also wisdom thinking, with its own commitments to creational themes and non-election specific revelation.

The tendency to view wisdom as its own unique entity within the Old Testament has carried on into our present season.[9] In fact, for very different reasons than von Rad, James Crenshaw prefers to reckon with wisdom as non-integrated to the very degree that it insists on this depiction itself and in so doing describes the true heart of Wisdom.[10] Wisdom is different and means to be different. It is a voice in objection.[11] Largely necessary for this depiction is the notion that the literary boundaries of wisdom are both clear and well-defined in terms of a sequential development.[12] Conservative wisdom in Proverbs is challenged by the dialogues of Job and deconstructed by Koheleth to the point of cynicism and dissolution. Wisdom ends up being epistemological despair and the rejection of historical thinking and indeed creation theology itself. God in the dock.[13]

---

of Gerhard von Rad and Beyond," in I. Fischer, K. Schmid, and H. G. M. Williamson, eds., *Prophetie in Israel: Beitrage des Symposiums "Das Alte Testament und die Kultur der Moderne" anlässlich des 100. Geburtstags Gerhard von Rads (1901–1971) Heidelberg, 18.–21. Oktober 2001*, ATM 11 (Munster: Lit-Verlag, 2003), 30–51.

[9] See the very helpful alternative position of Raymond C. Van Leeuwen, "Wisdom Literature," in Kevin Vanhoozer, ed., *Dictionary for Theological Interpretation of the Bible* (Grand Rapids: Baker Academic, 2005), 847–50.

[10] James Crenshaw, *Old Testament Wisdom: An Introduction* (Atlanta: John Knox, 1981).

[11] "Within Proverbs, Job, and Ecclesiastes one looks in vain for the dominant themes of Yahwistic thought . . . Instead, the reader encounters in these three books *a different thought world*, one that stands apart so impressively that scholars have described that literary corpus as an alien body within the Bible" (Crenshaw, *Old Testament Wisdom*, 29; emphasis original). One can find similar statements though with less urgency in the wisdom accounts of von Rad, Blenkinsopp, Zimmerli, and others. See the helpful evaluation of Mark Sneed, "Is the 'Wisdom Tradition' a Tradition?" *CBQ* 73 (2001): 50–71.

[12] Note how Crenshaw refers to "that literary corpus within the Bible" when of course there is no such thing, except by extraction.

[13] Gregory of Nyssa comments, "Let no one suppose that the words (of the

Some dissenting voices have recently questioned whether we are in any position to speak of a wisdom tradition in the Old Testament at all.[14] It is not clear that we really have the means by which to verify a development along these lines, from Proverbs to Job to Koheleth. The significance hermeneutically of associating three works with Solomon, including Song of Songs, and leaving Job to its own—internally complicated—side, must also be set to the side as a later distraction.[15]

It is at this point where the connection between Koheleth and the thinking of the Priestly writing may prove a fruitful alternative, both in refusing to declare Wisdom as an alternative literature closed off to itself or one impossible to integrate with other Old Testament traditions. Equally to be resisted is the idea that Koheleth is simply a literature of despair. When one studies the earlier history of interpretation this view of Ecclesiastes is completely missing. This prominent view of Koheleth is the consequence of certain strands of modernity, which are further reinforced when one imagines there is a significant developmental movement from Proverbs to Job to Ecclesiastes nowhere marked in any known canonical arrangement.

---

opening poem) are an indictment of creation. For surely the charge would also implicate him who has made all things" (Homily 1 on Ecclesiastes, from *Gregory of Nyssa: Homilies on Ecclesiastes*).

[14] Sneed, "Is the 'Wisdom Tradition' a Tradition?"

[15] "He wrote the *Song of Songs*, with its accent on love, in his youth; *Proverbs*, with its emphasis on practical problems, in his maturity; and *Ecclesiastes*, with its melancholy reflections on the vanity of life, in old age" (Midrash Shir Hashirim Rabba 1:1, sec. 10). "And let it not surprise you, seeing that our Lord and Savior is One and the Same, that we should speak of Him first as a beginner, in Proverbs; then as advancing, in Ecclesiastes; and lastly as more perfect in the Song of Songs" (Origen, *Prologue to the Song of Songs*, in *The Song of Songs: Commentary and Homilies*, ed. Johannes Quasten and Joseph C. Plumpe, Ancient Christian Writers 26 [Mahwah, N.J.: Paulist, 1957]).

Creational Order in Genesis 1–11: A Conceptual Backdrop

Reading carefully the canonical presentation of Genesis 1–11, without prioritizing the alleged episodes of a discrete J theologian, one senses the significance of the notice at Genesis 8:22: "As long as the earth endures, seedtime and harvest, cold and heat, summer and winter, day and night will never cease."

The creational order established by God in Genesis 1 will never again be tampered with. One hears very similar notes sounded in the Psalter. One can count on the creational stronghold that means storms, seasons, sun, moon, and the floods are all being governed such that they will never again be overthrown. Temporality is made possible because of these foundational realities.[16]

When it comes to the proper exegesis of Koheleth, then, and especially its opening and closing texts, whose significance as interpretive frames is often noted, one must contend against both an isolation of so-called wisdom literature and furthermore Koheleth within it. Ecclesiastes on such an account is in revolt not only against Proverbs and Job, but as such is a rogue witness within the canon, with no connective tissue except protest and objection. Koheleth's declaration of "vanity of vanities" is not condemnation of the fruitlessness of the created order and God himself, of equal character to his recognition about the limits of human faculties, epistemology, cognition, memory, and acquisition. In the opening poem the latter is being set in contrast to the mysterious sovereign ordering of creation, issuing forth in the acknowledgement that all is beyond human comprehension and human ordering. By setting Koheleth off against Proverbs and

---

[16] "Knierim rightly insisted that cyclical time (day and night, winter and summer) was for Israel more fundamental then linear time, for the simple reason that cyclical, cosmic time patterns are what make history, with its unique and contingent events, possible" (Raymond van Leeuwen, "Creation and Contingency in Qohelet," unpublished paper given at the Conference on Ecclesiastes, Wycliffe Center for Scripture and Theology, May 9 2014, Toronto, Canada).

Job and then creating a quasicanonical division called wisdom literature, we lose access to the account of creation and time we may fruitfully compare with what the Preacher has to say. In our view the opening poem of Koheleth can be properly understood only when it is placed in the correct context of comparison. But let us first start at the end.

At the close of the book we have a poem about death. It opens with "remember your Creator," a clear evocation of the presentation known in Genesis 1. Whatever the limits of human remembering chapter 1 may declare (v. 11), this does not apply to remembering God. In what follows the entropy of the human in death is depicted in the clothing of creational images. In this way the subjective experience of dying is described by means of the objective world of creation. As Fox puts it, "It is as if Koheleth is saying, when you die, a world *is* ending—*yours*."[17] For of course the world is not dying at all but lives on and carries on without us. The poem ends, "And the dust returns to the earth as it was, and the spirit returns to God who gave it." Of course this language is deeply evocative of the original act of creation of humankind, as declared in Genesis 2: "Then the LORD God formed man of dust from the ground, and breathed into his nostrils the breath of life; and man became a living being." This is here ending, finally and forever, for Koheleth. Remember your creator. Your spirit is now returning to God who gave it. The earth endures forever, from which you came.

The long Psalm 104 speaks in the same way in verse 29. "When thou hidest thy face, they are dismayed; when thou takest away their breath, they die and return to their dust." In Psalm 104 this statement is played out against a song of praise, extolling light, the stretching out of the heavens, beaming off the waters, making clouds as secure chariots, governing the winds, securing earth's foundations, rebuking flood waters, setting bounds for mountains

---

[17] Michael V. Fox, *Ecclesiastes*, The JPS Bible Commentary (Philadelphia: The Jewish Publication Society, 2004), 76.

and valleys, bringing forth springs and nourishment, ordering sun and moon, providing homes for the beasts. "O Lord, how manifold are thy works! In wisdom hast thou made them all; the earth is full of thy creatures." This is what an unburdened Job might have said under more graceful conditions when God appeared and showed him creation from the side of the divine council. And inside this paean to God the Creator there is as well the acknowledgement that we will die and return to the dust of Genesis 2 from whence we came, when God withdraws his spirit at the end of our days. The extolling of God as the ante- and still post-diluvian protector of creational order, bulwark against the floods of chaos, of course appears as a repeating theme in the Psalms, in the Psalms of Zion and in hymns like Psalm 104. Genesis 1–3 do not consist in rival and independent versions but together function as the backdrop of creational order and magnificence within which we mortals have the gift of God's spirit and life until he withdraws them.

In Genesis 2:4, sandwiched between two accounts of creation, we find the distinctive *toledoth* formula "these are the generations of the heavens and the earth when they were created." Like four others out of eleven in Genesis it introduces not genealogy as such but narrative accounts. Yet even these five instances (2:4; 6:9; 11:27; 25:19; 37:1) are not devoid of genealogical reference. Whether an original genealogical function of the *toledoth* has been modified (due to diachronic factors) to offer service as narrative introductions to what follows or whether the term itself is elastic and polysemous, as has been argued, meaning something like "anticipating active sequences of events," need not detain us here; both may be true.[18]

The heavens and the earth are not the generators of human life of course, but God, as we read in 2:7. "Now the LORD God formed man of the dust of the earth and breathed into him the breath of life." But the dust from which man is made is from the

---

[18] Sarah Schwartz, "Narrative *Toledot* Formula in Genesis: The Case of Heaven and Earth, Noah, and Isaac," *JHS* 16 (2016): 1–36; the quote is on p. 33.

earth, and the phrase may play on that. Perhaps this explains the reversed word order ("earth and heavens") in the second verse-half and the ensuing attention to earth items like irrigation and the tending of the land, noted as not possible without human superintendence. This creates a slightly awkward transition between stories with different origins and provenance but to the effect of enabling a complementary merging of two accounts with different sequencing and core interests. They now overlay one another in primeval time. The second account of course ends where it began, now with post-rebellion consequences such as the world of Koheleth presupposes, though of course for him under a post-flood rainbow:

> Cursed is the ground because of you;
>   in toil you shall eat of it all the days of your life;
> thorns and thistles it shall bring forth to you;
>   and you shall eat the plants of the field.
> In the sweat of your face
>   you shall eat bread
> till you return to the ground,
>   for out of it you were taken;
> you are dust,
>   and to dust you shall return. (Gen 3:17-19)

And so it is for Koheleth in the final poem of that book.[19] The sun and the light and the moon and the stars are darkened because subjectively we mortals see them at the end of life that way, through faculties now weakened with age, beyond the limitations already noted by the Preacher in preceding chapters. Sounds become low intimations, at times frightening in obscurity. Teeth and back and limbs weaken. Desire fails. Minor notes make themselves felt in snapped cords, broken bowls, pitchers, and wheels, in

---

[19] On the options for interpretation of the final poem (allegorical, literal, eschatological)—or probably some subtle combination of these given the subject matter—see the compact appraisal of Fox, *Ecclesiastes*, 76.

contexts where once they had functioned well. The grasshoppers and mourners will carry on after us.

Against the backdrop of the final poem and the other pertinent texts concerning creation and divine sovereignty over time we can enter the book of Ecclesiastes better prepared to hear its opening chapter. To place Koheleth on a sliding scale of wisdom's deterioration from Proverbs to Job to the despair of God and creation threatens to deprive the text of Koheleth of its own unique voice. An artificial context is inserted in the name of something called wisdom literature, rather than endeavoring to hear Koheleth's witness through the hermeneutical lens of an aged Solomon in a carefully constructed guise. It is beyond the scope of the present chapter to evaluate what is meant by use of the term "Koheleth" and the avoidance of actually naming the protagonist King Solomon. My own view is that what is being evoked by the name of the protagonist is collecting and acquiring (so frequent use of the term *qahal* in chapter 8 of 1 Kings). This accommodates the creation of a persona of aged wisdom on the other side of failure and achievement both: a Solomon who lost his name and his way due to excess, out beyond the diminished portrait beginning to emerge at the close of 1 Kings 13. The Koheleth of rabbinic evaluation.[20]

Above all, what needs to be avoided is prejudicing proper interpretation of the opening chapter by assuming preemptively

---

[20] See Christopher Seitz, "Koheleth and Canon," in S. A. Cummins and Jens Zimmerman, eds., *Acts of Interpretation: Scripture, Theology, and Culture* (Grand Rapids: Eerdmans, forthcoming). "When King Solomon of Israel was sitting on his royal throne, his heart became very proud because of his wealth, and he transgressed the degree of the Memra' of the Lord; he gathered many horses, chariots, and cavalry; he collected much silver and gold; he married among foreign peoples. Immediately the anger of the Lord grew strong against him. Therefore, He sent Ashmedai king of the demons, against him who drove him from his royal throne and took his signet ring from his hand so that he would wander and go into exile in the world to chastise him. He went about in all the districts and towns of the Land of Israel. He wept, pleaded, and said, 'I am Qohelet, who was previously named Solomon. I was king over Israel in Jerusalem'" (*The Targum of Qohelet*).

that the book of Ecclesiastes is a rogue witness. Here a turn to the history of interpretation is helpful, where the Preacher is typically viewed as a man of great wisdom penetrating to the heart of reality but never viewed through a lens of cynicism or abject despair about God's ways. His is the wisdom of having got it all and learned thereby that all is nothing. The function of the epilogue of Ecclesiastes and the sentence wisdom found in the latter half of the book is to relate Koheleth's sober wisdom to that of Proverbs, as "rules and exceptions."

In chapter 1 we are immediately introduced to the book's repeated phrase *hebel hebelim*. The phrase applies to life under the sun, and specifically to the toil immediately referred to under it, as Lohfink has argued.[21] Again the hardship of toil evokes the curse of the garden. A contrast is then developed: the generations of humankind, which come and go, consistent with the *toledoth* theme of Genesis, but here depicted in contrast to the enduring character of the earth and thus introducing a death motif. We come from the earth; we return there; but the earth endures forever. Again the theme is rooted in the ground assumptions of Genesis 1–3. Roland Murphy worries too much about the ever-standing earth and "the eternity of the world" when he cites Zimmerli: "The permanence of the earth is merely the foil against which the restless coming and going of human beings is outlined."[22] Why "merely" when we know that life under the sun will come to an end, but the sun will rise all the same? As we learn in Psalm 19, the sun's journey is that of a champion.

> He has set a tent for the sun,
> which comes forth like a bridegroom leaving his chamber,

---

[21] Norbert Lohfink, *Qoheleth: A Continental Commentary* (Minneapolis: Fortress, 2003; German original, 1980), 37.

[22] Roland Murphy, *Ecclesiastes*, WBC 23A (Waco, Tex.: Word, 1992), 7. It is a bit unclear where the English quote comes from; Zimmerli's main work on the subject is *Das Buch des Predigers Salomo*, ATD 16/1 (Göttingen: Vandenhoeck & Ruprecht, 1962).

>   and like a strong man runs its course with joy.
> Its rising is from the end of the heavens,
>   and its circuit to the end of them;
>   and there is nothing hid from its heat.

Murphy speaks of a "lively contrast" with Psalm 19, but it is hard to understand the distinction between "life under the sun" and the sun's own life as collapsing into parallel examples of futility.[23] The contrast would fall apart.

It may be that difficulty with understanding the implications of verses 5-7 has had the effect of destroying the contrast set up in verses 3-4, forcing an interpretation of the sun's mighty, regular circuit riding—so obviously Psalm 19, 104, Genesis 1, and elsewhere—as a negative occurrence. The main image is of created realities not overreaching bounds or dissipating. The rivers never overfill the sea—after Genesis 8:22 that is. The winds never blow themselves out but carry on endlessly and mysteriously. The "return" and the "again" are reliable according to God's purposes, much as is the daily repetition of the sun's tireless journeying to give light and heat without rest.

With this picture in place it is possible, then, to understand the ensuing contrast and to see it as consistent with what was said in verses 3-4: where the enduring of the earth is contrasted with the dust-returning generations, and the life of the sun and the life under the sun are differentiated.[24] Now we learn more about the contrast. Verses 8-11 concern themselves with the human faculties of, in order, speaking ("a man cannot utter it"), seeing, hearing, and remembering. Sandwiched between the first three and the last one in this series is a reflection on novelty (vv. 9-10). The point being registered is that things we think are new are things that existed once, but we have forgotten them. There are never genuinely new things, and if one says there are, they are merely

---

[23] Fox, *Ecclesiastes*, 7.

[24] Lohfink, *Qoheleth*, 41: "The sun, which sets, appears to be transient like humans, but it is not. It rises unchanged in its cycle."

a version of something forgotten, something truly forgotten, or something claiming to be genuinely new that is not of sufficient independent significance to count in life under the sun. The 8-track tape player, iPhone 3, the newest of this or that soon to be displaced.[25]

At issue throughout this section is the limited character of human perception, memory, epistemology, and the reliability of human faculties. They are what they are, but unlike the earth or sun or wind or rivers, are not calibrated to reach some kind of bounded limit of contented and effective execution. The ear never hears things up. The eyes do not see things up. The memory does not remember things up. All wording is wearisome. Unless one knows this truth about inability to reach a boundary, our faculties will generate restlessness. It is for this reason that the best translation of *kol debarim* at the opening of section 8-11 is "all words," thereby successfully anticipating the *ledabber* in the next phrase, "a man cannot speak."[26] Fox is here correct when he writes, "It is not the natural phenomena but rather human words that are 'weary'" (v. 6). Only this translation, furthermore, can successfully maintain the contrast found in the opening unit (vv. 2-7) and its depiction of what Fox calls "the natural phenomena" as over against "life under the sun," and allow for a consistent depiction of this same contrast in the final section (vv. 8-11) but keeping the focus on human limitation in speaking,

---

[25] "Rather, he seems to mean that of the things that matter in life, there is nothing truly new. For Qohelet what seems to be new (think of a newborn baby) is not really new, for babies are as old as humanity. Or perhaps the type of things humans label as new (computers!) are just not significant enough to matter. For Qohelet, the things that matter are life and death, the joys and pleasures of food and drink—which are always more that just food and drink—of married love and family" (Van Leeuwen, "Creation and Contingency").

[26] Gregory of Nyssa translates thus: "All words (*panta logoi*) are laborious, a man will not be able to speak, an eye will not have its fill of seeing, nor will an ear have its fill of hearing" (Homily 1). "The point is that human words never achieve their purpose" (Murphy, *Ecclesiastes*, 8). He translates, "All words are wearisome" and notes the anticipation of *dabar* in 8b (5–6).

seeing, hearing, and remembering. These do not run on tracks God has otherwise set up for earth, sun, rivers, and winds. That is life under the sun, and until one gets it, one will labor at that which does not profit and will fail to enjoy life on the terms God has set for its proper living. Since bounds do not arise on their own we may be tempted to think there are none. Koheleth has reached the bounds his great wealth and power enabled him to taste. So he is a reliable source of caution.

My goal in this brief section has been to keep Ecclesiastes within the proper context of interpretation its author shares, which I have argued involves the same conceptual backdrop as Genesis 1–11, various Psalms, and wider shared assumptions he shares with the Old Testament. Setting up a context for interpretation based upon a category wisdom literature simply ends up confirming the predispositions of interpreters who reject the wisdom of Proverbs, placing it on an artificial grid headed over the bumpy terrain of Job en route to Koheleth as cynic. Maybe the point of the book of Ecclesiastes is to push us and to expose our lurking predispositions by asking us to see if there is a wisdom genuinely linking texts like Genesis 1, Psalm 19, Psalm 104, the book of Proverbs, Job, 1 Kings 2–13, and Koheleth after all. Not by arguing for protest and opposition, but by seeing the maxims of the Preacher and the sentences of Proverbs and the commandments of the Pentateuch as equally "sayings of the wise," which like goads (12:11) demand of us a deeper wisdom, competent to guide in youth and in middle age and on the other side of excess and folly, at the portal of death itself. Then we might discover the Preacher of Gregory of Nyssa, Jerome, Martin Luther, and even Ernest Hemingway.

Creation is that which makes history and temporality possible. The Old Testament provides a rich array of texts that serve to describe creation post-flood as that which ensures a salvation history is possible, even when it has broken down in exile, or when at last it breaks down in our own personal historical life.

A musical text that I suspect has Ecclesiastes in its background captures the tone well. It serves to transition the discussion to our concern with ontology and its theological potential in the Elder Testament.

Up in the morning
Out on the job
Work like the devil for my pay
But that lucky old sun got nothing to do
But roll around heaven all day

Fuss with my woman
Quarrel with my kids
I sweat till I'm wrinkled and grey
But that lucky old sun got nothing to do
But roll around heaven all day

Good Lord of mine
Can't you see I'm tired
Tears are in my eyes
Send down that cloud with a silver lining
Take me to paradise

Show me that river
Take me across
Wash all my troubles away
Like that lucky old sun
Give me nothing to do but roll around heaven all day
Like that lucky old sun
Give me nothing to do but roll around heaven all day.[27]

---

[27] The 1949 song "That Lucky Old Sun" (Beasley Smith, words by Haven Gillespie) was popularized by Frankie Lane, Louis Armstrong, Ray Charles, Aretha Franklin, Frank Sinatra, and Paul Williams, among others. "Old Man River" (1927, Kern/Hammerstein) puts nature in a more detachedly oblivious role.

The Ontology of Genesis 1

In her thorough and often insightful essay on the *toledoth* in Genesis, Schwartz spends appropriate time evaluating the oddity of the *toledoth* that introduce not genealogies but narratives, and especially the intriguing case of 2:4, "these are the generation of the heavens and the earth when they were made, on the day the LORD God made the heavens and the earth."[28] She rightly concludes this is the introduction to the narrative that follows consistent with others who have argued for this. That is, its purpose is transitional and not summative. The second half of the verse clearly consists of a resumptive declaration based on Genesis 1:1, "In the beginning God created the earth and the heavens" and now with "LORD God" in anticipation of the usage in the narrative to follow. Mention was made above of the reverse order of "earth and heavens" as likely anticipatory of the focus on earth and the creation of humanity from it which follows. One take on the interpretation of this verse she clearly wishes to rule out.

> One possibility is that the word toledot means "descendants," depicting the works of creation as the metaphorical "children" of heaven and earth, as mentioned above. It can also be defined as "products," as Stordalen proposes, which implies that the narrative does not discuss creation of the world itself but what happened to the world after its creation. Again, this interpretation is problematic because the works of creation are not described as the products of heaven and earth, and this idea is opposed to the theological approach that God is the creator—although He uses the earth as raw material, the earth is by no means the "parent" of creation, not even metaphorically.[29]

Her own proposal is to read the word *toledot* as meaning "chronicles"/"story." Citing with approval Abravanel, "the formula

---

[28] Schwartz, "Narrative *Toledot* Formula."

[29] Schwartz, "Narrative *Toledot* Formula," 30–31. Cited is Terje Stordalen, "Genesis 2,4: Restudying a *locus classicus*," *ZAW* 104 (1992): 163–77.

introduces a narrative concerned with the creation of the world and the events that follow."[30] Yet because she also notes that the text to follow really makes only brief reference to "the creation of the world," she adjusts her position in this way: "the formula hints to identification of the creation of the world with the creation of humankind, and emphasizes the concept that the supreme objective of the creation of the world is the creation of humanity."[31] So in her own roundabout way, she views the *toledot* as indeed referring to the creation of humanity after all, insofar as it has collated (my term) creation of the world and creation of humanity, with a backward glimpse at Genesis 1:1 and a forward anticipation of the creation of humanity from the dust of the earth as the focus of the narrative to follow.

I stay with this close reading because within it may well be the seeds of what appears in the reception history of Genesis 1–3 in certain Jewish and especially Christian circles. A lot is compressed into what the brief and unusual *toledoth* at Genesis 2:4 is getting at. On the one hand, given the clearly significant repetition of the phrase as a structuring device in the canonical form of Genesis, we are right to believe that this is a phrase of some significance here. Elsewhere it would appear to insist that whatever damage humankind may seek to do—Adam, or Cain, or the evil heart of the imagination, or tower builders at Babel—God's charge to be fruitful and multiply and fill the earth is a persistent and overriding charge coming to fruition in historical time. The ontology of God's creative self in making humankind in his image and likeness stands as a fact that will perdure and make human history possible.

---

[30] Schwartz, "Narrative *Toledot* Formula," 31. She cites (31, n. 115) Abravanel to this effect: "And the text said, these are the chronicles and the events it will mention afterwards, they are the toledoth of the heavens and the earth when they were created, that is, from the day they were created, and from the day the Lord God made the earth and the heavens" (Yehuda Shaviv, ed., *The Commentary of Rabbi Isaac Abravanel on the Torah*, vol. 1, *Genesis* [Jerusalem: Horeb, 2007], 155; in Hebrew).

[31] Schwartz, "Narrative *Toledot* Formula," 31–32.

Even a flood of his own undertaking will not thwart it. Thistles and pain and labor that may produce ennui and death in humankind (Gen 3:14-19)—testified to in Koheleth's sustained somber acknowledgement—cannot offset the creative will grounded in God's self and God's promise. The earth endures forever (Eccl 1:4) even as *toledoth* generations come and go (Eccl 1:4) because God is the creator of the heavens and the earth. The heavens and the earth have "progeny" insofar as that signal act of creation remains as an ontological marker of God's self and God's will, and that self and will have created humankind in God's image and declared the matter very good. Generational time is made possible, and it will continue beyond the dying of this or the next individual generation.

It is here that we begin to see in the history of reception a probing of just what is at stake in the ontology of God economically assured and perduring through history. Philo sees in *bereshith* of Genesis 1 more than a single temporal marker trying to describe a moment in time. This is because he knows that this signal divine moment in creational time cannot only or primarily mean something "back then" but must rather have to do with the purpose of time and creation itself, ontologically understood. In something beyond his own divine self of transcendence and life God has reached out. The first word of God's wording is somehow his word and his own self at the same time, extruding into what we call "the creation of the world" yet without identifying himself through absorption with it. "In beginning"—in the divine *ad extra*—God created the heavens and the earth. Humankind alone can "read" this word because of the status God has given to him, which capacitates the hearing of his speaking. We are therefore "created" in the *reshith* that is God's signal act of creation. So the *toledoth* of Genesis 2:4 situates us at that moment so as to make clear what is being said in Genesis 1:1 as we await the "very good" address at 1:26. Philo calls this *reshith* God's torah. By this he means the eternal expression of God's will and self as made known to humankind.

By doubling back on Genesis 1:1 so as to lead into "the LORD God formed man of dust from the ground, and breathed into his nostrils the breath of life" (Gen 2:7), we see that the truly generational/generative act of creation is at the very first headed primarily toward day six. The heavens and earth do not create iterations of themselves but function as the stable universe within which human generating and human history is set into motion within the providence of God, who has made humanity male and female in his image. Philo sees in *bereshith* the torah of God's wording and sovereignty in history.

As noted above, Christian exegesis of Genesis 1 and kindred texts like Proverbs 8:22 saw in the substantive *arche/bereshith* of scripture's first word the Word of God. In *arche*, by his Word, God created the heavens and the earth. The motif finds confirmation in the simple and ensuing fact that God creates by speaking things into existence. His Word is his-self in creating outside of his own divine life. "And God said, let there be light" and so on for six successive days. John 1 states it clearly, "In *arche* was the Word, and the Word was with God and the Word was God. All things were made by Him and without him was not anything made that was made. In him was life and the light of men" (1:1-4). Genesis says that "the Spirit of God was moving over the face the waters" (1:2), and so the triune life is there as the eternal fellowship of creative love about to be made manifest: Elohim, Word, and Spirit, in whose image humanity is made (1:26-27). The Adam created on day six and again in 2:6 falls. But the Word who was beginning/ *arche* with God became flesh, and dwelt among us so as to show forth the power necessary to make Adam's children the children of God (1:12-13). Here Genesis and John rhyme.

The ceaseless coming and going of the generations represents creation's own groaning, and it finds its counterpart in the somber recognition of Koheleth that labor, achievement, generating children, and amassing goods is, east of Eden, no end in itself but an unhappy business under the sun. As Gregory of Nyssa saw in his homilies it took the true Ecclesiast to enter our human condition in all its brokenness and, suffering alongside Koheleth and surpassing his adamic plight, to set the course aright.[32] The generations come and the generations go, but not just the earth endureth forever, but also the redeeming work of the Word of God. There at beginning, at the most Elder of our time, and there at the end, calling us to a new heavens and a new earth.

> Show me that river
> Take me across
> Wash all my troubles away
> Like that lucky old sun
> Give me nothing to do but roll around heaven all day
> Like that lucky old sun
> Give me nothing to do but roll around heaven all day.[33]

---

[32] "Perhaps this inscription refers to the leader of the Church (*ecclesia*). The true Ecclesiastes (Christ) gathers into one assembly those persons who often have been scattered and frequently deceived. Who could he be except the true king of Israel to whom Nathaniel said, 'You are the son of God and the *king of Israel*'? If these words pertain to the king of Israel, the Son of God, as the Gospel says, then he is called Ecclesiastes. We will not deviate from the inscription's meaning provided that we learn about him who firmly establishes the Church through the Gospel and to whom these words apply. 'The words of Ecclesiastes, son of David': thus Matthew begins his gospel with the *name David and calls him Lord*" (Gregory of Nyssa; cited in J. Robert Wright, ed., *Ancient Christian Commentary of Scripture*, vol. 2 [Downers Grove, Ill.: InterVarsity, 2005]).

[33] Lyrics from "That Lucky Sun," a 1949 song written by Haven Gillespie and Beasley Smith.

15

"When Christ came into the world he said"
The Scriptural Christ in the Letter to the Hebrews

We have chosen in this chapter to look at a special case where the Elder Scripture is viewed as speaking forth mature Christian teaching. The Letter to the Hebrews is a New Testament witness of course, and so in some sense this chapter marks a departure from our procedure of attending to the Elder Scripture as such. What is striking, however, is the manner by which the letter has access to what the opening verses call "by the son speaking," which is set in contrast to "by the prophets' speaking." "Son speaking" is in fact a particular kind of Elder Scripture disclosure as the author of the letter conceives of this. Here we have a species of ontological reflection whereby the Son's speech is accessible to the Christian church directly from the first witness.

We will in the course of the examination look at one conceptually difficult instance of this manner of reflection, which appears to press it beyond its more obvious limits: son speaking in the incarnation itself. This exception only underscores how ambitious a conceptuality we encounter in the author's manner of setting forth "son speaking" in a new dispensation directly from the Elder one.

From beginning to end Hebrews demonstrates a thick reliance on/deployment of the Old Testament. But it would be wrong to think of this as a typical reliance, just with more density than other New Testament witnesses—important though that density is for how the letter manifests the use of the Old Testament compared with other books of the New Testament.[1]

It has been observed that one way Hebrews might be characterized is as negative toward the Old Covenant, to the point of supersessionism. The term is itself imprecise, it should be noted, insofar as one might also describe Judaism as supersessionistic, though on different terms, lacking as it does a priesthood, temple, land, prophecy, and various other aspects of Israelite faith and worship central to the Old Testament. But to say Hebrews views the Old Covenant negatively—a view we will test here—should not be confused with the main topic under discussion: namely, the use of the Scriptures of Israel.

The simplest way to illustrate this distinction would be to attend to those places where the criticism of sacrifice, for example, is based upon the old scriptures themselves (Heb 10:5 citing Ps 40). Or where Jeremiah's promise of a new covenant becomes central to

---

[1] See Christopher Seitz, "The Letter to the Hebrews, Biblical Theology and Identification," in my *The Character of Christian Scripture: The Significance of a Two-Testament Bible* (Grand Rapids: Baker Academic, 2011), 115–35. Andrew Lincoln views Hebrews as a particularly pertinent example of biblical theology arising within the Bible itself: "of all the New Testament writings Hebrews provides us with the most focused and explicit treatment of the relationship between the new revelation in Christ and God's previous disclosure" (Lincoln, "Hebrews and Biblical Theology," in Craig Bartholomew et al., eds., *Out of Egypt: Biblical Theology and Biblical Interpretation* [Grand Rapids: Zondervan, 2004], 313–38). Note how reflexively a contrast is presupposed between "new revelation in Christ" and "God's previous disclosures." As we shall see, in Hebrews revelation in Christ exists exclusively through the vehicle of previous disclosures.

the argument of the author of Hebrews. That is, the not A-but-B conceptuality of Hebrews seeks to ground itself within the Old Testament's own theological grammar.² The Old Testament itself does question sacrifice in relationship to other priorities that must be present: obedient wills and compliant hearts. Hebrews could quote Jeremiah 7:22: "For in the day I brought them out of the land of Egypt, I did not speak to your fathers or command them concerning burnt offerings and sacrifices. But this command I gave them, 'Obey my voice and I will be your God and shall be my people.'" So to declare Hebrews hostile to the Old Testament would be to roster it alongside Old Testament witnesses. The first and oldest word about sacrifice and obedience is not obsolete but remains normative.

Parenthetically, this is what makes the Old Testament the kind of astonishing literature that gives rise to the book of Jonah, which opens the entire life of Israel to a criticism—sympathetic and humorous all the same—that emerges from within its own self-monitoring. Hebrews isn't latter epoch, exterior criticism of an older and obsolete day, but one that insists it must rise up from within the scriptures' own voice. And so the paradox of particularly heavy citation in the service of declaring the Old Testament's own voice, this in turn being Christ's voice, or by-the-son speaking (Heb 1:2).

This raises an important hermeneutical question on two fronts at least. Does this use of the Old Testament happen in what we might call a proper—that is to say, accurate, responsible, comprehensive, non-specious—reading of the sense-making of the scriptures of Israel? And second, to what degree does Hebrews' use of the Old Testament offer a model for our own reading? This second question is tied up with the project of many recent New Testament scholars' efforts to explain how a New Testament author uses the scriptures of Israel, as a piece of historical re-description,

---

² Jeremiah 31 quoted for five verses and glossed, "in speaking of a new covenant, God makes the old obsolete."

also intended as a model for our emulation, once the historical specification of hermeneutical technique has been carried out.³ To illustrate the problematical character of this as a Christian reflex one need only turn to John Calvin, who routinely notes the flexibility of the New Testament's use of the Old Testament and judges it a free rendering that does not to tell us definitively/finally what the Old Testament as Scripture means to continue communicating now as Christian scripture.

Hebrews can also serve to frustrate this recent New Testament project in that (1) its link to Paul is unclear (typically, Paul-of-the-genuine-letters is the exemplar in this project), (2) it is a unique individual witness in the New Testament canon, and (3) the use of it on just these individualized terms can lead to a wrong kind of supersessionism, severed from any balance from the wider New Testament canon.⁴ So the emulation project, insofar as it is a proper hermeneutical position at all, begins to turn back on itself when it comes to reading Hebrews as an individual witness as against other parts of the New Testament canon.⁵

The canonical dimension has been raised by Childs and others. It asks whether and how far one can read any witness as a discrete testimony, independent of and indeed over against other witnesses,

---

³ See, for example, Richard B. Hays, *Echoes of Scripture in the Letters of Paul* (New Haven: Yale University Press, 1989). See Seitz, "Letter to the Hebrews," in *Character of Christian Scripture*, 93–113.

⁴ "The ending does not propose a direct link with Paul by attributing to him the authorship. Rather, it offers an indirect relationship through Timothy with whom the unknown writer shares a common ministry . . . it is significant that the letter to the Hebrews has not been brought within this circle (Paul and Pastorals). It has been assigned a position just outside this corpus" (Brevard S. Childs, *The New Testament as Canon: An Introduction* [Philadelphia: Fortress, 1984], see 417–18).

⁵ The problem has to be confronted by Lincoln in "Hebrews and Biblical Theology." The reader is free to "relativize" and "critique" the New Testament since that is the stance Lincoln views as operative by the author of Hebrews vis-à-vis the Old Testament. But then what of the supersessionism ingredient in this kind of hermeneutic? Lincoln at least sees the issue and tries to deal with it as a consequence of his reading stance.

precisely when the focus is on an author's redescribed intentions in the compass of a single witness. Further, one could ask if this how Paul, for example, wished his use of the Old Testament to operate. His is a model but not monolithic reading of the scripture he holds to be sacred and that will continue to sound forth its notes for Christian guidance and God's word, alongside whatever use he might wish to make of it or commend on more general terms. Single authorial intention ("I Paul mean this") is not so easily excavated, especially when recourse is being made by said author to scriptural witnesses that have their own order of ongoing divine authority and intentionality. More generally, inspired authors say more under inspiration than any account of single historical intention can comprehend and re-describe. Paul's reading of Deuteronomy, for example, belongs to the occasion of his letter's purpose, and its own canonical intentionality as Christian scripture is not thereby delimited. I take up these questions in some detail in the Brazos Colossians commentary.[6]

The question becomes even more acute when it comes to a witness like Hebrews, whose association with the Pauline Letter collection has always been questioned—if indeed that is what its position in the canon, usually following Philemon and preceding the Catholic Epistle, even means to communicate.[7] So who is the author and who is his audience and what does it mean to read Hebrews as a discrete witness? Questions like this become even more fraught when one seeks to compare, say, the use of the Old Testament in Romans and Colossians, thinking that comparisons are how one truly appreciates the witness, as against complementarity across differentiated books.

---

[6] Christopher Seitz, *Colossians*, Brazos Theological Commentary on the Bible (Grand Rapids: Brazos, 2014). See also my two-part "Jewish Scripture for Gentile Churches," *ProEccl* 23 (2014).

[7] On the movement of Hebrews in the New Testament canon, see David Trobisch, *Paul's Letter Collection* (Minneapolis: Fortress, 1994); Brevard S. Childs, *The Church's Guide for Reading Paul: The Canonical Shaping of the Pauline Corpus* (Grand Rapids: Eerdmans, 2008).

Childs pursues this angle of view when he discusses Hebrews' use of the old scriptures and reference to the Old Covenant both. He judges it as marking a kind of outer limit, beyond which the Letter of Barnabas goes. For Barnabas the giving of the Law has no constructive, enduring divine intention beyond preoccupying Israel with unimportant regulations. So Hebrews is bounded by its difference from Barnabas on one side and its location within the New Testament canon on the other, whose correlate witnesses prevent Hebrews from being read in isolation. Such is Childs' hermeneutical position on canon.[8]

There is another approach to Hebrews: its use of the Old Testament and its hermeneutical usefulness. This is the position of Andrew Lincoln. He judges Hebrews a uniquely significant example for biblical theology because of the numerous references it makes to the Old Testament. The author of Hebrews adapts the sense of the Old Testament to pastoral issues he is concerned to address, and in so doing, demonstrates the flexibility that any reader must bring to the Old Testament *and New Testament both*. As the author of Hebrews adjusted the Old word of scripture in the light of changed circumstances, so the Christian reader adopts the same hermeneutic when it comes to the second witness of the New Testament. So the supersessionism of Hebrews—the judgment is here largely correct according to Lincoln—is now not to be followed, because the flexibility of the author is what matters, not the content of his judgments. Just as the content of the Old Testament needed

---

[8] "Whereas the writer of Hebrews understood the old ordinances largely symbolically, Barnabas saw the Mosaic law as a pernicious delusion and the work of an evil power (IX.4). In sum, the book of Hebrews marked an outer limit within the early church in its appraisal of the Old Testament as mere 'shadow' of the New" (Childs, *Biblical Theology of the Old and New Testaments: Theological Reflection on the Christian Bible* [Minneapolis: Fortress, 1993], 312–13). Parenthetically, I do not know why the previous caution about avoiding use of the terms "Old" and "New Testaments" when speaking of Hebrews and the Old Covenant (at a time when there was no Old Testament and New Testament) is not observed. The Old Covenant might be viewed as "shadow" but not the Old Testament Scriptures (later so-called).

critical evaluation, which Lincoln judges Hebrews to major in, so too the modern reader faces the New Testament's own ethical injunctions with discrimination and correction.

It is here that our own account of Hebrews' use of the scriptures of Israel will take its departure. It is our judgment that there are places where the use of these scriptures is quite distinctive measured against what one sees in the Letters of Paul or the Gospels and Acts. Appreciating this unique vantage point and conceptuality will go a long way in refining how we understand the scriptures functioning in Hebrews, and also how we might responsibly learn to use them given now the presence of a second testament and two-volume Christian scripture.

Son Speaking

Given its position as a solemn preface (Heb 1:1-4), the opening verses of Hebrews likely intend to give us some important clue to how the author means to classify his understanding of divine revelation. There is on his account "by the prophets speaking" and "by the son speaking." That this is only partly a temporal distinction—"BC speech" and "AD speech"—is clear when one attends to three facets, borne out when one proceeds to track the use of scripture in Hebrews to follow, not least in the immediately ensuing collocation of Old Testament verses (1:5-13).

First, Hebrews wants to distinguish the category sonship from angelship. The son is superior. "For to which of the angels did God say . . ." (1:5)?

So too there is speaking by prophets (to the fathers) and speaking by a son (to us). The initial distinction is one of genre (plural speech to plural past audience; singular speech to us). It should be added that speaking by a son can also arguably include God's speaking to the Son. Hebrews 1:5-14 is just this kind of speech.

Secondly, the speaking by a son never takes the form of "AD speaking," that is, selections of citations from the earthly Jesus: distinctive teachings from the sermon on the mount, last supper, the passion narratives, and so forth. The author can characterize the earthly son, but he does not do this by recording his speaking. A good example is 5:7-10 ("in the days of his flesh Jesus offered up loud cries and tears"); incidentally this is one of the few places where the name Jesus appears at all in Hebrews, accompanied by the distinctive "in his earthly days." Son speaking is not this. The unusual case of 10:5 ("when Christ came into the world he said") is the subject of evaluation below.

Related to this and crucially, by-the-son speaking takes the form of citations from the Old Testament, either as speech from God to Christ or pertaining to Christ the son ("You are my son, today I have begotten you," Heb 2:5 and 5:5 [Ps 2:7]; "I shall be a father to him," Heb 2:5 [2 Sam 7:14]); from God to God the son ("Your throne O God, is forever and ever . . . God, your God, has anointed you," Heb 2:8-9 [Ps 45:6-7]); from God to the Lord Christ ("You, Lord, laid the foundations of the earth in the beginning, they will perish but you remain . . . you are the same and your years will have no end," Heb 1:10-12 [Ps 102:25-27]); from God and/or the Holy Spirit to the present generation ("Today, if you hear his, Christ's, voice, harden not your hearts," Heb 3:7; 3:15; 4:7 [Ps 95:7-11]; "This is the covenant I will make with them," Heb 10:16 [Jer 31:33]); or directly from Christ himself ("when Christ came into the world he said, 'sacrifices and offerings you have not desired, but a body you have prepared for me,'" Heb 10:5 [Ps 40:6-8]). The temporal audience is later (it is last days speaking as 1:2 has it; or the world to come, when considered from the temporal standpoint of the old), but the address, the son speaking, comes all the same from the old scriptures and not an AD, "in the days of his flesh," record. It can even be both by-the-prophets speaking, but now pertaining to last days by-the-son speaking, as in the case of Jeremiah 31 or as with the frequent recourse to David's speech in the Psalms. The audience of Moses was addressed with warning, which it did not heed, as Psalm 95 tells us, now in prophet David's psalmic speaking. But that word of prophet David's later rehearsal was always calibrated precisely to address the "today" of

"When Christ came into the world he said" 251

Hebrews' audience, and it is what the author would call by-the-son speaking, not retrospectively but *prospectively*. This is the point of the long argument in Hebrews 3–4 concerning David's later use of the Moses material, thus making "today" a future referent, and the promised rest not that of the time of Joshua (Heb 4:8-11). That is, the prospective hermeneutic is not invented from a retrospective stance, but rather the author of Hebrews seizes on a dynamic already present in the Elder Scripture. I will return to the final refrain that concludes the long disquisition on Psalm 95 in a moment. Here it is where the author declares the living and active character of God's word.

In the final chapters there is also direct divine speech to the present generation from the old scriptures that is a catena of prophetic declarations (10:37-38; Habakkuk and Isaiah) or wisdom (Job and Proverbs) that one might think is by-the-prophets speaking, and so it is. But it is speech directed to the audience of Hebrews and would not be able to be classified as other than by-the-son speaking also, to which response is made by the author and the present generation "we" in the words of Psalm 118 and Psalm 56, at Hebrews 13:6 ("so we can confidently say 'The Lord is my helper, I will not fear; what can man do to me?'"). The author of Hebrews sees by-the-son speaking emerging directly from the scriptures of Israel, as the speech of God, of Son, and of Holy Spirit; as speech of God to the Son as Lord and as God; and as speech of the incarnate one himself. As we shall see, the final one is the most ambitious, because it lacks the temporal moveable feast character of the others, where the colloquies have no fixed temporal framework but consist of divine dialogues of various kinds in their use by Hebrews.

The example of the last kind comes in clearest form in 10:5. In point of fact, this kind of by-the-son-speaking is the rarest of what we see in Hebrews. Here reference is specifically to the incarnate Son as incarnate. The other colloquies exist in the context of the exalted Son's eternal relationship to God—temporally unmarked, as it were. The example of 2:6-9, where Psalm 8 is drawn upon for by-the-son speaking, contrasts the promises of God to humanity in by-the-prophets-speaking as unfulfilled, but then as made effective in the Son, now "crowned with glory and honor." So even as it speaks of the son of man subjected—whether the reference is to the son of man contrasted with the God of creation in Psalm 8, or of the son of God in that role in his earthly life—this is to establish a contrast with the glory now beheld in him, to whom the church looks in hope.[9]

It may be for this reason that the use of Psalm 40 to speak of the actual incarnate life forced the author of Hebrews onto slightly more difficult terrain when it comes to using the Old Testament to enact son speaking.[10] In the other cases, the temporal flexibility of divine colloquy in the Old Testament allowed for an equally flexible deployment of them as speech from God to Son as last-days speaking in temporally unmarked form. The examples of 1:8-9 and 1:10-12 are no exceptions. Though arguably speech from David or Psalmist to God, they contain elements in that form that allow them to function now as speech from God to God the Son

---

[9] I deal with this subject at some length in *Character of Christian Scripture*, 118–27. See also the treatment of Psalm 8 and Hebrews' use of it in Childs, *Biblical Theology in Crisis* (Philadelphia: Westminster, 1970).

[10] In *The Birth of the Trinity: Jesus, God, and Spirit in New Testament and Early Christian Interpretations of the Old Testament* (Oxford: Oxford University Press, 2015), Bates writes, "Even if several enigmas exist" (1) but then initially hovers over them in the confident interpretation he adduces for Ps 40's use in Heb 10: "These prophetic visitors—here he means the David of Psalm 40—could listen as God the Father spoke with the preexistent Son, as the Father, for instance lovingly described the way he was preparing a human body for him" (5). But the father (using this conceptuality) is addressed in Ps 40; he does not describe anything. The preexistent Son is not being addressed in the psalm but is himself speaking, and he is clearly not preexistent—this is the challenge we are dealing with in the rubric, "when Christ came into the world he said. . . ." Later he clarifies that "the preincarnate Jesus Christ is thanking God the Father for the body God has made for him . . . just as Christ was entering the world." While plausible, this shows the absolute limit of what the use of a psalm in these temporal conditions could tolerate for true application. Harold W. Attridge speaks more generally of the significance of 10:5 "because it indicates the cosmos as the sphere of the decisive sacrifice of Christ" (Attridge, *Hebrews: A Commentary on the Epistle to the Hebrews*, Hermeneia [Philadelphia: Fortress, 1989], 273).

("therefore God, your God has anointed you") because the Psalm itself (45:6-7) masterfully shifts from doxology and praise to God for Israel's king (v. 6) to address to the king himself whom God has anointed. By allowing the single voice of the Psalm to be taken up by the God addressed in the Psalm, God now sings the praises of God the son. A version of the same thing occurs in the case of Psalm 102, where God addresses the Lord who laid the foundations of the earth and speaks of his eternal life, that Lord now being the *arche* through whom all things were made.[11]

The use of Psalm 40 to speak of the incarnation involves a more challenging case, even as a modest version of the colloquy element is present and available for creative hearing and re-use ("then I said, behold I have come to do your will, O God").[12] The psalm contains the important feature the author would be looking for in the context of an argument about sacrifice in the old covenant, now to serve the purpose of by-the-son-speaking. The Psalmist is in a moment of exhilaration and joy because God has delivered him. He cannot wait to speak of God's deeds and thoughts toward him/us. God has not desired sacrifices and yet has given him an open ear and enabled him to step forward in obedience. God's law is in his very heart.

We see a similar frame of reference in Psalm 51. The psalmist would be happy to provide sacrifices if God so willed it. But here what is of greater purpose is a broken and contrite heart. This itself is a kind of sacrifice: "the sacrifices of God are a broken spirit" (51:17). And so the Psalm ends by speaking of a repaired Zion,

---

[11] See the still highly significant overview by C. F. Burney, "Christ as the APXH of Creation (Prov. viii 22, Col. I 15–18, Rev. iii 14)," *JTS* 27 (1926): 160–77.

[12] For Luther's appeal to colloquies in the royal psalms to confirm proper Trinitarian exegesis, see Helmer, "Luther's Trinitarian Hermeneutic and the Old Testament," *Modern Theology* 18 (2002). My account is influenced by that essay's investigation of the royal psalms. Luther believes that the Old Testament has a Trinitarian pressure wherein David is gifted by the Holy Spirit to hear exchanges between the Father and the Son. No one is taking a role in a drama. For Luther, this is what the literal sense actually means.

and of sacrifices once again being pleasing, and once again being offered. This isn't an either-or, in other words, but a matter of the proper relationship between two things (heart and sacrifices), especially in deep brokenness and despair—the sin of David with Bathsheba—or in reflexive and deep joyful obedience (Ps. 40). In such an instance, the law can be said to be functioning within the heart.

It has been noted that the author of Hebrews has had to make some very minor changes occasioned by the use of Psalm 40 in order for the psalm to function well, even with its important colloquy language. That these are his own changes can be seen by their subtle departure from Greek translations we have in major uncial form. Instead of Greek "you did not seek" (*ouk 'ethelesas*) the author of Hebrews produces at verse 6 "you were not pleased" (*ouk eudodokesas*).[13] The final citation at verse 7 is shortened over against the Greek and rearranged. Left out altogether is "your law is in my heart." In the paraphrase the author himself provides at verse 8, all references to sacrifice are changed to plurals, while in the actual quotation "whole burnt offerings" is the departure from the Greek alone.

What, then, are we to make of the citation in Greek "a body thou hast prepared for me" instead of the admittedly interesting Hebrew: "ears you have dug out"?[14] It is assumed frequently that the author of Hebrews here follows a Greek translation available to him (the reading is found in major Greek translations dating in the fourth–fifth century). Attridge calls it an interpretive paraphrase in the Greek, one whose logic is not hard to follow.[15] To have an ear carved out, like a circumcised heart, is a way to speak of a receptive

---

[13] Attridge (*Hebrews*) wonders if other psalms have influenced the author's alteration, notably 51:16, 19. That makes it no less an adaptation. Is the problem that God does indeed seek/want sacrifices, and in Psalm 40, this is set aside because the Psalmist found that the law was in his heart and he was enabled to step forward in joy all the same?

[14] The Hebrew text has its own interesting history of interpretation.

[15] Attridge, *Hebrews*.

will, at the center of the bodily life. By *pars pro toto*, the ear dug out becomes a prepared body. One can see Jewish and Christian interpretation of Psalm 40 take this line even leaving aside the use made of the Psalm in Hebrews 10. Rashi speaks of a dug-out ear as a sign of total obedience.[16]

When one evaluates the creative use of the Psalm for the purpose of by-the-son speaking in Hebrews 10—including changing singular to plural, rearranging the phrases in 40:7-8, leaving out the final line—why would we credit an "interpretive paraphrase" to the Greek translation we are now able to consult, and which we are assuming the author of Hebrews is using, when he is quite happy to do his own interpretive paraphrasing and does quite clearly with Psalm 40? It is for this reason that one careful evaluation of the entire use of Psalm 40 by the author of Hebrews concluded that "it was he rather than the LXX translator who came up with the *pars pro toto* metonymy as a means of highlighting the messianic significance of the psalm."[17] This gets at the slippery business of what it means to refer to "the LXX" at all, as if every New Testament author had a single Greek Old Testament Bible on their shelves, and we can have that too. Jerome translated the Psalter on the basis of the Greek tradition/s available to him, and he rendered the phrase *aures autem perfecisti mihi* or "ears you perfected for me"; his second translation from the Hebrew has *aures* as well, so there is agreement with Greek and Hebrew over "ears" and no correcting the Greek on the basis of the Hebrew as we frequently see in Jerome's *iuxta hebraica* column. For this and other reasons Ralphs accepted "ears" for the Göttingen critical edition of the Greek Psalter. (Aquila, Symmachus, and Theodotion all have *otia* and not *soma*.)

To adapt a phrase. "The ears have it."

---

[16] Mayer I. Gruber, *Rashi's Commentary on the Psalms* (Leiden: Brill, 2003).

[17] Karen H. Jobes and Moisés Silva, *Invitation to the Septuagint* (Grand Rapids: Baker Academic, 2000), 195–99. See as well the earlier judgment of Pierre Grelot ("Le texte du Psaumes 39:7 dans la Septante," *RB* 108 [2001]: 210–13).

This particular psalm created some challenges for by-the-son-speaking even as it provided a marvelous occasion of joyful stepping forward to do the will of God, and the direct speech of the one who did so, "Behold, I have come to do you will, O God." The ready ear is a body prepared. And in the light of this we can probably understand the final challenge the psalm presented. On this occasion, the author of Hebrews wanted a dialogue that might be language of the incarnate Son, speaking to God, and not a colloquy whose temporal axis was far more open to movement through time, such that it might become by-the-son speaking in the variety we have observed elsewhere. Here it is that we find explanation I believe for the otherwise temporally more challenging introductory clause: "when Christ came into the world he said" followed by a citation from Psalm 40.[18] The author wants to speak about a ready will and an obedient heart from the standpoint of incarnate life and the bodily sacrifice of the earthly savior. Not sacrifices and offerings of old, but a new kind of bodily offering, once for all.

To try to locate the Elder Testament speech in a temporal frame that would allow it to be the speech of the incarnate one, and not divine speech to him as exalted, or speech by him at another moment in his (eternally) economic life, one needs a way to say this is speech by him "when he came into the world" even as it was, by another manner of reckoning, speech by him in David in the figural life of Israel. It may be that this conceptuality is more

---

[18] Bates wants this to be the preincarnate Christ speaking just at the moment of his entering the world. See *Birth of the Trinity*, 86–87. I can understand such a perspective but cannot see how it applies to the infant incarnate one in the economy and the preexistent Christ at the same time (". . . the Spirit is perceived to be speaking from the person of Jesus Christ, and the Christ is speaking to the Father when Jesus came into the world, that is, at the moment of the incarnation"). Or, I can see, but wonder if we are entering an odd—confusedly economic—frame of reference ("The Holy Spirit is not time-bound, and the Spirit can establish a different setting for the divine speech uttered through David as the prophet takes on different roles"). Psalm 40 of course says nothing about precise moments of entering the world, by David or by a *prosopon* to whom he is referring. This is the work of the author Hebrews.

difficult for the author of Hebrews to work with, since it sees the figural Christ fully alive within the scriptures' own forward-moving conceptuality, and not just in eternal colloquies otherwise compelling for what they may be said to contribute to Christian theology from within the *scopus* of the covenant life God has with Israel. A way to illustrate this, less compactly but more accurately, would be for him to say, "When Christ came into the world, he took up that language which he had given David to say on his behalf previously." This would allow for the temporal fixity of incarnation as a reality, but likewise the forward-moving declaration by David of his dug-out ear and joyful obedience as a figure of the man Christ. Psalm 40 is not an ambitious colloquy of the kind we see in royal psalms but a radiant individual proclamation. The author of Hebrews may have got used to accessing colloquies for Christian extension and application and tried to do the same thing here with his creative introductory rubric, pushing the economic and immanent dimensions to their limit if not straining them to overload.

Conclusion

To conclude, it is important to return to our entry point and the general observation that the author of Hebrews appears on the one had to speak of an obsolete era in the past and yet uses the scriptures of that time directly to convey the truth about Christ, *to the extent that all by-the-son-speaking is always only ever old-scripture speak and takes no other form in his discourse.*

It would be a peculiar species of supersessionism that claims the old witness is in fact truth-bearing beyond our wildest dreams and constitutive of what son speaking qua son speaking is. The old witness is not put in the past (superseded by X that follows). It is shown to be ahead of us in time. The reference in 10:5 is odd because the author of Hebrews has no way to speak about "Christ coming into the world speaking" that isn't the speaking from a past record. He wants to speak about the prepared sacrificial body of Christ, and he uses Psalm 40, with his own specific alterations, to this end. This instance is the *ne plus ultra* of Hebrews' audacious accessing of colloquies from the old witness: it is discourse in the realm of divine life now brought down into the earthly frame of incarnate reference. And vice versa. Or in between. In forcing his conceptual framework into the monologue of David-Psalmist become Incarnate Son he shows how far it is that son speaking from the old scriptures is prepared to be seen as significant by the author of Hebrews.

Returning finally to our other entry point. Fortunately it is the fact of a dual witness of Old Testament and New Testament that enables us to evaluate what he has done. The scriptures of Israel have in the meantime become the Old Testament of a two-testament canon. Far from becoming obsolete or indeed cast off in the name of a superior New witness, itself alone to be called scripture, it remains in place as both the venerable and abiding part one of the Christian Bible. As such it shows us how to understand the local move of an audacious apostolic witness who was bold to take it up and hear Christ, God, and Spirit all speaking from within its single, original, ambitious providential scope. To understand the bold move of Hebrews 10:5 and to make sense of it—both at the level of the Greek creativity he displays and in the peculiar "when Christ came into the world he said" rubric he deploys—is to bring us closer to the original form of the witness and its potential in that form.

Rashi once commented about the manna of Israel's sojourn in the wilderness that the fact of its surplus and its daily melting under the sun's heat meant that it ran into streams, the water thereof to be drunk by harts and roes. These in turn were hunted by the nations of the world, who "experienced through them the taste of the manna." Thereby, and in consequence, he said, "understanding how great was Israel's excellency." We can see the power of the testimony to Christ accessed from the old scriptures by the author of Hebrews precisely because we can see what "the manna of David" looks like in the form God first gave it. Without that, we cannot taste the excellency that is the manna or its distillate, both partaking the form of Christ, in the manner of God's economic disposing in prophet (Moses) and apostle (Paul): "all drank from the same spiritual drink, for they drank from the spiritual Rock that followed them, and the Rock was Christ." Would the author of Hebrews have been surprised that the old scriptures would continue to have their providential role as Christian scripture, standing alongside—should we say above—his own creative deployment? We cannot know.

But the inspired author can see only so far at any rate. God, who is the first word, has the last word. The canon of scripture in its comprehensive, mysterious totality allows the manna and the true bread from heaven to intersect and to reveal their full testimony by seeing them in accordance one with the other. When Christ came into the world he said what he had been saying figurally in David, now opened onto the horizon of Israel and church both, through the witness of prophet and apostle. Inspiration means being given more to say than any single age can comprehend, and canon is the means by which to see all that come true in accordance.

Or as the author of Hebrews himself put it at a moment of inspired insight, enclosing us and himself both.

> For the word of God is living and active, sharper than any two-edged sword, piercing to the division of soul and spirit, of joints and marrow, and discerning the thoughts and intentions of the heart. And before him no creature is hidden, but all are open and laid bare to the eyes of him with whom we have to do. (4:12)

16

Theophany and Trinity

We have looked at the variety of exegetical impulses vis-à-vis the Elder Testament that may be said to manifest a sustained interest in ontology in the theological interpretations of the early church. These give rise to the earliest Trinitarian reflections. The literal sense of the Old Testament pressures a theological appreciation of the ontology of the God of Israel and his Word made known through colloquies in the Psalms, divine agency in creation (Genesis, Proverbs, Ecclesiastes), the subtle out-workings of the name of God (YHWH Elohim), and son speaking from the scriptures of Israel as identified by the author of the Letter to the Hebrews. A rich figural repertoire likewise exists to bespeak the manifestation of the Word of God within God's life with his people Israel.

Theophanies were a classical locus for certain early church exegetes to think about the divine life in agency. The rich opportunities for this in the Elder Scripture did not come in one fixed form but in several. Yet the appearance of angels or other intermediaries did not translate immediately into credible articulations of the fully divine presence. One needed to exercise caution because of witnesses like the Letter to the Hebrews and other sources, which of course declared angelic agency a category not compatible with what one might mean on the same level of Elohim-YHWH-*kurios*.

In the name of relative completeness—for the richness of the Elder Scripture as funding Christian theology is simply organized here, not comprehended—this chapter looks at the theophany appearances and how they might be said to occupy an appropriate category for Christian Trinitarian reflection.

We start with some typical reflections from the early church to edge up to our concerns in this chapter. Note the recapitulative character of time that animates their perspective on Elder Scripture.

What makes the significance of incarnation and suffering/death/resurrection is the ability to argue this has been planned from long ago. Much like the speech of God to Moses, which explains that the contest with Pharaoh will be intentionally drawn out to God's larger purpose, and that the crossing at the Sea won't be a meteorological quirk but will show him to be "I am as I am," so that all may know that, so Melito writes of the Lord's temporal staging in this way:

> Indeed, the Lord prearranged his own sufferings in the patriarchs, and in the prophets, and in the whole people of God, giving his sanction to them through the law and the prophets. For that which was to exist in a new and grandiose fashion was preplanned in advance, in order that when it should come into existence one light attain to faith, just because it had been predicted long in advance. (Melito of Sardis, *On Easter* 57)

The manner of this disclosure is found in historical types. Chrysostom has his own way of stating this, as noted above.

> The fact that he has a Son, however, the inspired authors registered ahead of time in the Bible, neither speaking with complete clarity lest they fail to respect your limitations, nor concealing the truth so as to give you a chance later to come to your senses and to glean from your own Bible the teachings of truth.

In agreement with Melito, Clement of Alexandria sees in the preplanned character of the manifestation of the logos the entire key to what it means for there to be a fulfillment powerfully designed to give rise to faith.

> But on the Scriptures being opened up, and declaring the truth to those who have ears, they proclaim the very suffering endured by the flesh, which the Lord assumed, to be the power and wisdom of God. And finally, the parabolic style of Scripture being of the greatest antiquity, as we have shown, abounded most, as was to be expected, in the prophets, in order that the Holy Spirit might show that the philosophers among the Greeks, and the wise men among the Barbarians besides, were ignorant of the future coming of the Lord, and of the mystic teaching that was to be delivered by Him. Rightly then, *prophecy, in proclaiming the Lord, in order not to seem to some to blaspheme while speaking what was beyond the ideas of the multitude, embodied its declarations in expressions capable of leading to other conceptions* . . . Whence also Peter, in his Preaching, speaking of the apostles, says: But we, unrolling the books of the prophets which we possess, who name Jesus Christ, partly in parables, partly in enigmas, partly expressly and in so many words, find His coming and death, and cross, and all the rest of the tortures which the Jews inflicted on Him, and His resurrection and assumption to heaven previous to the capture of Jerusalem. As it is written, "These things are all that He behooves to suffer, and what should be after Him." Recognizing them, therefore, we have believed in God

in consequence of what is written respecting Him. (*Stromata* 6; emphasis added)[1]

The Elder character of the disclosed content means that God has been at work from eternity, so that when Christ comes in the flesh, he comes in accordance with a public record against which his climaxing work can be seen for what it is in God's superintendence of time: "I will be as I will be in my promise keeping with my people." One might mention as well the ongoing character of the word of the scriptures as directing the eschatological hopes of the church, making possible the calibration in faith of first and final Advents of the Lord.

Irenaeus sees the logos of God actively resident within the people of Israel. Thinking of the reverse direction, he understands Christ's incarnation as a reparticipation in the life of Israel within which he had previously been an actor *asarkos* and *incarnadans*, now accomplishing a final recapitulative salvation in his life amongst us, culminating in the cross and the defeat of Satan as the new Adam.

Our concern has been to argue that the Elder Testament had and has its own providential role in articulating the doctrine of God toward which Trinitarian confession is calibrated. The New Testament has no doctrine of God properly speaking. It assumes the theological framework of the Old Testament as describing the One God "with whom we have to do."

---

[1] I take the reference to mean: the literal/historical sense as uttered forth by the prophets, because divinely given, had to make sense to themselves and their contemporaries *so as not to blaspheme* and function properly as God's speech. Yet, God *embodied its declarations in expressions capable of leading to other conceptions* so that it would serve the confirming role in showing the accordance between the logos of God in Israel and in the incarnation. *Expressions leading to other conceptions* is a nicely turned phase. Chrysostom's language above is similar, though more negatively framed given his interlocuters: "neither speaking with complete clarity so as to respect . . . limitations, nor concealing the truth." This is an important conceptual framework.

Justin Martyr

The one major figure not taken up in any detail thus far is Justin Martyr, and his special contribution to our topic found in the *First Apology* and the *Dialogue with Trypho*. His work has been the subject of several significant explications recently by Bogdon Bucur.[2] A scholar of the early church, Bucur notes at present the beginning of an important collapse of the borderline one might have tried to maintain for scholarly precision between patristics and early Christian origins. He has in mind the New *Religionsgeschichtliche Schule*, as he calls it, composed of New Testament scholars like Hurtado, Gathercole, Boyarin, and others.[3] One should include here work not so narrowly classifiable, in my judgment, such as contributions from Richard Bauckham, Kavin Rowe, David Yeago, and others.[4] The first studies the religious phenomenon of worship and early Jewish varieties of monotheism, and the second works more specifically on the pressure said to be arising from the Elder Scriptures given the need to articulate the work of Christ in invariable relationship

---

[2] Bogdan G. Bucur, "Justin Martyr's Exegesis on Biblical Theophanies and the Parting of the Ways between Christianity and Judaism," *TS* 75 (2014): 34–51; also relevant is his " 'Early Christian Binitarianism': From Religious Phenomenon to Polemical Insult to Scholarly Concept," *MT* 27 (2011): 102–20; and "Clement of Alexandria's Exegesis of Old Testament Theophanies," *Phronema* 29 (2014): 61–79.

[3] Larry Hurtado, "The Binitarian Shape of Early Christian Worship," in Carey C. Newman, James R. Davila, and Gladys S. Lewis, eds., *The Jewish Roots of Christological Monotheism* (Leiden: Brill, 1999), 187–213; Simon J. Gathercole, *The Preexistent Son: Recovering the Christologies of Matthew, Mark, and Luke* (Grand Rapids: Eerdmans, 2006); Daniel Boyarin, *The Jewish Gospels: The Story of the Jewish Christ* (New York: The New Press, 2012).

[4] Richard Bauckham, *God Crucified: Monotheism and Christology in the New Testament* (Grand Rapids: Eerdmans, 1998); C. Kavin Rowe, "Biblical Pressure and Trinitarian Hermeneutics," *ProEccl* 11 (2002): 295–312, and "Romans 10:13: What Is the Name of the Lord?" *HBT* 22 (2000): 135–73. See also the comments on Yeago in the following note.

to the descriptions of God inherited from the scriptures. Of course there is overlap.[5]

That New Testament and early church scholarship begin to encounter one another ought to come as no surprise because both are recognizing the significant role the Elder Testament has on the texts in question: second century interpreters like Justin, Melito, and Irenaeus, and the New Testament sources themselves. Bucur is keen to establish that the achievement of Justin when it comes to articulating the binitarian conception of theology shared by varieties of Jews and Christians—the terminology is anachronistic and too binary—belongs "in the air," as it were. It is not the particular achievement of Justin but one that predates him and with which he works. "The argument from theophanies did not derive *from* Justin's second-century antidualistic polemics but was the extension *to* such a purpose of a much older exegetical tradition belonging to the Christian discourse *ad intra*, in the context of worship and celebration."[6]

Here one notes the specific attention paid to what earlier he calls "history of religion." To speak of "the context of worship and celebration" via the language of "a *much older* exegetical tradition" (emphasis added) is however to raise a question about the form, provenance, and date of this "exegetical tradition" strictly speaking. The "exegetical tradition" he is referring to is presumably the particular handling of the Elder Scriptures Justin and the apostolic writings (to be referred to as New Testament scripture in time) both may be said to share. That is to say, for Justin and for the apostolic writings of the period *both* the same scriptural pressure from a single authoritative Testament is at work. The "much older exegetical" reality is indeed much, much older: it is the scriptures of Israel themselves. Justin's arguments for how one might appreciate the theological claims pressuring forth and challenging him

---

[5] See the perceptive comments of David Yeago regarding the distinction between judgments and concepts in David Yeago, "The New Testament and the Nicene Dogma: A Contribution to the Recovery of Theological Exegesis," *ProEccl* 3 (1994): 152–64.

[6] Bucur, "Justin Martyr's Exegesis," 47.

and Trypho in respect of proper evaluation spring from a single source, equally old and equally contemporary in terms of its claim to be the sole arbiter of the truth of the matter. Here they agree entirely. There can be no doubt that Justin's arguments are later than the earliest Christian *kerygma*. But Justin is not arguing with Trypho on that basis. If he did, citing a New Testament of equal authority as the Elder Testament, Trypho would simply conclude that Justin has changed the subject and left the field of play. What is required is a persuasive claim to the truth of this single witness shared by them both.

At stake here is the observation of von Campenhausen and others that in the earliest Christian commentary the only scripture cited as scripture is the Elder Testament.[7] One can see evidence of the apostolic arguments, but they have not yet been cited *as scripture*. The observations of Irenaeus and Clement and others about the rule of faith presuppose that the rule intends to constrain how a single scripture is properly to be heard.[8] In this sense, Irenaeus and Justin share the same basic field of play. Both are endeavoring to hear the single scripture as pressuring forth the theological position of God's relationship to the logos, who has been made flesh, over against rival claims by various kinds of "Jewish" and "Christian" interlocutors.

---

[7] Hans von Campenhausen, *The Formation of the Christian Bible* (Philadelphia: Fortress, 1972). "We must remember that by 'Scripture' the Fathers, up to Irenaeus, Hippolytus, and Theophilus of Antioch, usually meant the Old Testament. At first this was the only approved and recommended collection of writings. But the paradosis of the Church, faithful to that of the apostles, was precisely the transmission of the Christ-event, as based documentarily on the Old Testament writings, and at the same time, explaining the meaning of these writings" (Yves Congar, *Tradition and Traditions* [London: Burns and Oates, 1966], 31). Similar quotes from von Campenhausen, John Behr, and Ellen Flesseman-Van Leer can be seen in Christopher Seitz, *The Character of Christian Scripture: The Significance of a Two-Testament Bible* (Grand Rapids: Baker Academic, 2011), 191–203.

[8] Seitz, "The Rule of Faith, Hermeneutics, and the Character of Christian Scripture," in *Character of Christian Scripture*, 191–203.

What Bucur and others helpfully show is that the position of Trypho would appear to admit of an exegetical take on the shared scriptures in which conceded is that the One God has an active agency that is equally divine.

> The God who communed with Moses from the bush was not the Maker of all things, but He who has been shown to have manifested Himself to Abraham and to Isaac and to Jacob; who also is called and perceived to be the Angel of God the Maker of all things, because He publishes to men the commands of the Father and Maker of all things. (Justin, *Dial.* 60)

The position had been regarded as so rogue that no Jew possibly could have held it, or alternatively the figure of Trypho is simply a cipher to set up Justin's counterfactuals for his audience. Bucur, by contrast, locates a realistic Trypho within the range of Judaisms at the time, which now complicate our picture, not unlike what it means to speak of "Christians" given the internal debates, disagreements, and polemics which we also know mark the period. While Trypho, he believes, can and does hold such a view—and he would not be alone from outside the "Christian" circle—at the same time Trypho clarifies in what way he disagrees vehemently with Justin over Justin's own conclusion in favor of Christ as God. On Trypho's lips is placed the Christian position, which he judges blasphemous and not within the scope of his own rather audacious description of God the Manifestor (if one may call it that, as distinct from God the Creator, Father and Maker of all things). The Christian position he avers is this:

> This crucified man was with Moses and Aaron, and spoke with them in the pillar of the cloud; . . . he became man, was crucified, and ascended into heaven, and will return again to this earth; and . . . he should be worshipped. (*Dial.* 38.1)

and

Theophany and Trinity 269

> Jesus Christ is Son of God and Apostle, and was formerly Logos and was sometimes revealed in the form of fire and sometimes in an incorporeal image. But now, having become a human being by the will of God for the sake of the human race . . . (*Apol.* 63.10)

Based upon the content as provided, these views are representative of the contemporaneous writings of Irenaeus, Clement, and others more than a "much older exegetical tradition" we can identify in the New Testament. This is not a major point. At issue is the existence of a form of binitarianism based upon a reading of the shared Elder Testament that Justin and Trypho, and other early Christian exegetes, could actually share. The ontological space is there for development. The place where the disagreement manifests itself is whether Christ incarnate and crucified is this "God Manifestor" in his life in Israel. Bucur refers to the Elder Scriptures as "the rewritten Bible" in Christian handling. Yet the Elder Scriptures are not being "rewritten" in the view of early and later Christian exegetes. They are delivering their essential literal sense in an extensional mode of reference. Justin and Trypho share the same scripture—this is what makes charges to the contrary when they occasionally appear sensible—but they disagree over whether the space open for "God Manifestor" is held by Jesus Christ, who is the logos made flesh and crucified under Pontius Pilate. Moses and the prophets are not for Trypho "men of Christ" (*Apol.* 63:17). There are indeed such for the early exegetical tradition of the Fathers.

We hope this limited glimpse into the arguments of Justin and others in respect of theophanies serves to give indication of this further extensional reach of the Elder Testament in Christian exegesis. In each and every case we have examined in part 3, the context of argument and the literal sense itself is not lifted arbitrarily into a realm other than its rootedness in Israel's real life in time with God as testified to publicly in the texts of the Elder Scripture. The historical sense, as we mean it, remains. To be sure this historical sense is not a realm of reconstructed authors and audiences en route to a final literary stopping point, but is rather the canonical presentation as we mean that in the late-modern, critically informed dress of canonical interpretation. The fact that Trypho and Justin are fighting over just this common witness, and the latter insists with vigor this must be so, means that neither are permitted to access a different kind of sense-making except one that is persuasive to both, or argued ought to be.

Conclusion

Such, then, is their system, which neither *the prophets* announced, nor *the Lord* taught, nor *the apostles* delivered . . . They endeavour to adapt with an air of probability to their own peculiar assertions the parables of *the Lord*, the sayings of *the prophets*, and the words of *the apostles*, in order that their scheme may not seem altogether without support. In doing so, however, they disregard *the order and connection* of the Scriptures, and so far as in them lies, dismember and destroy the truth. By transferring passages, and dressing them up anew, and making one thing out of another, they succeed in . . . adapting the oracles of the Lord to their opinions. Their manner of acting is just as if one, when a beautiful image of a king has been constructed by some skilful artist out of precious jewels, should then take this likeness of the man all to pieces, should rearrange the gems, and so fit them together as to make them all into the form of a dog or a fox, and even that but poorly executed; and should then maintain and declare that this was the beautiful image of the king which the skilful artist constructed, pointing to the jewels which had been admirably fitted together by the first artist to form the image of the king, but have been with bad effect transferred by the latter one to the shape of a dog, and by thus exhibiting the jewels, should deceive the ignorant who had no conception what a king's form was like, and persuade them that the miserable likeness of the fox was, in fact, the beautiful image of the king. In like manner do these persons patch together old wives' fables, and then endeavor, by violently drawing away from their proper connections, words, expressions, and parables whenever found, to adapt the oracles of God to their baseless fictions.

Irenaeus, *Against Heresies* 1.8.1

In the literal meaning of Scripture, the logos is not, properly speaking, incarnated as he is in the humanity of Jesus, and this is what allows us to speak of a comparison: he is, nevertheless, already truly incorporated there; he himself dwells there, not just some idea of him, and this is what authorizes us to speak already of his coming, of his hidden presence.

Henri de Lubac, *History and Spirit*[1]

In the realm of biblical commentary, the interpreters of the School of Antioch (chiefly Diodore of Tarsus, Theodore of Mopsuestia, and Theodoret of Cyr) are often considered the most historically oriented of the period. They could also be characterized as concerned with single-sense making, which they believed preserved a proper approach to scripture as against the School of Alexandria and the allegorical approach adopted there.[2] They all wrote commentaries on the Psalms that we can

---

[1] Henri de Lubac, *History and Spirit: The Understanding of Scripture According to Origen* (San Francisco: Ignatius, 2007), 389.

[2] Christopher Seitz, "Psalm 2 in the Entry Hall of the Psalter: Extended Sense in the History of Interpretation," in Ephraim Radner, ed., *Church, Society, and the Christian Common Good* (Eugene, Ore.: Cascade), 97–104.

consult, and the latter two also completed full commentary treatments of the Book of the Twelve. Theodoret is conscious of the charges leveled at Theodore, and though he does not refer to him by name, a careful reader can see where he creates distance between himself and his prolific predecessor.

For a time modern interpreters looked at the Antiochenes as something like the precursors of historical-critical method. Bultmann wrote his dissertation on the (then newly discovered) writings of Theodore of Mopsuestia.[3] Their fashionable status in this respect has had to be adjusted, however, as scholars over time accepted that the similarities were overdrawn.[4] Antiochene exegesis may be interested in single-sense making and history, but it is a very simple account of historical reference over against the vastly different species at work from the eighteenth century on in the critical biblical studies with which we are familiar. The David of the Psalter is the David of Samuel and Chronicles simpliciter. The books of the Twelve minor prophets belonged to them as their authors, and the idea of *vaticinium ex eventu* would have struck them as eccentric or heretical or both. But the idea of redactional additions would never have occurred to them. Single authorial minds address single audiences on single themes. On occasion the Psalms address future events and in so doing may be called prophecy as prediction. Usually these are events within the history of Israel (Hezekiah, exile), sometimes the Maccabean period, and rarely but nevertheless on occasion the New Testament era, as with Psalm 2.[5]

In the case of a psalm like 22, Theodore prefers to speak of it offering a past example in the life of Israel that the Incarnate One

---

[3] Rudolf Bultmann, *Die Exegese des Theodor von Mopsuestia*, ed. Helmut Feld and Karl Hermann Shelke (Stuttgart: W. Kohlhammer, 1984).

[4] Brevard S. Childs, "Allegory and Typology," in Christopher R. Seitz and Kent Harold Richards, eds., *The Bible as Christian Scripture: The Work of Brevard S. Childs* (Atlanta: SBL, 2013), 299–311; Robert Louis Wilken, *The Spirit of Early Christian Thought: Seeking the Face of God* (New Haven: Yale University Press, 2003), 94–120.

[5] Seitz, "Psalm 2 in the Entry Hall of the Psalter," 95–106.

drew upon during his passion on the cross.[6] The single sense of the past offered a fitting moral example from out of Israel's storehouse, but the psalm's single sense was not referring to Christ directly. Aquinas will refer to this exegesis of Psalm 22 by Theodore quite explicitly as deficient and warranting the condemnation he would in time receive. For Aquinas the literal sense of the psalm is, he says, its spiritual sense.[7] Any reading in the name of an "historical sense" that cannot reach toward a wider extended sense is too restrictive and misjudges what is meant by literal. One can see here how remarkably different this take on the literal sense is than the one we have come to reflexively declare the same as the historical sense over the past 150 years.

The playing surface on which the Antiochenes sought to harness the literal sense and protect it from the excesses of allegory was not always smooth, however. Theodoret has already begun to sense the need for something like an extensional sense that is embedded in the literal sense and must be accounted for as well alongside the historical setting. Though he is correctly viewed as the strong opponent of Theodore, Cyril of Alexandria seems closer in his handling of the literal sense to Theodoret than his Alexandrian forebears, so one can perhaps see how several generations of working at this question has begun to create a more flexible handling. There is even an interesting case of Theodore's own wrestling with the limits of a too-restrictive single-sense limitation in his commentary on Zechariah. In some way the problem tracks as well in modern commentary treatments. Is the royal referentiality in the book to be seen consistently as focused on Zerubbabel, or is there more than one referent on this score; and how are these two dimensions related? Is "the Branch" of 3:8 Zerubbabel, who is named specifically in 4:6-10? The question becomes more acute

---

[6] Christ cannot, moreover, be thought of as referring to his sins (so the Greek text of Ps 22:1).

[7] Christopher Seitz, "Psalm 34: Redaction, Inner-Biblical Exegesis and the Longer Psalm Superscriptions—'Mistake' Making and Theological Significance," in Seitz and Richards, *Bible as Christian Scripture*, 279–98.

as one reads into chapters 9–14, where the named figure drops out but the Davidic hopes do not. This has led in the modern period to dividing the book into sub-sections and arguing for no overall consistency at this point, but instead a changing perspective given dashed hopes on the firm ground of Persian period realities.

Theodore has no recourse to theories about different authors of the book, however, again making the point that the Antiochenes are not modern historical critics. When he comes to chapter 9 and its redolent language picked up in the Gospels ("lo, your king comes to you; triumphant and victorious as he is, humble and riding on an ass, on a colt the foal of an ass"), having thus far kept the single sense on Zerubbabel and historical events associated with him, he senses a problem. He is aware of appeals to sense-making that he does not believe are justified, and so he must push back against them but also his own preferences.

With reference to Zechariah 9:9, Theodore comments, "I am amazed at those adopting farfetched ideas, applying part to Zerubbabel and part to Christ the Lord, which results in nothing else than their dividing the prophecy between Zerubbabel and Christ the Lord." He then continues,

> The Law (by this he means the Old Testament as a whole) contained an outline of everything to do with Christ the Lord. Many things that happened in unlikely fashion, therefore, affecting either the people or the individuals chosen for some tasks, Scripture expresses in a rather hyperbolic manner in these same cases, the expression at face value not doing justice to the reality. Such things are found to achieve reality, however, when looked at in reference to the person of Christ the Lord, who in every case brings the outline of the Law to a close and ushers in the reality in its place, rightly demonstrating the reality of such statements.[8]

---

[8] Theodore of Mopsuestia, *Commentary on the Twelve Prophets*, trans. Robert C. Hill (Washington, D.C.: The Catholic University of America Press, 2004), 366–67.

This is a remarkable comment given the way Theodore has consistently sought to uphold a single, historical sense. It begins to move toward what will be called in the period *theoria*, but it is directed against a different kind of double literal sense—something one can see in the commentary of Didymus on Zechariah, for example. Theodore is trying to negotiate a view in which the literal sense has only one sense, not two, but the same single sense (in "outline") points to a second fulfillment ("reality"). His historical orientation does not admit of a sense that would have made no sense to Zechariah or his real audience in time. In his language, that would "divide" the prophet and his speech. The "unlikely" and the "hyperbolic" in fact make historical sense but pressure forth a second referentiality with which the language will find accordance. They "achieve reality" due to a providential oversight and final denouement.

The term "theoria" cannot be held to have a single definitional meaning wherever we see it referred to in this period.[9] It can, indeed, refer to the capacity of the words to have an extensional meaning, an endowment of the biblical author as inspired, or a quality of the interpreter's grasp of things in the light of other things. That is just as well, for some combination is likely the case. In this book we have emphasized the first of these dimensions. Whether in the dynamics of Elder Scripture monotheism; or in the account it gives of God through the divine naming and disclosing; or in the agency it bespeaks whereby the transcendent God shares himself really and fully through time with a people; or in the exalted nature of its speech in respect of earthly referents like King David, each of these in their own way contribute to the ontological ambition of the Elder Testament's literal sense witness.

Our goal in this book would be misunderstood if it was viewed as a rejection of historical interest or the critical reconstructions of the past centuries and the insights they have brought to bear. For it

---

[9] See the excellent survey of Bradley Nassif, "'Spiritual Exegesis' in the School of Antioch," in Bradley Nassif, ed., *New Perspectives on Historical Theology: Essays in Memory of John Meyendorff* (Grand Rapids: Eerdmans, 1996), 343–77.

is precisely in its historical situatedness that we argue the literal sense has this larger canonical coefficient. In its claim to be grounded in a real past, and spoken with the literal precision that now comes down to us, is the sense-making that speaks and continues to speak through time. Here is the conjunction of theological and literary and historical extravagance, all daring to claim to speak of God and to be God's speech and to incarnate God's self and presence.

In what we are endeavoring to set forth here one should find an appeal to conceptual breadth. By the very means with which Theodore came to understand that there appeared to be a built-in limitation to single-sense interpretations—either on the plane of allegorical or historical reading—he was simply encountering the extravagance built into what it means for the Elder Scripture to speak of God, in its own idiom, as the same God to be confessed as Father, Son, and Holy Spirit. I am not claiming he understood this on these terms, but that he was being properly stretched to ask about a different kind of conceptuality.

To conclude then.

The theological exegete Karl Barth is known in part for "trinitarian hermeneutics" in his engagements with the historical and literal sense-making of his own day in the name of a church dogmatics.[10] Whatever the limitations to be noted in some places

---

[10] See the evaluation and criticisms of R. Kendall Soulen, "YHWH the Triune God," *Modern Theology* 15 (1999): 36–41. Certainly it is a fateful move to say that the divine name means "I am He whose proper name no one can repeat" or the name Yahweh is "in content, a refusal of any name" just to the extent it could lead to an account where the personal revelation is apophatically diminished as it waits for the name of Jesus Christ to fill it with content (Barth, quoted on p. 37). But I suspect Barth's rhetoric sometimes gets out in front of more carefully formulated statements. This is not to diminish the critique of Soulen, though I find his own proposal limited for other reasons. There needs to be a careful reciprocity in the theological evaluation of the revelation of YHWH and Jesus Christ. Soulen's worries about supersessionism frequently flatten the discussion. See now Michael G. Azar, "Origen, Scripture, and the Imprecision of 'Supersessionism,'" *JTI* 10 (2016): 157–72. I have an earlier discussion in "Handing Over the Name: Christian Reflection on the Divine Name YHWH,"

of his work, he does grasp there is something to the YHWH-*kurios* identity that says a great deal of what needs to be said at the heart of Christian reading of the scriptures as a whole. He writes,

> It cannot possibly have happened unawares and unintentionally that this word (*kurios*) was at any rate used to translate the Old Testament name of God Yahweh-Adonai, and was then applied to Jesus. We are pointed in the same direction by the practical meaning of the name Jesus as the name in which they prophesied, taught, preached, prayed and baptized, in which sins were forgiven, demons driven out, and other miracles done, in which his followers were to gather, in which they were to receive one another, in which they were to believe, on which they were to call, in which they were to be upheld, for the sake of which they were to be hated and despised, to renounce all worldly possession and even perhaps to die, in which again they are washed, sanctified and justified (1 Cor. 6:11), and which is, so to speak, the place, the sphere, in which all they say and do is to take place (Col. 3:17). *The name of Yahweh has precisely the same comprehensive and pervasive meaning in the Old Testament. The name of Yahweh is simply Yahweh revealed to men.*[11]

What is referred to here as "precisely the same comprehensive and pervasive meaning" is otherwise the historical sense of the Elder Testament's own world of reference, in which YHWH-Elohim's life with a people is that life which figures forth a later testament's own understanding of how it might be said to live before the God of Israel, under the Lordship of Jesus Christ, and within the life of the triune God. "The place, the sphere, in which all they say and do" is that Name disclosed in the life of the first covenant people now finding

---

and "Our Help Is in the Name of the LORD, the Maker of Heaven and Earth," in my *Figured Out: Typology and Providence in Christian Scripture* (Louisville, Ky.: Westminster John Knox, 2001), 131–44; 177–90. I treat the worship dimension for the Christian church above in chapter 11.

[11] Barth, *Church Dogmatics* I/1, ed. G. W. Bromiley and T. F. Torrance (London: T&T Clark: 2010), 400; emphasis added.

accordance in time to confirm, enclose, uphold, direct and deliver the Elder Testament's adopted family, the Israel of God, the church.

Early in our work we asked about the kind of readership the Elder Testament could be said to anticipate. It is a question posed in our present period where books and reading are universal realities. To be noted in the early church, by contrast, is a sense of reading as embarking on a privileged journey. This is especially true for Gentile readers of the first scripture. Two reasons account for this. The first is their recognition that the first scripture is a unique literature in its attachment to and incubation within a people God spoke to and to whom he entrusted these same oracles of God. A bridge had to be crossed to come into such a frame of reference for others. The second factor ties directly to this. The Risen Lord's own long life with the first scripture was a life within, arising from, ingredient in that same testament. That he opened that life to the first witnesses had an analogy for what it meant for next witnesses as well to have access on kindred terms: their significance lay in their everywhere having to do with him, such that he became the door opening onto their testimony, previously held in trust in a different frame of privileged reference.

"Elder Testament" was chosen as a term of reference to avoid the sense of an "old witness" being now improved upon in some essentially chronological sense, moving as first episodes toward a more significant finale that put them in a fresh and appropriate shade, itself to be called the New Testament. We have sought to slow down that movement by paying attention to the way the First and Only Testament did its proper work in the early church and also to interrogate it altogether. The problem with an historicizing of the first witness was both its failure to attend to the canonical sense toward which it gives account for its theological ontology and its tendency to "honor" the first witness by distancing it from claims being made about its crucial role as Christian Scripture. Our hope is that the conceptual lens on the Elder Scripture has been widened so that as canon it may properly speak of One God: the Father, the Son, and the Holy Spirit.

Bibliography

Adam, A. K. M., Stephen E. Fowl, Kevin J. Vanhoozer, and Francis Watson, eds. *Reading Scripture with the Church: Toward a Hermeneutic for Theological Interpretation.* Grand Rapids: Baker, 2006.

Anderson, Bernhard. *Understanding the Old Testament.* 1966. 5th ed. Upper Saddle River, N.J.: Prentice-Hall, 2006.

Anderson, Gary. "Joseph and the Passion of Our Lord." Pages 198–215 in *The Art of Reading Scripture.* Edited by Richard B. Hays and Ellen F. Davis. Grand Rapids: Eerdmans, 2003.

Astruc, Jean. *Conjectures sur les mémoires originaux dont il paroit que Moyse s'est servi pour le livre de la Genèse.* Brussels, 1753.

Athanasius. *A Defense of the Nicene Definition* and *Letters on the Synods.* NPNF 2nd series, vol. 4. Translated by John Henry Newman and Archibald Robertson. Edited by Philip Schaff and Henry Wace. Grand Rapids: Eerdmans, 1991.

Attridge, Harold W. *Hebrews: A Commentary on the Epistle to the Hebrews.* Hermeneia. Philadelphia: Fortress, 1989.

Auerbach, Eric. *Mimesis: The Representation of Reality in Western Literature.* 50th anniversary edition. Princeton: Princeton University Press, 2003. German original, 1946.

Azar, Michael G. "Origen, Scripture, and the Imprecision of 'Supersessionism.'" *JTI* 10 (2016): 157–72.

Baden, Joel. *The Composition of the Pentateuch: Renewing the Documentary Hypothesis.* New Haven: Yale University Press, 2012.

Barr, James. *History and Ideology in the Old Testament: Biblical Studies at the End of a Millennium.* Oxford: Oxford University Press, 2005.

———. *Old and New in Interpretation: A Study of the Two Testaments.* New York: Harper & Row, 1966.

Barth, Karl. *Church Dogmatics* I/1. Edinburgh: T&T Clark, 1936.

———. *Church Dogmatics* I/2. Edited by G. W. Bromiley and T. F. Torrance. London: T&T Clark, 2010.

———. *The Word of God and the Word of Man.* Gloucester, Mass.: Peter Smith, 1978.

Bartholomew, Craig, and Michael Goheen. *The Drama of Scripture: Finding Ourselves in the Biblical Story.* Grand Rapids: Baker Academic, 2004.

Bartholomew, Craig, and Heath Thomas, eds. *A Manifesto for Theological Interpretation.* Grand Rapids: Baker Academic, 2016.

Barton, John. *Reading the Old Testament: Method in Biblical Studies.* 2nd ed. London: Darton, Longman & Todd, 1996.

Bartsch, Hans-Werner. "Rudolf Bultmann: An Attempt to Understand Him." Pages 2:83–132 in Karl Barth, *Kerygma and Myth.* Edited by Hans-Werner Bartsch. London: SPCK, 1962.

Bates, Matthew W. *The Birth of the Trinity: Jesus, God, and Spirit in New Testament and Early Christian Interpretations of the Old Testament.* Oxford: Oxford University Press, 2015.

Bauckham, Richard. *God Crucified: Monotheism and Christology in the New Testament.* Grand Rapids: Eerdmans, 1998.

Behr, John. *The Way to Nicaea.* Vol. 1 in *The Formation of Christian Theology.* Crestwood, N.Y.: St. Vladimir's Seminary Press, 2001.

Black, C. Clifton. "Trinity and Exegesis." *ProEccl* 19 (2010): 151–80.

Blenkinsopp, Joseph. *A History of Prophecy in Israel.* Rev. and enlarged edition. Louisville, Ky.: Westminster John Knox, 1996.

Boyarin, Daniel. *The Jewish Gospels: The Story of the Jewish Christ.* New York: The New Press, 2012.

Braaten, Carl E., and Christopher Seitz, eds. *I Am the Lord Your God: Christian Reflections on the Ten Commandments*. Grand Rapids: Eerdmans, 2005.

Bray, Gerald. "The Church Fathers and Biblical Theology." Pages 23–40 in *Out of Egypt: Biblical Theology and Biblical Interpretation*. Edited by Craig Bartholomew et al. Grand Rapids: Zondervan, 2004.

Brion, Marcel. *Provence*. Artaud, 1960.

Brueggemann, Walter. *Theology of the Old Testament: Testimony, Dispute, Advocacy*. Minneapolis: Augsburg Fortress, 1997.

Bucur, Bogdan G. "Clement of Alexandria's Exegesis of Old Testament Theophanies." *Phronema* 29 (2014): 61–79.

———. "'Early Christian Binitarianism': From Religious Phenomenon to Polemical Insult to Scholarly Concept." *MT* 27 (2011): 102–20.

———. "Justin Martyr's Exegesis on Biblical Theophanies and the Parting of the Ways between Christianity and Judaism." *TS* 75 (2014): 34–51.

Bultmann, Rudolf. *Die Exegese des Theodor von Mopsuestia*. Edited by Helmut Feld and Karl Hermann Shelke. Stuttgart: W. Kohlhammer, 1984.

Burney, C. F. "Christ as the APXH of Creation (Prov. viii 22, Col. I 15–18, Rev. iii 14)." *JTS* 27 (1926): 160–77.

von Campenhausen, Hans. *The Formation of the Christian Bible*. Philadelphia: Fortress, 1972.

Cassuto, Umberto. *The Documentary Hypothesis and the Composition of the Pentateuch: Eight Lectures by U. Cassuto*. Translated by Israel Abrahams. Jerusalem: Shalem Press, 2006. Hebrew original, 1941.

Chapman, Stephen. "The Canon Debate: What It Is and Why It Matters." *JTI* 4 (2010): 273–94.

———. *The Law and the Prophets: A Study in Old Testament Canon Formation*. Tübingen: Mohr Siebeck, 2000.

———. "The Old Testament Canon and Its Authority for the Christian Church." *ExAud* 19 (2003): 125–48.

Childs, Brevard S. "Allegory and Typology." Pages 299–311 in *The Bible as Christian Scripture: The Work of Brevard S. Childs*. Edited by Christopher R. Seitz and Kent Harold Richards. Atlanta: SBL, 2013.

———. *Biblical Theology in Crisis*. Philadelphia: Westminster, 1970.

———. *Biblical Theology of the Old and New Testaments: Theological Reflection on the Christian Bible*. Minneapolis: Fortress, 1993.

———. *The Book of Exodus: A Critical, Theological Commentary*. OTL. Philadelphia: Westminster, 1974.

———. "The Canon in Recent Biblical Studies: Reflections on an Era." *ProEccl* 14 (2005): 26–45.

———. *The Church's Guide for Reading Paul: The Canonical Shaping of the Pauline Corpus*. Grand Rapids: Eerdmans, 2008.

———. *Introduction to the Old Testament as Scripture*. Philadelphia: Fortress, 1979.

———. *The New Testament as Canon: An Introduction*. Philadelphia: Fortress, 1984.

———. "Psalm Titles and Midrashic Exegesis." *JSS* 16 (1971): 137–50.

———. "The Sensus Literalis of Scripture: An Ancient and Modern Problem." Pages 80–93 in *Beiträge zur alttestamentlichen Theologie: Festschrift für Walther Zimmerli zum 70. Geburtstag*. Edited by Walther Zimmerli, Herbert Donner, Robert Hanhart, and Rudolf Smend. Göttingen: Vandenhoeck & Ruprecht, 1977.

Clement of Alexandria. *Stromata*. In vol. 2 of *The Ante-Nicene Fathers*. Edited by Alexander Roberts, James Donaldson, and A. Cleveland Coxe. Translated by William Wilson. Buffalo, N.Y.: Christian Literature, 1885. Repr., Peabody, Mass.: Hendrickson, 1994.

Collett, Don. "A Place to Stand: Proverbs 8 and the Construction of Ecclesial Space." *SJT* 70 (2017): 166–83.

———. "Reading Forward: The Old Testament and Retrospective Stance." *ProEccl* 24 (2015): 178–96.

Congar, Yves. *Tradition and Traditions*. London: Burns & Oates, 1966.

Crenshaw, James. *Old Testament Wisdom: An Introduction*. Atlanta: John Knox, 1981.

Dohmen, Christoph. *Exodus 1–18*. HThKAT. Freiburg: Herder, 2005.

Dozeman, Thomas B., and Konrad Schmid, eds. *Farewell to the Yahwist?: The Composition of the Pentateuch in Recent European Interpretation*. SBLSS 34. Atlanta: Scholars, 2006.

Dozeman, Thomas B., Konrad Schmid, and Baruch J. Schwartz, eds. *The Pentateuch: International Perspectives on Recent Research*. Tübingen: Mohr Siebeck, 2011.

Elliott, Mark W. *The Heart of Biblical Theology: Providence Experienced*. Surrey, UK: Ashgate, 2013.

Feldmeier, Reinhard, and Hermann Spieckermann. *God of the Living*. Waco, Tex.: Baylor University Press, 2015.

Finn, Leonard G. "Reflections on the Rule of Faith." Pages 221–42 in *The Bible as Christian Scripture: The Work of Brevard S. Childs*. Edited by Christopher R. Seitz and Kent Harold Richards. Atlanta: SBL, 2013.

Fitzmyer, Joseph A. *The Gospel According to Luke X–XXIV*. AB. New Haven: Yale University Press, 2005.

Fowl, Stephen E., ed. *The Theological Interpretation of Scripture: Classic and Contemporary Readings*. Cambridge, Mass.: Blackwell, 1997.

Frei, Hans. *The Eclipse of Biblical Narrative: A Study in Eighteenth and Nineteenth Century Hermeneutics*. New Haven: Yale University Press, 1974.

Fox, Michael V. *Ecclesiastes*. The JPS Bible Commentary. Philadelphia: The Jewish Publication Society, 2004.

Gathercole, Simon J. *The Preexistent Son: Recovering the Christologies of Matthew, Mark, and Luke*. Grand Rapids: Eerdmans, 2006.

Gilkey, Langdon. "Cosmology, Ontology, and the Travail of Biblical Language." *JR* 41 (1965): 194–205.

Grabbe, Lester, ed. *Can a "History of Israel" Be Written?* JSOTSup 245. Sheffield: Sheffield Academic, 1997.

Green, Joel. *Practicing Theological Interpretation*. Grand Rapids: Baker Academic, 2011.

Gregory of Nyssa. *Gregory of Nyssa: Homilies on Ecclesiastes: An English Version with Supporting Studies*. Edited by Stuart George Hall. Proceedings of the Seventh International Colloquium on Gregory of Nyssa (St. Andrews, 5–10 September 1990). Berlin: de Gruyter, 1993.

Grelot, Pierre. "Le texte du Psaumes 39:7 dans la Septante." *RB* 108 (2001): 210–13.

Gruber, Mayer I.. *Rashi's Commentary on the Psalms*. Leiden: Brill, 2003.

Halpern, Baruch. "The Ritual Background of Zechariah's Temple Song." *CBQ* 40 (1978): 167–90.

von Harnack, Adolf. *Bible Reading in the Early Church*. London: Williams & Norgate, 1912.

Hays, Richard B. *Echoes of Scripture in the Letters of Paul*. New Haven: Yale University Press, 1989.

Hays, Richard B., and Ellen F. Davis, eds. *The Art of Reading Scripture*. Grand Rapids: Eerdmans, 2003.

Helmer, Christine. "Luther's Trinitarian Hermeneutic and the Old Testament." *Modern Theology* 18 (2002): 49–70.

Hill, Robert Charles, trans. with introduction. *St. John Chrysostom Commentary on the Psalms*. Vol. 2. Brookline, Mass.: Holy Cross Orthodox Press, 1998.
Hurtado, Larry W. "The Binitarian Shape of Early Christian Worship." Pages 187–213 in *The Jewish Roots of Christological Monotheism*. Edited by Carey C. Newman, James R. Davila, and Gladys S. Lewis. Leiden: Brill, 1999.
Irenaeus. *Against Heresies*. Edited by Alexander Roberts and James Donaldson. *ANF* 1. 1885. Grand Rapids: Eerdmans, 1986.
———. *The Demonstration of the Apostolic Preaching*. Translated by Armitage Robinson. London: SPCK, 1920.
———. *On the Apostolic Preaching*. Translated and introduction by John Behr. Crestwood, N.Y.: St. Vladimir's Seminary Press, 1997.
Jeremias, Jörg. "The Interrelationship between Amos and Hosea." Pages 171–86 in *Forming Prophetic Literature: Essays on Isaiah and the Twelve in Honor of John D. W. Watts*. Edited by James W. Watts and Paul House. JSOTS 235. Sheffield: Sheffield Academic, 1996.
Jobes, Karen H., and Moisés Silva. *Invitation to the Septuagint*. Grand Rapids: Baker Academic, 2000.
Jowett, Benjamin. *Essays and Reviews*. London: Parker, 1860.
Justin. *Dialogue with Trypho the Jew*. In vol. 1 of *The Ante-Nicene Fathers*. Edited by Alexander Roberts and James Donaldson. New York: Scribner's, 1903.
———. *Justin's Apology on Behalf of Christians*. Edited by Denis Minns and Paul Parvis. Oxford: Oxford University Press, 2009.
Keck, Leander E. *Christ's First Theologian: The Shape of Paul's Thought*. Waco, Tex.: Baylor University Press, 2015.
———. *Why Christ Matters: Toward a New Testament Christology*. Waco, Tex.: Baylor University Press, 2015.
Van Leeuwen, Raymond C. "Scribal Wisdom and Theodicy in the Book of the Twelve." Pages 31–49 in *In Search of Wisdom: Essays in Memory of John G. Gammie*. Edited by Leo Perdue, Bernard Brandon Scott, and William Johnston Wiseman. Louisville, Ky.: Westminster John Knox, 1993.
———. "Wisdom Literature." Pages 847–50 in *Dictionary for Theological Interpretation of the Bible*. Edited by Kevin Vanhoozer. Grand Rapids: Baker Academic, 2005.
Legaspi, Michael. *The Death of Scripture and the Rise of Biblical Studies*. Oxford: Oxford University Press, 2010.

Lenzi, Alan. "Proverbs 8:22–31: Three Perspectives on Its Composition." *JBL* 125 (2006): 687–714.

Levenson, Jon D. *The Death and Resurrection of the Beloved Son: The Transformation of Child Sacrifice in Judaism and Christianity.* New Haven: Yale University Press, 1995.

———. *The Hebrew Bible, the Old Testament, and Historical Criticism.* Louisville, Ky.: Westminster John Knox, 1993.

Lewis, Jack P. "Jamnia, Council of." Pages 634–37 in *The Anchor Bible Dictionary*, vol. 3. Edited by David Noel Freedman. New York: Doubleday, 1992.

Lincoln, Andrew. "Hebrews and Biblical Theology." Pages 313–38 in *Out of Egypt: Biblical Theology and Biblical Interpretation.* Edited by Craig Bartholomew et al. Grand Rapids: Zondervan, 2004.

Lindbeck, George. *The Nature of Doctrine: Religion and Theology in a Postliberal Age.* Louisville, Ky.: Westminster John Knox, 1984.

Lohfink, Norbert. *Qoheleth: A Continental Commentary.* Minneapolis: Fortress, 2003. German original, 1980.

Longman, Tremper. *How to Read Proverbs.* Downers Grove, Ill.: InterVarsity, 2002.

———. *Proverbs.* Grand Rapids: Baker, 2006.

de Lubac, Henri. *History and Spirit: The Understanding of Scripture According to Origen.* San Francisco: Ignatius, 2007.

Luther, Martin. *D. Martin Luthers Werke* [WA]. 120 vols. Weimar, 1883–2009.

MacDonald, Neil. *Metaphysics and the God of Israel: Systematic Theology of the Old and New Testaments.* Grand Rapids: Baker, 2006.

McDonald, Lee, and James A. Sanders. *The Canon Debate.* Peabody, Mass.: Hendrickson, 2002.

McKenzie, Steven, and M. Patrick Graham, eds. *The History of Israel's Traditions: The Heritage of Martin Noth.* London: Bloomsbury, 1994.

Melito of Sardis. *On Easter.* Quotations from "A New English Translation of Melito's Paschal Homily." Translated by Gerald F. Hawthorne. In *Current Issues in Biblical and Patristic Interpretation: Studies in Honor of Merrill C. Tenney*, edited by G. F. Hawthorne. Grand Rapids: Eerdmans, 1975.

Moberly, Walter. "'Interpret the Bible Like Any Other Book?' Requiem for an Axiom." *JTI* 4 (2010): 91–110.

———. *The Old Testament of the Old Testament.* OBT. Minneapolis: Fortress, 1992.

Murphy, Roland. *Ecclesiastes*. WBC 23A. Waco, Tex.: Word, 1992.
———. *Proverbs*. WBC 22. Waco, Tex.: Word, 1998.
Nassif, Bradley. "'Spiritual Exegesis' in the School of Antioch." Pages 343–77 in *New Perspectives on Historical Theology: Essays in Memory of John Meyendorff*. Edited by Bradley Nassif. Grand Rapids: Eerdmans, 1996.
Newman, Murray Lee, Jr. *The People of the Covenant*. Nashville: Abingdon, 1962.
Noth, Martin. *A History of Pentateuchal Traditions*. Englewood Cliffs, N.J.: Prentice-Hall, 1972. German original, 1948.
———. *The Deuteronomistic History*. 2nd ed. Sheffield: JSOT, 1991.
Olson, Dennis. *The Death of the Old and the Birth of the New: The Framework of the Book of Numbers and the Pentateuch*. BJS. Atlanta: Scholars, 1985.
———. *Deuteronomy and the Death of Moses*. OBT. Minneapolis: Augsburg Fortress, 1994.
Origen. *The Song of Songs: Commentary and Homilies*. Edited by Johannes Quasten and Joseph C. Plumpe. Ancient Christian Writers 26. Mahwah, N.J.: Paulist, 1957.
Perdue, Leo. *The Collapse of History: Reconstructing Old Testament Theology*. OBT. Minneapolis: Augsburg Fortress, 1994.
Propp, William. *Exodus 1–18*. AB. New Haven: Yale University Press, 1997.
von Rad, Gerhard. *Old Testament Theology*. 2 vols. London: Oliver & Boyd, 1962, 1965.
———. *The Problem of the Hexateuch and Other Essays*. Edinburgh: Oliver & Boyd, 1966. German original, 1938.
———. *Weisheit in Israel*. Neukirchen-Vluyn: Neukirchener, 1970. English translation: *Wisdom in Israel*. Translated by James D. Martin. Harrisville, Penn.: Trinity International, 1972.
Rendtorff, Rolf. "Genesis 8,21 und die urgeschichte des Jahwisten." *KuD* 7 (1961): 69–78.
———. *The Old Testament: An Introduction*. Philadelphia: Fortress, 1991.
———. *The Problem of the Process of Transmission in the Pentateuch*. Sheffield: JSOT, 1990.
Reventlow, Henning Graf. *The Authority of the Bible and the Rise of the Modern World*. Philadelphia: Fortress, 1985.
Rowe, C. Kavin. "Biblical Pressure and Trinitarian Hermeneutics." *ProEccl* 11 (2002): 295–312.
———. "Romans 10:13: What Is the Name of the Lord?" *HBT* 22 (2000): 135–73.

Saebo, Magne, ed. *Hebrew Bible/Old Testament: The History of Its Interpretation*. 3 vols. Göttingen: Vandenhoeck & Ruprecht, 1996–2014.
Sailhamer, John H. "Biblical Theology and the Composition of the Hebrew Bible." Pages 25–37 in *Biblical Theology: Retrospect and Prospect*. Edited by Scott Hafemann. Downers Grove, Ill.: InterVarsity, 2002.
Sand, Alexander. "Überlieferung und Sammlung der Paulusbriefe." Pages 11–24 in *Paulus in den neutestamentlichen Spätschriften*. Edited by K. Kertelge. Freiburg: Herder, 1981.
Schmid, Konrad. *Genesis and the Moses Story: Israel's Dual Origins in the Hebrew Bible*. Winona Lake, Ind.: Eisenbrauns, 2010.
Schwartz, Sarah. "Narrative *Toledot* Formula in Genesis: The Case of Heaven and Earth, Noah, and Isaac." *JHS* 16 (2016): 1–36.
Seitz, Christopher R. "Canon, Narrative, and the Old Testament's Literal Sense: A Response to John Goldingay." *TynBul* 59 (2008): 27–35.
———. *The Character of Christian Scripture: The Significance of a Two-Testament Bible*. Grand Rapids: Baker Academic, 2011.
———. "Christological Interpretation of Texts and Trinitarian Claims to Truth." *SJT* 52 (1999): 209–26.
———. *Colossians*. Brazos Theological Commentary on the Bible. Grand Rapids: Brazos, 2014.
———. "The Crisis of Interpretation over the Meaning and Purpose of the Exile." *VT* 35 (1985): 78–97.
———. *Figured Out: Typology and Providence in Christian Scripture*. Louisville, Ky.: Westminster John Knox, 2001.
———. *The Goodly Fellowship of the Prophets: The Achievement of Association in Canon Formation*. Grand Rapids: Baker Academic, 2009.
———. "How Is Isaiah Present in the Latter Half of the Book? The Logic of Isaiah 40–55 within the Book of Isaiah." *JBL* 115 (1996): 219–40.
———. *Isaiah 1–39*. IBC. Louisville, Ky.: John Knox, 1993.
———. "Isaiah 40–66." In *The New Interpreters Bible*, vol. 6. Edited by Leander E. Keck. Nashville: Abingdon, 2001.
———. "Jewish Scripture for Gentile Churches: Human Destiny and the Future of the Pauline Correspondence—Part 1: Romans." *ProEccl* 23 (2014): 294–307.
———. "Jewish Scripture for Gentile Churches: Human Destiny and the Future of the Pauline Correspondence—Part 2: Colossians." *ProEccl* 23 (2014): 457–70.

———. "Job: Full Structure, Movement, and Interpretation." *Int* 43 (1989): 5–15.

———. *Joel*. ITC. London: Bloomsbury, 2016.

———. "Ketuvim and Canon." In *The Shape of the Writings*. Edited by Julius Steinberg and Timothy J. Stone. Winona Lake, Ind.: Eisenbrauns, 2015.

———. "Koheleth and Canon." In *Acts of Interpretation: Scripture, Theology, and Culture*. Edited by S. A. Cummins and Jens Zimmerman. Grand Rapids: Eerdmans, forthcoming.

———. "Old Testament or Hebrew Bible? Some Theological Considerations." *ProEccl* 5 (1996): 292–303.

———. "On Not Changing Old Testament to Hebrew Bible." *ProEccl* 6 (1997): 136–40.

———. "The Place of the Reader in Jeremiah." Pages 67–75 in *Reading the Book of Jeremiah: A Search for Coherence*. Edited by Martin Kessler. Winona Lake, Ind.: Eisenbrauns, 2004.

———. *Prophecy and Hermeneutics: Toward a New Introduction to the Prophets*. Grand Rapids: Baker Academic, 2007.

———. "Prophecy in the Nineteenth Century Reception." Pages 556–81 in *Hebrew Bible/Old Testament: The History of Its Interpretation*. Vol. 3: *From Modernism to Post-Modernism*. Edited by Magnus Saebo. Göttingen: Vandenhoeck & Ruprecht.

———. "Prophecy and Tradition-History: The Achievement of Gerhard von Rad and Beyond." Pages 30–51 in *Prophetie in Israel: Beitrage des Symposiums "Das Alte Testament und die Kultur der Moderne" anlässlich des 100. Geburtstags Gerhard von Rads (1901–1971) Heidelberg, 18.–21. Oktober 2001*. Edited by I. Fischer, K. Schmid, and H. G. M. Williamson. ATM 11. Munster: Lit-Verlag, 2003.

———. "The Prophet Moses and the Canonical Shape of Jeremiah." *Zeitschrift fur die alttestamentliche Wissenschaft* 101 (1989): 1–15.

———. "Prophetic Associations." Pages 156–66 in *Thus Says the Lord: Essays on the Former and Latter Prophets in Honor of Robert R. Wilson*. Edited by John J. Ahn and Stephen L. Cook. LHBOTS 502. London: T&T Clark, 2009.

———. "Psalm 2 in the Entry Hall of the Psalter: Extended Sense in the History of Interpretation." Pages 95–106 in *Church, Society, and the Christian Common Good*. Edited by Ephraim Radner. Eugene, Ore.: Cascade, 2017.

———. "Psalm 34: Redaction, Inner-Biblical Exegesis and the Longer Psalm Superscriptions—'Mistake' Making and Theological Significance." Pages 279–98 in *The Bible as Christian Scripture: The Work of Brevard S. Childs*. Edited by Christopher R. Seitz and Kent Harold Richards. Atlanta: SBL, 2013.

———. "Reconciliation and the Plain Sense Witness of Scripture." Pages 25–42 in *The Redemption: An Interdisciplinary Symposium on Christ as Redeemer*. Edited by Stephen T. Davis, Daniel Kendall, and Gerald O'Collins. Oxford: Oxford University Press, 2004.

———. "Scriptural Author and Canonical Prophet: The Theological Implications of Literary Association in the Canon." Pages 176–88 in *Biblical Method and Interpretation: Essays in Honour of John Barton*. Edited by Katharine J. Dell and Paul M. Joyce. Oxford: Oxford University Press, 2013.

———. "The Ten Commandments: Positive and Natural Law and the Covenants Old and New." Pages 18–40 in *I Am the Lord Your God: Christian Reflections on the Ten Commandments*. Edited by Carl E. Braaten and Christopher Seitz. Grand Rapids: Eerdmans, 2005.

———. *Theology in Conflict: Reactions to the Exile in the Book of Jeremiah*. BZAW 176. Berlin: de Gruyter, 1986.

———. "The Trinity in the Old Testament." Pages 28–40 in *The Oxford Handbook of the Trinity*. Edited by Gilles Emery and Matthew Levering. Oxford: Oxford University Press, 2011.

———. "The Unique Achievement of the Book of the Twelve: Neither Reactional Unity Nor Anthology." In *The Book of the Twelve: An Anthology of Prophetic Books or the Result of Complex Redactional Processes*. Edited by Heiko Wenzel. Göttingen: Vandenhoeck & Ruprecht, forthcoming.

———. *Word without End: The Old Testament as Abiding Theological Witness*. Waco, Tex.: Baylor University Press, 2005.

———. *Zion's Final Destiny: The Development of the Book of Isaiah: A Reassessment of Isaiah 36–39*. Minneapolis: Fortress, 1991.

Seitz, Christopher R., and Kent Harold Richards, eds. *The Bible as Christian Scripture: The Work of Brevard S. Childs*. Atlanta: SBL, 2013.

Shaviv, Yehuda, ed. *The Commentary of Rabbi Isaac Abravanel on the Torah*. Vol. 1, *Genesis*. Jerusalem: Horeb, 2007. In Hebrew.

Sneed, Mark. "Is the 'Wisdom Tradition' a Tradition?" *CBQ* 73 (2001): 50–71.

Soulen, R. Kendall. *The God of Israel and Christian Theology.* Minneapolis: Fortress, 1996.

———. "YHWH the Triune God." *Modern Theology* 15 (1999): 36–41.

Spinks, D. Christopher. *The Bible and the Crisis of Meaning: Debates on the Theological Interpretation of Scripture.* T&T Clark Theology. London: T&T Clark, 2007.

Steinberg, Julius, and Timothy J. Stone, eds. *The Shape of the Writings.* Winona Lake, Ind.: Eisenbrauns, 2015.

Steins, Georg. *Die Chronik als kanonisches Abschlußphänomen. Studien zur Entstehung und Theologie von ½ Chronik.* Bonner Biblische Beiträge 93. Weinheim: Beltz Athenäum Verlag, 1995.

Sternberg, Meir. *The Poetics of Biblical Narrative: Ideological Literature and the Drama of Reading.* Bloomington: Indiana University Press, 1985.

Stone, Timothy J. *The Compilational History of the Megilloth.* FAT. Tübingen: Mohr Siebeck, 2013.

Stordalen, Terje. "Genesis 2,4: Restudying a *locus classicus.*" *ZAW* 104 (1992): 163–77.

Strawn, Brent A. "And These Three Are One: A Trinitarian Critique of Christological Approaches to the Old Testament." *PRSt* 31 (2004): 191–210.

Sweeney, Marvin. "Tanak versus Old Testament: Concerning a Foundation for a Jewish Theology of the Bible." Pages 353–72 in *Problems in Biblical Theology: Essays in Honor of Rolf Knierim.* Edited by Henry T. C. Sun and Keith L. Eades. Grand Rapids: Eerdmans, 1997.

Terrien, Samuel. *The Elusive Presence: Toward a New Biblical Theology.* San Francisco: Harper & Row, 1978.

Theodore of Mopsuestia. *Commentary on the Twelve Prophets.* Translated by Robert C. Hill. Washington, D.C.: The Catholic University of America Press, 2004.

Trebolle-Barrera, Julio. "Qumran Evidence for a Biblical Standard Text and for Non-Standard and Parabiblical Texts." Pages 89–106 in *The Dead Sea Scrolls in Their Historical Context.* Edited by Timothy H. Lim. London: T&T Clark, 2000.

Treier, Daniel J. *Introducing Theological Interpretation of Scripture: Recovering a Christian Practice.* Grand Rapids: Baker, 2008.

Trobisch, David. *Paul's Letter Collection.* Minneapolis: Fortress, 1994.

Utzschneider, Helmut, and Wolfgang Oswald. *Exodus 1–15.* IEKAT. Stuttgart: Kohlhammer, 2013.

Vanhoozer, Kevin J., gen. ed. *Dictionary for Theological Interpretation of the Bible*. Grand Rapids: Baker Academic, 2005.
Vanhoozer, Kevin J., Craig Bartholomew, and Daniel J. Treier, eds. *Theological Interpretation of the Old Testament: A Book-by-Book Survey*. Grand Rapids: Baker Book House, 2005, 2008.
Vanhoozer, Kevin J., Daniel J. Treier, and N. T. Wright, eds. *Theological Interpretation of the New Testament: A Book-by-Book Survey*. Grand Rapids: Baker Book House, 2008.
Waltke, Bruce. *The Book of Proverbs: Chapters 1–15*. Grand Rapids: Eerdmans, 2004.
Watson, Francis. *Paul and the Hermeneutics of Faith*. London: T&T Clark, 2004.
———. *Text and Truth: Redefining Biblical Theology*. Grand Rapids: Eerdmans, 1997.
Weeks, Stuart. "The Context and Meaning of Proverbs 8:30a." *JBL* 125 (2006).
Wellhausen, Julius. *Prolegomena to the History of Israel*. Edinburgh: Adam & Charles Black, 1885. German original, 1883.
Westermann, Claus. *Genesis 1–11: A Continental Commentary*. Minneapolis: Augsburg, 1984. German original, 1974.
Wilken, Robert Louis. *The Spirit of Early Christian Thought: Seeking the Face of God*. New Haven: Yale University Press, 2003.
Wolff, Hans Walter. "The Kerygma of the Deuteronomistic Historical Work." Pages 83–100 in *The Vitality of Old Testament Traditions*. By Hans Walter Wolff and Walter Brueggemann. Atlanta: John Knox, 1975.
Wright, G. Ernest. *The God Who Acts: Biblical Theology as Recital*. SBT. London: SCM, 1964.
Wright, J. Robert, ed. *Ancient Christian Commentray on Scripture*. Vol. 9. Downers Grove, Ill.: InterVarsity, 2005.
Yeago, David. "The New Testament and the Nicene Dogma: A Contribution to the Recovery of Theological Exegesis." *ProEccl* 3 (1994): 152–64.
Young, Frances. "Augustine's Hermeneutics and Postmodern Criticism." *Int* 58 (2004): 42–55.
———. *Biblical Exegesis and the Formation of Christian Culture*. Cambridge: Cambridge University Press, 1997.
———. "Exegetical Method and Scriptural Proof: The Bible in Doctrinal Debate." StPatr 19. Leuven: Peeters Press, 1989.

———. "Proverbs 8 in Interpretation." Pages 102–15 in *Reading Texts, Seeking Wisdom*. Edited by David F. Ford and Graham Stanton. Grand Rapids: Eerdmans, 2004.

Zimmerli, Walther. *Das Buch des Predigers Salomo*. ATD 16/1. Göttingen: Vandenhoeck & Ruprecht, 1962.

Scripture Index

Genesis	2, 7, 70, 73–74, 81n11, 86–87, 89, 89n8, 90–94, 97–106, 108, 132, 134–35, 143, 157–58, 164, 168, 170, 174, 223, 225, 230, 233, 238–39, 241, 261	1:12-13, 26-27	241
		2	229–30
		2:4	93, 222, 225, 230, 238, 239–40
		2:4a	103
		2:6, 7	241
1–3	230, 233, 239	3:14-19	240
1	7, 61, 73, 92, 102, 104–5, 195, 208, 210, 215–16, 225, 228–29, 234, 236, 238, 240–41	3:17-19	231
		4	209
		4:4	116
		4:26	88, 90n10, 94
1:1-11	56, 91–93, 104, 219, 221–22, 228, 236	5:1	105
		8:22	93, 228, 234
1:1-2	241	10:1-32	74n6
1:1	27, 102, 210, 215, 215n22, 219, 238–40	11:1-9	74n6
		15:2, 7	102n7

15:13	81n11	21–34	136
16:2, 5	102n7	Deuteronomy	87, 88n5, 121, 132–34, 134n4, 135–37, 140, 143, 146, 247
17:1	90, 93, 106		
18	116, 195–96		
18:14	102n7	5:3	137
18:27, 31, 32	102n7	6	92
20:4	102n7	6:4	198
22:12	67	6:20-25	133
24:3, 12, 31, 35	102n7	26	92
24:40, 42, 48, 56	102n7	26:5-11	133
26:28-29	102n7		
32:13–33:20	18	Joshua	73, 88, 120–21, 134–36, 139–42, 160
Exodus	2, 30, 75, 77, 81n11, 83, 87–88, 90, 93–95, 101–3, 105, 110, 132, 134–35, 135n6, 137, 147, 158	Judges	120–23, 125, 136, 139–40, 169–70
		Ruth	73, 122–23, 125, 140, 162–65, 169–71
1:8	81n11		
3	93–94, 102, 109–11, 113, 115, 117	3:11	125
3:13	90	1 Samuel	121–22, 125, 164, 169, 211
4:1-17	91		
4:1	90	16–31	18
4:24-36	79	2 Samuel	121, 164, 166, 211
4:29-31	91	7:14	250
6	89–91, 93, 102, 135	23:2	192
6:2	94		
6:14-25	81n11	1 Kings	121, 141, 164–65
12:23	79	2–13	236
12:40-41	81n11	8	232
15:27	28	13	232
23–34	77, 79	2 Kings	88, 121, 141–42, 164, 171
23	79	18–20	139n1, 143
25–31	136	22–23	133
25	117	1 Chronicles	74, 120, 122, 127, 140, 162–63, 164, 171–72, 174, 273
35–40	136		
Leviticus	59, 132, 134–35, 137		
Numbers	88, 132–36, 137, 146	3:1-24	173
1–10	136	6:15	173

Scripture Index 297

2 Chronicles	73–74, 120, 122, 127, 140, 162–63, 164, 164n3, 166, 171–72, 174, 273	40	244, 252, 252n10, 253–54, 254n13, 255–56, 256n18, 257
36	172	40:6-8	250
Ezra	55, 122, 127, 140, 162–64, 169, 171–72, 174	45:6-7	250, 253
		51	253
		51:16	254n13
Nehemiah	55, 122, 127, 140, 162, 164, 169, 171, 174	51:17	253
		51:19	254n13
Esther	120, 122–23, 125, 140, 162–63, 171	56	251
		95	184, 250–51
		95:7-11	250
Job	2, 67, 96, 122, 132, 162–64, 166–69, 171, 226, 226n11, 227–29, 232, 236, 251	100	184–85
		102	253
		102:25-27	250
1–2	95	103	186
1:6-12	96	104	186, 229–30, 234, 236
1:21	95	104:29	229
38:1	56n7	110	7, 193–95, 197–98, 205–6, 214
42:7-17	95	110:1	193, 198
Psalms (Psalter)	2, 18n4, 22, 27n11, 43–44, 87, 122, 132, 158n26, 162–64, 166, 166n5, 167–68, 183–85, 190–91, 193–94, 199, 212–13, 228, 230, 236, 250, 255, 261, 272–73	110:2	198
		110:3	205
		118	251
		134	186
		137	151
		144	186
1	211	147:12	60
2	7, 195, 197, 211–14, 216, 273	147:19-20	55n5
2:7	250	Proverbs	122, 125, 132, 162–68, 170, 204–6, 208, 213, 215, 226, 226n11, 227, 227n15, 228, 232–33, 236, 251, 261
3	211		
8	214, 251–52, 252n9		
19	233–34, 236		
22	44, 101, 211, 273–74	1	213
22:1	274	8	7, 203, 206–8, 210–11, 213–16, 218
23	199		
25	151	8:22-31	29n15, 201–2, 213, 218
34	166n6	8:22	27n11, 204, 219, 241

9	213	31	245n2, 250
31:10	125	31:33	250

Ecclesiastes (Qoheleth) 2, 122, 125, 132, 162–65, 167–68, 219, 221–22, 226n11, 227, 227n15, 228, 228n16, 232–33, 236–37, 261

1	222
1:4	240

Song of Songs (Solomon) 122, 125, 162–63, 165, 168, 170, 227, 227n15

Isaiah 2, 18n4, 36, 66, 74, 108, 123, 126, 139–41, 141n3, 142, 144–48, 157–59, 189, 251

2	143, 159
2:1-5	158
6	117
8:16-20	159
29:11-12	159
30:8	159
36–39	139n1, 143
40–55	158
40:31	153
44:6	61
45	117, 216
45:20-25	187
45:23-24	216
53	44
55:11	159
60:3-4	60
66	144

Jeremiah 2, 27n11, 73–74, 123, 126, 139, 141, 143–46, 150, 153, 157, 159, 171, 244

7:22	245
26:18	143

Lamentations 123, 125, 132, 162–64, 171

4:21–22	151

Ezekiel 2, 74, 108, 123, 126, 139, 141, 144, 146–47

1	117
14:20	96

Daniel 120, 122–23, 140, 158, 162–63, 171

1:4	140
8:17, 27	158
10:8-12	158
13:42	67

Hosea 124n8, 139, 141, 148–50, 150n18, 151, 154, 159

14:1-8	149
14:9	151

Joel 66, 124n8, 148–51, 154, 156, 158–59

3:16, 19	150

Amos 66, 124n8, 148–49, 150n18, 151, 159

1:2	150
1:3–2:16	150
1:11-12	150

Obadiah 124n8, 148, 151, 159

1–4	151
10–14	151

Jonah 56, 124n8, 142, 148, 151–52, 152n20, 153, 158–59, 245

1:6-10, 15-16	152
3:3-4	152

Micah	124n8, 141, 143, 148, 152–53, 159	10:5-6	58
		22:45	194
4	143, 159	Mark	177, 198
4:1-4	152, 158	12	198
Nahum	148, 153–54	16:12	177
1:3	153	Luke	2, 42, 115, 177–80, 185, 189
Habakkuk	148, 153, 153n21, 154, 251	1:35	114
		1:46, 68	185
1:1	154n22	15	152n20
2:1-4	154n22	15:11-32	18
3:1-19	154, 154n22	19:32-37	178
3:8-20	154	20:8	178
3:19	154n22	24	175
Zephaniah		24:1-11, 13-14	177
1:1-6	154	24:19-27	178
		24:27-47	5
Haggai	154–55, 171–72	24:27	178–79
1:1	154	24:29	180
2:2, 10, 18, 20	154	24:44	22, 179
Zechariah	142, 148, 154–55, 157, 171–72, 185–86, 274, 276	John	23, 178–80
		1	216, 241
1–8	158	1:1-4	241
1	66	1:1	107, 195, 215–16, 241
1:1-6	142	1:2	241
1:4-6	155	1:12-13, 26-27	241
7:7, 12	142, 155	2:6	241
9–14	158	2:22	23n4
9:9	275	5:39	23n4
9:23	60	7:38-39	23n4
12:10	178	12:16	23n4, 179
Malachi	66, 70, 73n3, 120, 120n1, 122–23, 126, 139, 140–42, 148, 156, 159	19:35-37	23n4
		20:8	23n4
		20:9	23
3:16-18	156	20:15	178
Matthew	120, 122, 127, 174, 242n32	20:16	178
		Acts	59, 142, 180, 195, 211, 249
5:17-48	60	2:34-35	194

7	58n8	1:15	215
8:34	59	3:17	278
10:41	181	2 Thessalonians	
13	212	1:11	67
15	59	2 Timothy	
17:2	22	3:15, 16	23
Romans	145, 247	3:16	23
9–11	18	Philemon	247
15	23	Hebrews	123, 243–44, 244n1, 245–46, 246n4, 246n5, 247, 247n7, 248, 248n8, 249–52, 252n9, 254–56, 256n18, 257–59, 261–62
1 Corinthians			
2:10	192		
6:11	278		
8:6	188		
15:3	23	1:1-4, 5-14	249
Galatians	158	2:6-9	251
Ephesians		3–4	251
2:11-22	5	4:8-11	251
2:12	58	4:12	259
3	50	5:7-10	250
Philippians	187–89	10	255
1	117, 216	10:5	250–51, 257–58
2:5-11	187	10:37-38	251
Colossians	2, 158, 247	13:6	251
1	216		
1:15-18	219		

Author Index

Adam, A. K. M., 49n22
Anderson, Bernhard, 63, 63n15, 104n11
Anderson, Gary, 19n5
Astruc, Jean, 3, 89n8, 99
Athanasius, 4, 202–8, 208n11, 208n12, 210n17, 217
Attridge, Harold W., 252, 254, 254n13, 254n15
Auerbach, Eric, 41n10, 70, 79–84
Azar, Michael G., 277n10

Baden, Joel, 100n3
Barr, James, 64n18, 64n19
Barth, Karl, 33n22, 53n4, 72, 83, 277, 277n10, 278n11

Bartholomew, Craig, 15n1, 48n22, 49n22, 58n8, 244n1
Barton, John, 22n1, 30n17, 159n27
Bartsch, Hans-Werner, 54n4
Bates, Matthew W., 197n16, 252n10, 256n18
Bauckham, Richard, 42n12, 187, 187n4, 265, 265n4
Behr, John, 32n20, 33, 47, 116n21, 187–88, 188n5, 189, 202n2, 204n3, 267n7
Black, C. Clifton, 184n1
Blenkinsopp, Joseph, 226n11, 141n4
Boyarin, Daniel, 265, 265n3
Braaten, Carl E., 24n6, 61n12

Bray, Gerald, 15n1
Brion, Marcel, 113n20
Brueggemann, Walter, 37n2, 38n2, 121n3, 183n1, 184n1
Bucur, Bogdan G., 117n22, 265n2, 266, 268–69
Bultmann, Rudolf, 54n4, 273, 273n3
Burney, C. F., 27n11, 209n13, 209n14, 209n15, 210n17, 215, 215n20, 215n23, 218, 219n29, 253n11

von Campenhausen, Hans, 267 267n7
Cassuto, Umberto, 102, 203–4
Chapman, Stephen, 8n7, 22n1, 25n7, 88n5, 121n5
Childs, Brevard S., 2, 2n1, 3, 3n2, 3n3, 8n7, 22n1, 23n2, 28, 30, 33n22, 37–38, 38n3, 39, 39n5, 40, 40n7, 40n9, 41–42, 42n14, 43, 43n15, 43n16, 44, 44n17, 45, 45n19, 46–47, 62n13, 75, 75n8, 76, 103–4, 104n9, 104n11, 106n13, 121, 121n4, 125n9, 136n8, 166n6, 186, 189, 191n6, 203, 216n26, 225, 225n6, 246, 246n4, 247n7, 248, 248n8, 252n9, 273n4
Clement of Alexandria, 9, 16, 16n2, 34, 46, 46n21, 117, 117n22, 263, 265n2, 267, 269
Collett, Don, 37n2, 58n8, 60n11, 129n11, 202n1, 206n5, 207n8
Congar, Yves, 267n7
Crenshaw, James, 226, 226n10, 226n11, 226n12

Davis, Ellen F., 19n5, 58n8

Dohmen, Christoph, 31n18, 75, 75n8
Dozeman, Thomas B., 91n13, 135n6

Elliot, Mark W., 217n27

Feldmeier, Reinhard, 38n2
Finn, Leonard G., 217n27
Fitzmyer, Joseph A., 178–79, 179n1
Fowl, Stephen E., 49n22
Frei, Hans, 3, 36n1, 39n5, 41n10
Fox, Michael V., 229, 229n17, 231n19, 234n23, 235

Gathercole, Simon J., 265, 265n3
Gilkey, Langdon, 62n13, 63n17
Grabbe, Lester, 64n18
Green, Joel, 49n22
Gregory of Nyssa, 209, 222, 222n1, 226n13, 227n13, 235n26, 236, 241, 242n32
Grelot, Pierre, 255n17
Gruber, Mayer I., 194n11, 255n16

Halpern, Baruch, 155n23
von Harnack, Adolf, 24, 24n6
Hays, Richard B., 19n5, 58n8, 246n3
Helmer, Christine, 191, 191n7, 192, 192n8, 193n9, 193n10, 194, 194n12, 195n13, 196, 198, 198n17, 199n19, 253n12
Hill, Robert Charles, 218n28, 275n8
Hurtado, Larry W., 265, 265n3

Irenaeus, 4, 11, 25–26, 26n10, 27, 27n11, 27n12, 28, 28n13, 29, 29n14, 30–31, 32n20, 33n24,

40n8, 45–46, 69n1, 108, 115, 203–4, 204n3, 218, 264, 266–67, 267n7, 269, 272

Jeremias, Jörg, 148n16, 150, 151n19
Jobes, Karen H., 255n17
Jowett, Benjamin, 52n2, 53n3
Justin (Martyr), 45–46, 204, 265–70

Keck, Leander E., 3, 18n4

van Leeuwen, Raymond C., 147n17, 226n9, 228n16, 235n25
Legaspi, Michael, 89n8, 98n1
Lenzi, Alan, 206n5
Levenson, Jon D., 18n5, 104n10
Lewis, Jack P., 24n5, 265n3
Lincoln, Andrew, 244n1, 246n5, 248–49
Lindbeck, George, 3, 53n2
Lohfink, Nobert, 233, 233n21, 234n24
Longman, Tremper, 30n17, 64n18, 206n5
de Lubac, Henri, 181n2, 272, 272n1
Luther, Martin, 5, 39n6, 67, 96, 120n1, 184, 190–91, 191n7, 192–93, 193n10, 194–95, 195n13, 196–99, 201, 212, 214, 236, 253n12

MacDonald, Neil, 225n6
McDonald, Lee, 73n3, 123n7
McKenzie, Steven, 88n5
Melito of Sardis, 262–63, 266
Moberly, Walter, 53, 53n4, 67n22, 90n12, 94, 101, 101n5, 134n5
Murphy, Roland, 206n5, 233, 233n22, 234, 235n26

Nassif, Bradley, 29n16, 276n9
Newman, Murray Lee, Jr., 87n1, 265n3
Noth, Martin, 87, 87n2, 88, 88n5, 120, 121n2, 133, 134n4, 136

Olson, Dennis, 121n4, 136n8, 146n13
Origen, 4, 16n2, 46, 67, 68n23, 137, 203–4, 215n22, 227n15

Perdue, Leo, 64n18, 149n17
Propp, William, 87, 87n3, 109n17

von Rad, Gerhard, 63n14, 87, 87n2, 88, 88n4, 91–92, 92n15, 93, 103–4, 121, 121n3, 133, 133n3, 223, 223n2, 224–26, 226n8, 226n11
Rendtorff, Rolf, 28, 87, 87n2, 88, 92n16, 223n2, 224, 224n4, 224n5
Reventlow, Henning Graf, 99n2, 224
Richards, Kent Harold, 43n16, 166n6, 191n6, 216n26, 217n27, 273n4, 274n7
Rowe, C. Kavin, 33, 33n22, 33n23, 41n11, 265, 265n4

Saebo, Magne, 89n9, 99n2
Sailhamer, John H., 164n3
Sand, Alexander, 23n2
Sanders, James A., 22, 28, 73n3, 123n7
Schmid, Konrad, 87n4, 91n13, 92n15, 134n5, 135n6, 226n8
Schwartz, Baruch J., 91n13
Schwartz, Sarah, 104n9, 230n18, 238, 238n28, 238n29, 239n30, 239n31

Seitz, Christopher R., 23n3, 27n11, 29n16, 37n2, 43n16, 44n18, 59n9, 60n10, 61n12, 64n20, 83n13, 108n16, 125n9, 143n8, 145n11, 146n12, 146n14, 158n25, 159n26, 159n27, 163n2, 166n6, 167n7, 167n8, 171n10, 184n1, 185n2, 186n3, 191n6, 195n14, 211n19, 215n23, 216n24, 216n26, 217n27, 225n8, 232n20, 244n1, 246n3, 247n6, 267n7, 267n8, 272n2, 273n4, 273n5, 274n7
Shaviv, Yehuda, 239n30
Sneed, Mark, 224, 226n11, 227n14
Soulen, R. Kendall, 186, 186n3, 189, 277n10
Spieckermann, Hermann, 38n2, 224
Spinks, D. Christopher, 49n22
Steinberg, Julius, 25n8, 74n5, 125n10, 162n1
Steins, Georg, 164n3
Sternberg, Meir, 110n18
Stone, Timothy J., 25n8, 74n5, 125n10, 162n1
Stordalen, Terje, 238, 238n9
Strawn, Brent A., 39n4, 184n1
Sweeney, Marvin, 120n1, 122n6

Terrien, Samuel, 87n1
Theodore of Mopsuestia, 4, 211, 272–75, 275n8, 276–77
Trebolle–Barrera, Julio, 141n3
Treier, Daniel J., 49n22
Trobisch, David, 247n7

Utzschneider, Helmut, 76n8

Vanhoozer, Kevin J., 48n22, 49n22, 226n9

Waltke, Bruce, 206n5
Watson, Francis, 39n4, 153n21, 154n22
Weeks, Stuart, 162, 206n5
Wellhausen, Julius, 3, 85–89, 92, 100, 103, 143n7, 150
Westermann, Claus, 90n10, 94, 94n17, 106, 106n12
Wilken, Robert Louis, 202n1, 273n4
Wolff, Hans Walter, 121n3
Wright, G. Ernest, 62n13
Wright, J. Robert, 242n32
Wright, N. T., 49n22, 58n8

Yeago, David, 42n12, 187, 187n4, 216, 216n25, 265, 265n4, 266n5
Young, Frances, 8n7, 69n1, 202n2, 204n4, 206, 206n6, 207, 207n7, 207n8, 207n9, 208, 208n10, 209n16, 210n17, 216, 216n26, 217n27, 218

Zimmerli, Walther, 39n5, 226n11, 233, 233n22

www.ingramcontent.com/pod-product-compliance
Lightning Source LLC
Chambersburg PA
CBHW021346300426
44114CB00012B/1105